mv pathfinder field guide

MV Pathfinder
FIELD GUIDE

By LAWRENCE MAXWELL

*with the assistance of
more than a score of
naturalists and youth leaders
for
the Missionary Volunteer Department
of the General Conference
of Seventh-day Adventists*

REVIEW *and* HERALD
PUBLISHING ASSN.

WASHINGTON, D.C.

foreword

God's outdoors beckons youth to adventure and unhurried living. In these days of urbanization the *MV Pathfinder Field Guide* is a valuable aid in helping young people and their leaders—Master Guides, Pathfinder directors, teachers, et cetera—become acquainted with the skills necessary to make the most of an outdoor environment. As the Pathfinder Club program continues to escalate all over the world the contents of this book become of increasing value.

The *MV Pathfinder Field Guide* is the work of many youth leaders and contributors. A committee consisting of W. D. Blehm, Miller Brockett, F. W. Foster, Harry Garlick, John Hancock, J. R. Nelson, Donald M. Palmer, Clark Smith, and T. V. Zytkoskee, with L. A. Skinner as chairman, was appointed by the General Conference MV Department to outline the objectives and contents of the book. Resource material was also submitted by Fred Beavon, W. E. Burns, Lee Carter, H. W. Clark, E. D. Clifford, Desmond Cummings, Paul DeBooy, Lew Johnson, Boyd E. Olson, Edward Oliver, B. H. Phipps, D. I. Shaw, Grant Tolles, Ray Underhill, Jack Darnell, and Eugene Winter. Grateful thanks are due E. S. Booth and Lester E. Harris, Jr., for making valuable contributions in the field of science and for reading and correcting portions of the manuscript.

We are also indebted to the *Scout Field Book* published by the Boy Scouts of America for much of the material which appears in this volume.

Mildred Lee Johnson prepared the index and was responsible for securing many of the illustrations.

When the work of preparing the volume was begun, it became apparent that one individual must be appointed as general editor to unify the style. Lawrence Maxwell, editor of the *Guide* magazine, had a deep interest in the Pathfinder work and accepted the big task of editing the *MV Pathfinder Field Guide*. He did extensive research on the project, wrote much of the manuscript, and photographed nearly half of the pictures that appear.

The *MV Pathfinder Field Guide* was first published in 1962 under the direction of Theodore Lucas, secretary of the General Conference MV Department. This 1970 edition has been revised and brought up to date to keep pace with the changing times. It is our wish that this *Field Guide* may not only give many hours of enjoyable reading, but may serve as a practical guide and companion to those who seek the high road to adventure in our Father's world.

General Conference Missionary Volunteer Department

contents

getting in on the fun

PART ONE

it's great to be a pathfinder!

A CANOE trip tomorrow . . . a hike to the falls next week . . . a cookout the fifteenth.

There's always something doing in the Pathfinder Club. And all of them mean FUN!

Perhaps it's star study tonight, or a deep-sea diver showing his equipment. Perhaps it's cooking pancakes, or taking apart an automobile engine. Perhaps it's skiing down a wintry slope with snow flying everywhere.

This is Pathfinders. And yet there's more—

Hayrides in the moonlight . . . trips to famous battlegrounds . . . fairs and contests and games.

And more—

Missionary work and good turns . . . and weekend camping. Camping! Stories and songs around the campfire Friday night, church in the woods Sabbath morning, hike to Black Rock or Horsetail Falls Sabbath afternoon, games in the evening, swimming Sunday morning.

This, too, is Pathfinders? Yes, sir!

It's great to be a Pathfinder!

THE PATHFINDER CLUB

All this action takes place in the Pathfinder Club. Probably most of the fellows and girls you know are members already. If you aren't one yet, you're wishing you could know more about the club and how you can join.

The Unit's First

Everything in the Pathfinder Club turns around the unit. And the unit is six to eight boys or girls who like to do things together.

Leading the fun is the unit *captain*. He's the member of the unit with the best ideas, plenty of good judgment, and abundant energy for getting things done. He's elected by the other members of the unit at a regular meeting, but he gets the unit together as often as possible between times for hikes and cookouts and working on Pathfinder skills.

When the club goes camping, the unit members stick together, pitching their tents as a group. And when there are contests such as string-burning and knot-tying races, they make up a team.

The captain represents the unit on the club's steering committee. He makes sure too that when there's something doing, every member of the unit gets in on it. And of course all the members of the unit respect him when he calls for order.

Another officer in the unit is the *scribe,* who has the very important job of collecting dues and keeping the unit records. He has a list of all the members of the unit, and at every regular meeting he marks down who is present. He keeps the unit logbook too, and that's a real honor, for the log contains a brief description of all the extra special things the unit does, and it may go back many years. The scribe guards the log with great care.

Then there is the *guidon bearer,* who has the very special honor of carrying the guidon, the small flag that belongs to the unit and goes everywhere the unit goes.

Units that are especially active have other officers, such as *assistant captain* and *assistant scribe* and *supply keeper* (in charge of the unit's equipment), and *chow master* (sees there is plenty of food on hikes and campouts), *transportation agent* (to make sure there are cars for long trips), and *chief telephoner* (to call all unit members when big news has to go out fast). These officers and others are elected by the unit, permanently or just when needed.

Those Adults

Leading the club is the *Pathfinder director,* who is assisted by other adults who serve as *deputy director, counselors* and *instructors.* They are all busy people and they aren't paid a penny for the work they do for the Pathfinder Club. There aren't nearly enough adults like them to go around. That's why so many boys and girls like you who would like to have a Pathfinder Club can't have one. It's just playing it smart to give your directors and counselors 100 per cent cooperation. "Keep the Counselors Happy" is a very wise slogan!

Clubs Around the World

Your club may have a dozen units, or it may have only two, but it is part of an organization that circles the world.

Beyond your club are the clubs in your conference. You get to meet their members when you go to a Pathfinder Fair or a conference-wide camporee. Directing all the clubs in the conference is the conference youth director.

Work on **MV HONORS** and crafts at Pathfinder meetings! Flower arrangement, tumbling, and auto mechanics are only three of the many there are to choose.

Beyond the conference is the union, covering several States or provinces. The Pathfinders of the union get together at union-wide camporees. They are directed by the union youth director.

And beyond the unions lies the whole wide world; for Pathfinders are part of the Seventh-day Adventist Church, and there is hardly an organization anywhere that operates in so many different countries as does the Adventist Church. And where the Adventist Church goes, there go the Pathfinders. There are Pathfinders in England and Africa, in South America and the islands of the Pacific, far back in the jungles of Borneo and high in the hills of Burma. Nearly everywhere you go you'll find Pathfinder Clubs. And they're growing fast.

If you aren't already a member, do you want to join such a friendly, active, rollicking-good-time club? Sure as living, you do!

Here's how you can:

11

HOW TO JOIN

Three things must happen before you join. You must be between ten and fifteen years old, you must know the Pathfinder Pledge, Law, and Song, and you must fill in an entry blank.

Your Age

If you are ten or more, or in the fifth grade or above, you can join as soon as you've met the other requirements. If you're not, you'll just have to wait. But cheer up! Nature will take its course! You'll be the right age soon even if you do nothing about it. And you're bound to pass into the fifth grade as soon as you finish the fourth. Of course, you who are already in the higher grades won't have to wait at all.

If you must wait, learn the Pledge and Law and Song, so you can join without delay when the time comes. And there are many MV Honors you can be working on too, so you can fit into the swing of things as soon as you're a member.

The Pathfinder Pledge

Joining the Pathfinder Club is not like joining just any club. Pathfinders live by the Pathfinder code. When you join the club you start living by that code too. And it sets some very high standards.

The code is contained in the Pledge and the Law. The Pledge says:

By the grace of God,
I will be pure and kind and true.
I will keep the Junior Missionary Volunteer Law.
I will be a servant of God and a friend to man.

"By the grace of God." Right at the start Pathfinders show that they believe in God and need His help to live right. The Pledge is a prayer for that help and a promise to use it.

"I will." The will is the most important thing a human being possesses. With it we choose to do right or agree to do wrong. God does not force the will, Satan cannot. Pathfinders put their will on God's side.

"Be pure." A Pathfinder is clean inside and out.

"And kind." A Pathfinder is kind to everyone, especially to women and children, the sick, and the weak. He is kind to animals. He never knowingly hurts another's feelings, or laughs at another's misfortune.

12

Climax of the year is the annual **PATHFINDER FAIR**. Pathfinders from all over the conference demonstrate skills and show what they have made.

Once a year, at Halloween, many clubs take part in the **TREATS FOR THE NEEDY** campaign (above). Hundreds of thousands of cans of food are collected for Thanksgiving baskets. Another annual affair is the conference-wide **CAMPOREE** (below), when hundreds of Pathfinders camp together.

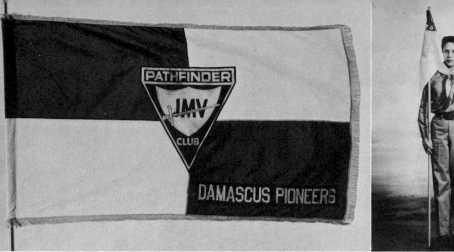

THE PATHFINDER FLAG, with the sword of God's Word and the shield of truth on a blue-and-white field of courage and purity, stands for the high ideals of the Pathfinder Club. The GUIDON goes wherever your unit goes.

"And true." A Pathfinder is trustworthy. What he promises to do, he carries out. He is strictly honest, never tells a lie, and always leaves other people's things alone. If he were ever to cheat or lie or steal he would expect to be asked to turn in his Pathfinder badge.

"Keep the Junior Missionary Volunteer Law." The Pathfinder Club is part of the Missionary Volunteer program of the Seventh-day Adventist Church, but a Pathfinder does not have to be a member of that church to belong to the club. He keeps the Law, not because he *must,* but because he *wants* to.

"A servant of God." A Pathfinder believes that God is the Master of his life, and he lets God tell him what to do.

"A friend to man." A Pathfinder is friendly to everyone. It's a part of being kind. He has his special friends, of course. But he seeks out the lonely and discouraged students in his class and makes friends with them too. He is always ready to contribute to a needy cause.

The Pathfinder Law

Every game has its rules. No one would want to play in one that didn't. And every member on the team is expected to obey. Pathfinders is a game, part of the greater Game of Life. So it has its Law, and every member tries his best "by the grace of God" to keep it.

He may not always manage to live up to it the way he feels he should, any more than a batter always hits home runs. But he keeps on, knowing that if he never gives up, the grace of God will surely

14

JMV Pledge

By the grace of God—
I will be pure and kind
and true
I will keep the JMV
Law
I will be a servant of God
and a friend to man

JMV LAW

The Junior Missionary
Volunteer Law is for me to—
1. Keep the Morning Watch
2. Do my honest part
3. Care for my body
4. Keep a level eye
5. Be courteous and obedient
6. Walk softly in the sanctuary
7. Keep a song in my heart
8. Go on God's errands

Every would-be Pathfinder must repeat from memory the **JMV PLEDGE AND LAW** before being admitted to membership. These are high standards that make Pathfinders the finest teen-age club anywhere in the world.

make him pure and kind and true, a servant of God and a friend to man. Someday he will be able to keep the whole Junior Missionary Volunteer Law, which is the same as the Pathfinder Law. He keeps as much of it as he can now, and tries each day to do better than yesterday.

The Junior Missionary Volunteer Law is for me to—
1. Keep the Morning Watch.
2. Do my honest part.
3. Care for my body.
4. Keep a level eye.
5. Be courteous and obedient.
6. Walk softly in the sanctuary.
7. Keep a song in my heart.
8. Go on God's errands.

"Keep the Morning Watch." A Pathfinder starts every day with prayer and Bible study.

"Do my honest part." A Pathfinder is helpful. He does his share of the work at Pathfinders, he carries his part of the load at home and school. And he does *a little bit more.*

"Care for my body." A Pathfinder believes that God has called him to help take the gospel message to all the world in this generation. It is the greatest challenge ever given to young people. He knows he'll need a healthy body to do it. He gets enough sleep at night and plenty of exercise during the day, and he's particular about what he eats—plenty of fruits and nuts and vegetables and

PATHFINDERS IN GRADES FIVE AND SIX: Boys wear sun-tan shirt and trousers, overseas cap, black tie, belt, socks, shoes. Girls wear one- or two-piece forest-green dress, one patch pocket on blouse, A-line skirt; green overseas cap; white or green socks; black shoes. Boys and girls wear gold neckerchief.

THE
PATHFINDER
Wear It

RIGHT SLEEVE: Club name is ½ inch below shoulder seam. Pathfinder emblem is ½ inch below name. **LEFT SLEEVE:** "MV World" goes 2 inches below seam. Chevron for highest class attained is ½ inch below world, with chevrons of lower classes ⅛ inch apart. (Bottom to top: blue, red, green, black, gold.)

16

PATHFINDERS IN GRADES SEVEN AND EIGHT are distinguished at once by the forest-green epaulets on the shoulders of the boys, and by the white blouse, which is optional for these older girls. The color of the slide that holds the neckerchief is that of the highest MV Class attained.

OFFICIAL
UNIFORM

Proudly!

ACROSS CHEST: Badge of office, good-conduct ribbon, and strip for highest class attained center above the pockets. Buttons for all classes earned are centered across flap, highest nearest left arm. ("MV World" on cap is 1½ inches back from the front, centered between top and bottom of flap.)

17

whole-grain cereals. He goes easy on soft drinks and candy, steers clear of meat, and takes nothing between meals. No tobacco or alcohol, of course. And he keeps happy. Laughter, he knows, is the world's best medicine.

"Keep a level eye." Shifting eyes are often the mark of secret sins. A Pathfinder keeps his eye level. No sneaking glances at sexy pictures for him, no dirty stories, either, or unclean jokes. When he's tempted to secret vice he runs from it, literally, knowing that vigorous outdoor exercise is the best safeguard of purity. He knows that a firm handclasp and a level eye are the sure signs of clean, courageous living, and that's the way he wants to be.

"Be courteous and obedient." A Pathfinder is respectful to everyone, and obedient to all whom it is his duty to obey, including his Pathfinder director and counselors, his parents, and his teachers at school. And he's glad to obey with a smile.

"Walk softly in the sanctuary." A Pathfinder is reverent. He attends church regularly. He never speaks lightly of religious things. He knows what he believes, and why, and he respects others whose religion is different from his own.

"Keep a song in my heart." A Pathfinder is cheerful. He greets people with a friendly smile and he does his duties cheerfully. When things go wrong, he doesn't let it get him down but bounces back and keeps going.

"Go on God's errands." A Pathfinder willingly takes part in missionary activities—giving out handbills, going Ingathering, collecting food for the needy at Halloween, or whatever it may be. He takes part in religious services too when asked, offering prayer, playing the piano, reading the Scripture, according to his abilities. He plans on a career that will give him the most possible opportunities to work for God when he grows up.

The Pathfinder Song

Oh, we are the Pathfinders strong,
The servants of God are we—
Faithful as we march along,
In truth and purity.

A message to tell to the world,
A truth that will set us free,
King Jesus the Saviour's coming back
For you and me.

When at last you are qualified to become a Pathfinder you will be welcomed into the club at a colorful and impressive **INDUCTION CEREMONY.**

Find the tune in *Singing Youth,* page 177. You'll like it. The music and words were written by Henry T. Bergh, who is an Adventist minister. Most clubs sing the Song at the beginning of every meeting.

Applying for Membership

When the time comes that you can join the Pathfinder Club, talk to the director of the club in your church. He will tell you what you need to know and give you an application blank.

If there is no Pathfinder Club in your church, talk to your pastor and ask him to get one started.

Fill in the application blank, answering all the questions, and get your parents to sign. Then give the blank back to the director.

When the big day comes for you to join, there will be a special induction ceremony. There will probably be candles and speeches and prayer. It will be very impressive. You'll be asked to repeat the Pledge and Law to prove to the members you really mean to live up to all that Pathfinders stand for. Then the director will shake your hand, the scribe will give you a membership card, and you will be . . . a Pathfinder!

UNIFORMS AND FLAGS

The Pathfinder Uniform

Right away, of course, you'll want to get the uniform. You weren't allowed to wear it before, but you can now.

Wear it proudly. It shows you belong to the best youth program in the world. Keep it clean and neat. Wear it to all Pathfinder meetings and outings. It's made of strong permanent-press material, built to stand rough usage. Wear all the insignia you are entitled to. They show the tests you've passed, and they make the uniform more colorful. The whole club looks better.

Never wear the uniform when you are selling candy or magazines to make money for yourself. But you may wear it when selling to make money for the club.

All Kinds of Flags

Your first glance over the Pathfinder Club will leave you thinking there are all kinds of flags. When you look closer you'll see that there are two large flags, the national flag and the Pathfinder flag.

The others are guidons and belong to the units. You'll be part of a unit. Probably the name has been chosen long ago and the guidon has a picture that represents the name. If you join the Panthers, the guidon will have the picture of a panther. If it's the Bluebirds, there will be a bluebird. The guidon is at the end of the unit during opening exercises, held by the guidon bearer. It leads the way when the unit hikes. It stands at the head of the tents when the unit camps. It says, "Here are the Panthers!" And every member of the unit works to make it the proudest guidon in the club.

SOMETHING HAPPENING ALL THE TIME

There's always something happening at Pathfinders. For instance—

Regular Meetings

Regular meetings come once a week, maybe once every two weeks. They begin right on time with the call "Fall IN!" and units form straight lines beside their guidons.

"ATTENTION!" Everyone snaps to it. "Color Guard, Forward MARCH!" Up come the national and Pathfinder flags from the back, through the center aisle, accompanied by trumpets and drums. "Salute the National Flag. Present ARMS!" Everyone re-

There is always something interesting at Pathfinder meetings. Here a couple of experts tell about Indian customs. At other meetings there may be a policeman, fireman, missionary, deep-sea diver, mountain climber. You can never tell who may come!

peats the Pledge of Allegiance. "Order ARMS! Salute the Pathfinder Flag. PLEDGE!" Right hand on heart, everyone repeats the Pledge and Law. "At EASE!"

Then follows the Pathfinder Song and prayer, and the scribes take the record. So much for the opening exercises.

Next comes the special feature. It may be given by an air pilot or a frogman or a detective or a naturalist, or somebody else with an interesting experience to tell.

After that there may be marching, which is always fun, or time spent on JMV Class requirements. And after that there is forty-five minutes or more of crafts, and at last the closing exercise.

"Fall IN!" calls the director. There's a mad scramble for positions. "Color Guard, Forward MARCH!" The color guard come up and take the flags, everyone salutes as the colors go by, there's a brief prayer, and all too soon, "Dis-MISSED!" Before you realize it the meeting's over.

Special Meetings

There are special meetings. The night a newcomer is voted in, there will be a special welcoming ceremony.

Investiture is very colorful. You may make it into something really big with a banquet and parents and after-dinner speeches and special demonstrations.

21

High light of the year is SUMMER CAMP—a week of swimming, boating, hiking, horseback riding, outpost camping, crafts, campfires, and consecration.

Outings

And very frequently there will be outings—hiking, canoeing, camping, cooking, swimming, and many others.

There really *is* something happening all the time at Pathfinders!

ON TO MASTER GUIDE

Yet Pathfinders is only part of the program the Seventh-day Adventist Church offers young people. There are all the JMV Classes, some of which you will do in church school. There are JMV meetings in church school too that help you learn to be leaders.

And, say, don't overlook that church school. It's part of the Adventist program for young people also. And so is the Sabbath school, with all the thrilling mission stories, and more opportunities for you to lead, and teachers that help answer your questions and get you ready for heaven.

So on through Pathfinders and JMV—Friend, Companion, Explorer, Ranger, today leading a little and learning much more. Tomorrow—Guide and Master Guide, a leader of men, perhaps a Pathfinder director, perhaps a missionary in a distant land, blazing trails for God.

And all this begins in the fun and activity and reverence of the Pathfinder Club.

It really *is* GREAT to be a Pathfinder!

always something happening

happening

PART TWO

hiking along together

"We feel the thrill of the winding trail,
And the lure of the waterfalls;
And the starry blue seems nearer too,
As the night bird softly calls." *

WHEN you've toiled all the way up a mountain trail and stand on the summit at last, you sense in your heart that there's nothing in the world that cannot be conquered by the man who has learned to hike.

And that's no fancy feeling. The world has been conquered again and again by tough-sinewed men who could hike. Jesus smashed the kingdom of darkness hiking around Palestine with His "unit" of twelve disciples. Paul and the other apostles turned the world upside down by hiking everywhere preaching the gospel. Martin Luther hiked from Wittenburg to Rome and back and upset the whole Roman Catholic Church. David Livingstone hiked 30,000 miles through Africa and opened the continent to missionaries and shattered the slave trade. It was hikers, hundreds of thousands of them, who braved the prairies and the Rocky Mountains to establish the western extremities of the United States and Canada. Herbert Hoover and Harry S Truman regularly hiked certain distances every day, and both became President of the United States; President Eisenhower became famous for his many miles of hiking on the golf course.

A hike is not a walk. A walker may shuffle along all day, scarcely knowing where he's going, and come home at night without knowing where he's been. But a hiker steps along with a purpose in view. He knows where he's going—and why. He keeps right on till he gets there, and when he comes home he's satisfied.

There are all sorts of hikes for Pathfinders to enjoy.

All Sorts of Hikes

There is the *skills hike*. The club sets out for a spot not more than two or three miles away. On arriving, they practice some Path-

* Poem is from the camp song of Wawona Camp in Yosemite, written by Vernon Berry.

finder skill such as fire building, cooking, first aid, or campcraft. Many requirements for JMV Classes can be satisfied quickly this way.

Friend-to-man hike. The Pathfinders set out by units to see how many good deeds they can accomplish in a given length of time. If they see a woman struggling with a heavy shopping bag, they politely offer to carry it for her; if they see a little child trying to cross a street, they help him over. The units will have many an interesting experience to report when they reassemble at the clubhouse!

Communications hike. Units set out along different trails. They stop at predetermined positions and signal back to base camp or to other units with flags or lights or mirrors. The messages contain problems to solve or directions on how to get to the next stop on the hike, where other instructions will be given.

Nature-Bible treasure hike. Treasure—preferably Pathfinder equipment or a good book—is tucked away at the foot of a tree or buried in a hole in the ground. Pathfinders set out by units to find it. Clues stapled to trees may say, "If this tree is an oak, look for next clue on a maple; if it is a pine, find next clue on a hickory." Or they could say, "If John 3:16 starts with 'whosoever,' find next clue under stone fifty yards west." Again, "Go as many yards east as Joseph's age when he went into Egypt (see Gen. 37:2)."

Paul-the-apostle Share-Your-Faith hike. On a Sabbath afternoon, Pathfinders hike to a nearby town where there is no Adventist church and distribute tracts, just as Paul hiked into various towns where there was no church and shared his faith.

First-aid hike. A Pathfinder lies moaning somewhere in the woods. The Pathfinders set out to help him, led on by the sound of his pitiful cries. On reaching him, they find a label that says what is wrong with him, and apply appropriate first aid. For variation the Pathfinder can lie quietly unconscious, and the club can find him by following a series of clues based on a knowledge of first-aid facts.

Lost-child hike. The telephone rings in the Pathfinder clubhouse—or a messenger runs breathlessly in—and everything suddenly stops as the announcement is made, "A child is lost in the woods. The frantic mother has asked whether the Pathfinders will please organize a search party and try to find him." Of course, you explain at once it is only make-believe—the child is a little girl's life-size doll that she has let the director hide in the woods—but it's still a lot of fun organizing the party and conducting the search.

These hikes are good for all the units of the club to go on together. Others are better for smaller groups, such as one or two units.

On a **GREAT EXPLORERS HIKE** follow the compass in a straight line, crossing all obstacles you come to. Take no foolish risks.

Or you may collect ancient sharks' teeth on a beach well known for its fossils on **FAMOUS PLACES HIKE.**

BEACH HIKES may turn up all sorts of creatures as interesting as this crab.

Nature hike. Each Pathfinder is given a list of things to find—6 pine needles, 3 acorns, 1 oak leaf, up to about twenty different items. Then all set out to see who can find everything first. When the whole club participates, each *unit* can be given a list.

Great-explorers hikes. These hikes take considerable courage and persistence. On them, you follow the routes of the famous explorers, going in a straight line up hill and down, regardless of brambles, rocks, or streams. *Columbus hike.* Set your compass and go due west. *Admiral Peary hike.* Go due north—to the North Pole, if you can. Peary did. Or head for the South Pole, on a *Roald Amundsen hike.* In summer do a *Lewis and Clark hike.* Follow a stream all the way up to its source or down to its mouth, as Lewis and Clark followed the Missouri and Columbia rivers. On the compass hikes follow the course in a straight line without deviating, so far as is *sensible.* Do not take foolish risks. The great explorers never did.

Hare-and-hounds hike. This is an ancient one, but as thrilling as ever. Two Pathfinders lead off, laying a handful of grain or cereal every fifty feet. Ten minutes later the rest of the unit set out in pursuit. At night the "hares" carry a flashlight. When they are a thousand feet away they yell, and the hounds give chase. The hares have a certain destination (their burrow) that they must reach before being caught; but every minute they must flash their light as a signal to the hounds.

You can think of a great many more hikes. Just the names of some will start your imagination going: *Star hike, long-distance hike, mountain-climbing hike, survival hike, photography hike, conservation hike, father-son hike, Marco Polo hike* (going due east).

Planning Hikes

Hikes like these don't just happen. They have to be planned carefully. When the unit expects to hike alone, all the members of the unit get together to discuss the plans, with the captain as chairman. When the whole club is going together, the unit captains meet with several of the counselors, and the counselor-in-charge-of-hiking is chairman.

The committee will: (1) Consider the interests and ability of the hikers; (2) decide on the kind of hike; (3) plan the route, make a list of items to be taken, work out any necessary hiking rules, and provide for transportation if it is needed; and (4) see that every hiker is fully informed concerning the nature of the hike, the time and place of meeting and returning, the hiking rules, and any food or equipment he should bring with him.

28

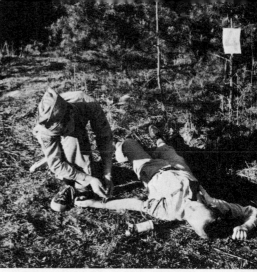

A SKILLS HIKE is full of surprises. Somewhere on the way you may have to pitch a pup tent or apply first aid. At the end there may be some prizes.

What to Take

Take as little as possible. The lightest load grows heavy if the trail is long. By all means keep your hands empty. You may need them for emergencies. Besides, carrying anything in the hands throws the body off balance and makes walking harder. Put all you can in pockets, the rest in a light packsack.

The equipment you take will depend upon the kind of hike and the weather. For clothes, wear your *Pathfinder Uniform* or the official *camping clothing*. Take a *sweater* for cool evenings and to keep you from chilling when you stop. Have a *raincoat* or *poncho* if rain threatens.

No matter what the hike, a *pocketknife* will be useful, so will a short piece of *strong string* or *rope*, a few *matches*, and a *notebook* and *pencil*. Someone certainly should have a *first-aid kit*. Never go without one. Always take a *flashlight*.

Other equipment such as *compass, maps,* and *cooking gear* should be light and compact. You will not need them on every hike.

Shoes and Socks and Blisters

Nothing can spoil the best-planned hike so thoroughly as one little blister. But fortunately, blisters can be avoided. They are usually caused by poorly fitted shoes, the wrong socks, or wet feet.

Your feet make it possible for you to hike, so give them the care they deserve. Choose the right *shoes*. They should be smooth inside and fit snugly in the heel, but with plenty of room for the toes to

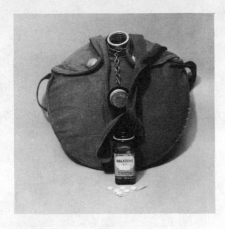

Never drink WATER on a hike unless you are sure it is pure. It is best to fill your canteen at home before starting. If you must drink strange water, always add tablets of Halazone or other guaranteed water purifier.

wriggle. The sole should be strong but pliable; the uppers soft and flexible. Leather is the best material, with broad, low rubber or composition heels. Leave sneakers at home.

Thick wool socks are best, preferably white, and a little too big. Many hikers like nylon socks against the skin. Experiment with cushion sole orlon socks for the girls. Keep feet comfortable!

Damp socks make for soft skin and tender feet. For frequent hiking through swamps and bogs, shoes can be *waterproofed* with a mixture of one part paraffin to two parts vaseline. But this may keep the feet damp with perspiration. Neatsfoot oil or silicone lets the shoes breathe, drying the feet. For all-round hiking do not attempt to waterproof. Simply shine your shoes frequently with ordinary shoe polish. *Wet shoes* should be dried slowly, turned upside down at night on two stakes several yards from the campfire, or stuffed with warmed pebbles or newspaper.

If you have to wade a creek or if you get caught in a downpour, stop afterward and dry your feet and put on the other pair of socks you brought. It is invigorating to bathe your feet in a stream two or three times on an all-day hike. Take your socks off at rest stops and turn them inside out before putting them on again. It will put new life into your feet.

Blisters, while still in the red stage, should be protected with a Band-Aid. Protect *fully-formed blisters* by building a ring of cotton around them, or applying a corn plaster. Put antiseptic on a *burst blister* and cover with a Band-Aid.

If you suffer from *cold feet* while hiking, remember that it is your blood that keeps you warm. Check to see that there is nothing around your legs or feet that is squeezing the flesh and cutting down

30

A CAVE HIKE offers thrills all its own! Put on old clothes, go down a small hole on a rope ladder, and walk (or crawl!) through narrow passages, see fantastic formations. Always take an experienced guide with you.

the blood flow. If something is, loosen it. If feet remain cold wear two pairs of socks (be sure to keep them dry); and improve your circulation by getting more exercise between hikes.

Wash your feet well the night before a hike, and trim the toenails square. If the skin has a tendency to be soft, soak your feet alternately in tubs of hot and ice-cold water, one minute each for ten minutes. Add a handful of salt to the water first.

Go All the Way

Every Pathfinder wants to *go all the way,* and every Pathfinder can. Start out slowly, even if you feel like a just-launched rocket. The fellow who starts out like a jet frequently comes home like a tortoise, ashamed that someone else is carrying his pack.

Bill Emmerton, of Australia, has walked one hundred miles in less than twenty-four hours nonstop at least six times, and he has gone twelve miles in just one hour two minutes and two seconds.

31

But records like those take a lot of working up to. Plan your first hikes at three or four miles an hour, twenty miles a day.

You can check your speed and your distance by counting your steps. First measure your stride from heel to heel. If it is 30 inches, then 35 steps per minute is one mile per hour. Seventy steps is two miles an hour; 106 steps, three; 141 steps, four. If your step is 24 inches, the number of steps per minute is 44 for one mile per hour, 88 for two, 132 for three, and 176 for four.

Count your steps by putting 18 pebbles in your left pocket. If your step is 30 inches, 120 steps make 100 yards. Every time you count 120, put a pebble in your right pocket. When the left pocket is empty, you will have gone a mile (1,760 yards). For a 24-inch step, count 150 steps for every 100 yards.

In level country, walk comfortably upright, your toes pointing straight ahead or, Indian fashion, slightly inward, with the heel coming down first and the big toe of the back foot pushing you forward.

On hills, use the bent-leg technique. Lean forward, bend the knees, and set the foot down almost flat.

Swing your arms gently to keep yourself in balance.

Rest when you are tired. A good plan is to hike twenty-five minutes and rest five. Get down on your back and put your feet up. Don't lie too long, or muscles will stiffen. Let slow hikers catch up, and wait while they rest. To push on as soon as they arrive is the height of cruelty. Slow hikers need more rest than fast hikers do.

Safety Pays

Drink only water that you know is pure, and not much of that. If there is any doubt, purify the water either by dissolving one Globaline (iodine) or two Halazone (chlorine) tablets to a quart, and letting the water stand twenty to thirty minutes; or by adding three drops of 2 per cent tincture of iodine to a quart and letting it stand thirty minutes; or by boiling the water five minutes and pouring it back and forth between two containers until it is cool.

Better yet, take water in a canteen. Don't drink it. Just moisten your mouth occasionally and spit the water out. Veteran missionaries on safari in Africa sometimes return the water from the mouth to the canteen.

A fairly large pebble in the mouth helps some hikers. By all means stay away from soda water and pop. They will bloat you.

Walk on the left of a highway, facing traffic. Go single file if you must travel on the road surface. Stay off the road, if possible. The shoulder is softer and safer.

WALK on the left in single file, facing traffic, and stay together. At night tie a white handkerchief around your right leg to help drivers see you.

Always RESPECT private property. Get permission ahead of time if you must cross someone's land. Leave your dinner area TIDY. Bury all garbage.

At night, wear a white handkerchief around your right leg. Act at all times as though car drivers cannot see you, for most likely they can't.

Be especially careful in rain or snow, for cars will need more space to stop and may skid off curves and hit you.

Courteous and Cheerful

Respect all "No Trespassing," "Keep Off," and "Private" signs. Always get a farmer's permission before crossing his land. He'll probably appreciate your asking him and be very cooperative. He could have you arrested otherwise!

Police your rest stops for paper and other litter before moving on.

If you must "go to the toilet," walk far from the trail, dig a hole about eight inches deep, and fill it in afterward. Keep back from streams so you won't pollute them.

Be kind to your counselors! Follow the pattern set up for the hike. If you have a number, say it loud and clear when you're asked to "sound off." If your unit is assigned a place in line, stick to it cheerfully. Places will be rotated, and you will have to eat the dust at the tail for only your share of the time.

And if there are chores, tackle them with a smile. All the world loves a cheerful hiker, and somehow, they are the ones who love hiking the most.

IF YOU ARE LOST

Control Your Panic

Someday you may suddenly realize that you are lost. No doubt a terrible wave of panic will sweep over you. You will think of many fearful things—like being attacked by a wild animal or slowly dying of starvation. Most people think such thoughts during the first anxious moments after they realize they don't know where they are. But suppress them as quickly as you can, for they are foolish. You are certain to be found. As soon as you are missed a search party will be organized and friends will come looking for you.

Pray

Kneel down and talk to God. Remember some of His promises —"I am with you alway." "The angel of the Lord encampeth round about them that fear him, and delivereth them." Jesus is watching over you. The angels are taking care of you.

REST when you rest, but not for too long—about five minutes in every half hour. DRINK also, but not too much, or you may become waterlogged.

Think

Sit down on a log and think. How did you get here? With your panic gone and your mind clear, you will probably remember exactly how you got where you are. If you do, and if you are *sure* which way to go, get up and walk back to the trail.

But if you are not sure, STAY WHERE YOU ARE. Wandering aimlessly will tire you, and you need all the strength you have. Chances are, too, that walking will take you farther and farther away from that search party that will be coming soon.

Climb a Hill

From the log where you are still sitting, look around. Is there a hill nearby? If so, climb it. From the top you may see a landmark that you recognize. If so, and if you are now *sure* which way to go, walk down the hill back to the trail.

But if you are not *sure*, STAY WHERE YOU ARE.

WET SHOES lead to cold feet and blisters. Dry the shoes overnight on sticks near the campfire—but not too close, for the leather may burn or crack.

Use Map and Compass

If you were smart enough to bring a map and a compass, use them. Spread out the map and orient it, either with the compass or by checking landmarks.

Think of the last landmark you passed—that bridge, perhaps an old cabin, a hill, a sharp turn in the trail—and find it on the map.

How long ago were you there? You have probably been traveling not more than three miles an hour. If you passed that landmark an hour ago, you are almost certainly less than three miles away from it now. Study the scale of the map, then draw a circle with a *radius* of three miles around that landmark. *You are somewhere inside that circle.*

Look for landmarks printed on the map—hills, rivers, gullies, old buildings, et cetera. Can you see them now? Have you passed any of them? Where are they in relation to where you are now? By such a study you narrow down the size of the area in which you probably are. When you have got it down to the smallest possible circle, imagine you are in the middle of it and mark that spot on the map. *This mark is where you probably are.*

What is the best route to the trail from this point? With your compass, mark out a route, follow the compass to the trail—and be back in camp before you are missed!

POUR WARM PEBBLES heated over the campfire into your wet shoes, or stuff newspaper into them if you have it, and they should be dry by morning.

Trust Your Compass

Before we go further, a word about that compass. Trust it! Unless you have dropped it, believe in it, even if it does say the north is where you are sure the west is. You are much more likely to be mixed up about directions than the compass is. If you have no compass, use your watch to find north. (See page 46.) You can use the watch to check the compass if you wish.

Enjoy Yourself

If all these suggestions fail—if you cannot possibly think which way you came, if there are no hills to climb and no landmarks you recognize, if you have neither map nor compass—STAY WHERE YOU ARE. And plan to enjoy yourself. Here is a chance for some real pioneering!

Begin at once to look for wild food and eat it. A full stomach can endure almost any hardship.

Then find a sheltered spot for the night and gather bedding.

Finally—if you have matches—gather wood, clear an area, and light a fire. Or light two fires a few feet apart. Two fires mean "I am lost." But they take more wood to keep them burning. In the daytime put wet leaves on the fire to make smoke. All North American forests are surveyed by watchers in fire towers, or are patrolled by forestry planes. Your smoke will soon be seen.

You won't get lost if you stay alert for TRAIL MARKERS. Paint on the tree at left marks the Appalachian Trail. Indians bent tree limbs to make trail signs. This marked tree is in Illinois. Today a railroad follows the Indians' route.

At night the flames will cheer you and keep you company. Sit down beside them and think of the story you will be able to tell the fellows when you get back to camp.

Remember that if you know the things that are written in this book about how to live in the wilderness, being lost does not need to be a terrifying experience. It can be a wonderful opportunity to put into practice what you have learned. It could be the greatest adventure of your life.

HOW MANY OF THESE CAN YOU DO?

Check each one when you finish it.

☐ 1. Go on a *Paul-the-apostle hike*. Report the number of tracts given out at your next JMV meeting in school.

☐ 2. Take a *hares-and-hounds hike*.

☐ 3. Do a *friend-to-man hike*. Report the good deeds as "errands" and the time as "hours of Christian help work."

☐ 4. At a club meeting demonstrate how to purify water with Halazone, Globaline, and iodine. Show what to do for blisters.

☐ 5. Earn the MV Honor award in *Hiking*.

INTERESTING BOOK ON HIKING

A Manual of Walking, Elon Jessup (E. P. Dutton & Co.).
An interesting book with many suggestions.

if you get lost

By all means, DON'T RUN! It will only make you tired when you need all the strength you can muster.

DO sit on a stump and THINK, and bow your head and PRAY.

If you can't remember how you got here, get busy and GATHER UP some wood for an overnight fire.

CLIMB a hill and look around. Chances are you'll recognize a landmark that will be of help.

For directions, narrow rings on a tree stump are usually NORTH.

find your way

THE missionary doctor swung his bag of medicines into the single-engine plane and climbed aboard. He read again the note that had been handed him. "Come at once. Little girl dangerously sick." The address was a lonely village in a valley across the mountain.

With a cough and a splutter the motor came to life, and the plane raced down the runway and bounced into the air. The Adventist physician circled the field, gaining altitude. Then, which way to go? How could he find that lonely community where the girl lay ill? Easy for him—he knew how! He found the village on his map, then took a reading on the compass, and in thirty-five minutes he was coming in for a landing down the main street of the town.

Someday you too may save a life because you know how to find your way with map and compass. In the meantime, you can have a lot of fun on map-and-compass cross-country hikes with the Pathfinder Club.

For although it's fun to hike along a well-marked trail, it's nothing compared to the thrill of striking off across the country with not a mark of a trail in sight and only your map and your compass and your skill to steer you right. That's *real* pathfinding!

The Compass

The compass is a simple instrument, just a magnetized needle turning on a pivot. No one knows who made the first one. It may have been a piece of magnetized iron ore hanging from a string.

But simple as the compass is, it was the key to the discovery of America and the exploration of the world. We still need one when we explore. A compass points only north. Starting there, the four *cardinal points* are north, south, east, and west. The in-between points are northeast, southeast, southwest, northwest. Ordinarily, in a place we are familiar with we can tell these directions without using a compass, but out in the woods or in strange mountain territory it is easy to become confused, and a compass is necessary.

The most important part of a compass is the magnetized needle. When the compass is moved, the needle swings until it comes to

MAKE A COMPASS by stroking a needle one way several times with one end of a magnet. Float needle on water. Use paper "boat" if necessary.

rest pointing north. But it is not pointing to the North Pole. Rather, it points to the magnetic North Pole, which is located near to Hudson Bay, fourteen hundred miles south of the North Pole. More on this later when we talk about *declination*.

Around the edge of the compass housing you will find marked the 360 degrees of a circle. These degrees are used to indicate a direction expressed in a number of degrees. When a direction is expressed in degrees it is usually called a magnetic *azimuth,* or magnetic *heading.* For instance, it might be "azimuth 85°." This term *azimuth* comes from the Arabic words *al,* meaning "the," and *sumūt* meaning "way." It means "the way" to go. The 360 degrees on the compass dial represent 360 "ways" to go. An azimuth is merely one of the 360 ways, or directions.

The cardinal points of the compass could be expressed as east—azimuth 090°, south—180°, west—270°, north—360° or 0°.

Using a Compass Is Easy

There is nothing difficult about using a compass if you remember a few simple principles. The easiest compass to use is the Pathfinder compass made by Silva, Incorporated. It has the compass

HOW TO USE THE COMPASS

If you are at A, the end of the dirt road, and want to go cross-country to B, mark the two points clearly and lay the map out flat. Then do STEP 1. Lay the compass so that the plastic base touches both A and B.

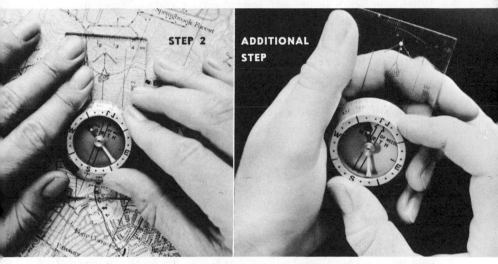

STEP 2. Turn the compass housing until the printed arrow lines up with the north-south lines on the map. (ADDITIONAL STEP. Turn the housing the correct number of degrees left or right to allow for declination.) STEP 3. Hold compass so direction-of-travel arrow points in front of you. Hold steady, turn your whole body till the magnetic arrow rests above the printed arrow. Look ahead, find a landmark, and walk toward it.

mounted on a plastic plate that has a direction arrow marked on it. Three steps make it easy to use.

Step 1. Place the edge of the plastic plate along the line on the map you wish to travel.

Step 2. Turn the compass housing until the arrow printed inside the housing is parallel with the NS lines on the map. Adjust for declination. (See section on declination.)

Step 3. Now turn the entire compass and plastic plate horizontally until the magnetic needle points in exactly the same direction as the printed arrow inside the compass dial. To travel your desired course, follow the direction-of-travel arrow on the base plate. Sight along this arrow to a tall tree or other landmark and go to it. When you reach it, get out your compass and sight again.

One, two, three—easy, isn't it? With these three basic steps mastered you can go cross country wherever you please.

Adjusting for Declination

There are some other things, however, that you should know about your compass. To orient the compass, turn it until the magnetic needle lies on top of the arrow printed in the compass housing. The north end of the magnetic needle and the arrow head of the printed arrow point in the same direction when the compass is correctly oriented.

But the compass is not now pointing to true north. It is only pointing to the magnetic north, and you must make a correction to allow for this variation. Variation, or *declination* as it is called, is the number of degrees that the compass needle points east or west of true north. In eastern United States the compass points west of true north, and in the west it points east of true north. If you live on a line running near the east shore of Lake Michigan on down along the east coast of Florida you are very fortunate. Your compass will point true north. Everywhere else you will have to correct it. But it is easy to make this correction.

After doing steps one and two, look at the degrees marked on the outside of the compass housing. Read the degree beside the direction-of-travel arrow on the plastic base. Let us suppose it is 64°. Your Pathfinder unit is hiking around a mountain in New England where the declination is 16° west. To correct for this west declination, add the 16° to the 64°, making 80°. Turn the housing so that the direction-of-travel arrow on the base plate is opposite 80°.

If you had been hiking near Los Angeles, where the declination

44

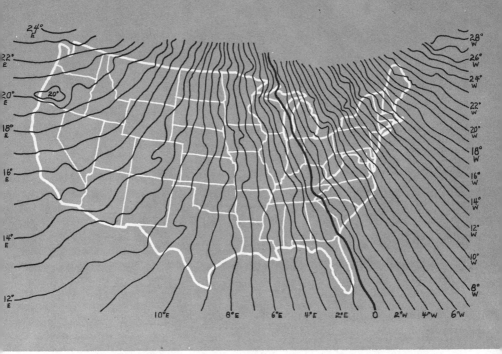

This is a **DECLINATION MAP. If you live in North America, find your home and its declination. Then write here, I must (add, subtract)** _____ °.

is 16° east, you would have subtracted 16° from the 64° leaving an adjusted azimuth of 48°.

A simple rule for remembering how to compensate for declination is: *Add west—Subtract east.* The corrected heading gives you your true direction. Now go on to step 3.

Suppose you are on a cross-country map-and-compass race. You find a card under a stone and it says, "Go 215 yards on azimuth 105° and look for directions on oak tree." What do you do? You turn the compass housing until 105° lines up with the shaft of the direction-of-travel arrow on the base plate. Then you correct for declination and proceed as in step 3. But hurry. The Pathfinders behind may be catching up!

How to Take an Azimuth Reading

You are out on the trail and see a lake off to one side. You decide to go off through the woods to it, but you want to be sure you get back to the main trail. Now your compass is all important.

Point the direction-of-travel arrow on the plastic base toward the point you want to reach. Orient the compass by turning the

USE THE SUN AND A WATCH to find true north. Hold the watch flat in your hand. Place a straw upright along the edge of the watch. Turn the watch until the shadow of the straw falls directly along the hour hand, that is, until the hour hand points directly at the sun. Between the hours of 6 A.M. and 6 P.M. (standard time, by day) a line from the center of the watch, dividing the SMALL angle between the hour hand and the figure 12 will point true south. Between 6 P.M. and 6 A.M. (standard time, at night) divide the LARGE angle to find south. (If you have summer time on your watch, turn it back one hour before figuring.) North is opposite south. Pictures show, left, watch at 9 A.M.; right, at 5 A.M.

housing until the arrow inside the housing is pointing in the same direction as the magnetic needle. Read the azimuth on the housing at the center line of the direction-of-travel arrow and remember it. Write it down. Take a sighting on your destination and go to it. Return by adding 180 degrees to your azimuth reading. If after reaching the lake you walk around it a bit, *return to the exact spot* where you first reached the lake and walk back toward the trail *from there*. Otherwise, you may miss the trail completely.

Find North Without a Compass

You may lose your compass, or damage it by dropping it. How can you find directions now? The sun, the moon, and the stars will tell you.

During the day use the sun and a watch to find true north. Study the pictures at the top of this page.

At night the North or Pole Star is always to your north, and you can find it by sighting along the pointers of the Big Dipper. The pointer stars are the two stars on the outer edge of the bucket of the Dipper. They are *not* in the handle. The Pole Star is about 1° away from true north.

46

RACE TO THE POLES! Be like the early explorers and see who can reach the poles first. Have a counselor mark an X at least a mile away on the map. This is the "North Pole." Each unit or two-man team gets a marked map, and at a signal the race is on. When a team thinks they have reached the pole, they plant their flag. The team that reaches the pole first, or the one closest to it when the time runs out, is the winner.

HOW MANY OF THESE CAN YOU DO?

Check each one when you finish it.

- ☐ 1. Using a watch, lay out eight directions, then check with a compass.
- ☐ 2. Make a compass by stroking a needle (in one direction only) with a magnet and floating the needle on a bit of wood or paper in a glass of water.
- ☐ 3. Go on a map-and-compass hike.
- ☐ 4. Play "Rescue Dr. Livingstone." Dr. Livingstone (a Pathfinder) is somewhere more than a mile away, within a circle marked on a map. Pathfinders set out (like Henry M. Stanley) to rescue him. Take "supplies" along, and have a feed when you find him.
- ☐ 5. Earn the MV Honor award in *Orienteering*.

INTERESTING BOOKS ON COMPASSES

From Lodestone to Gyro-Compass, Captain H. L. Hitchins (Philosophical Library)
All about how the compass was developed, and what kinds of compasses are used on ships.

mapping's fun

AMERICA might not have been discovered when it was if it hadn't been for the fact that Columbus had a faulty map. Most of the educated people of his day knew that the world was round, and many of them had a very good idea about how large it was. When Columbus said he was going to cross the Atlantic to China, these men tried to discourage him by telling him of the immense distance he would have to travel. But he wouldn't listen to them. His maps showed the world as being much smaller than their maps did, and he believed his own. So he set sail—and America turned out to be not very far away from where his maps said China was.

The Accurate Missionary

Map making was one of the chief reasons that kept Livingstone tramping through Africa. He wanted to persuade missionaries to come and preach to the heathen. He wanted to be able to tell them exactly where the tribes lived, and where the ground was fertile enough for mission stations. Everywhere he went he carried a compass and a sextant. Every time he camped, if the sky was clear, he would figure out his position and write it down. When he climbed a mountain he would boil water and take its temperature to find out how high the mountain was. He noted all the details, such as trees and fruits and grass and deserts.

He sent his notes to England, to the learned map makers of the Royal Geographical Society, and those distinguished men read the notes and laughed. For Livingstone said there was a river right where their map of Africa said there was a desert; his notes said there were mountains exactly where their map showed a plain. They almost threw the notes away. Then one of the scientists, more sensible than the rest, said, "We've never been to the interior of Africa ourselves, and neither has any other white man. Livingstone's the first one there. Let's check his letter more carefully." So they marked Livingstone's positions on their map, and the marks formed a definite, distinct line. The learned men were impressed. No traveler ever sent them records as good as these! This preacher was more accurate than the great explorers!

CAMP AU SABLE, the MV Summer Camp in Michigan, looks like this in an air photo. Turn back to page 48 and see how it looks on a U.S. Government topographic map. Notice the lake and how far apart the contour lines are, indicating the land around is flat. There is a closer view on page 22.

And that's the first reason why the world came to honor this missionary. He made his maps so well.

Maps Are Fun

You probably will not walk 30,000 miles through Africa, making maps as Livingstone did—though you may be a missionary someday —and America has already been discovered. Still, you'll be glad many times you know how to make a map.

A newcomer to town may ask you the way to church, the fellows back home will want to know all about the setup at summer camp, you'll want to show them where you went on the four-day pack trip. And you may be asked to map out the territory for the Ingathering campaign. Besides, map making is fun.

Maps Are Pictures

A map is a picture of the ground seen from above.

There are many different kinds of maps for many different purposes. A car driver wants an automobile map because it shows where the roads are. Soldiers want military maps because they show where bridges and forts and factories are. Firemen use public utility maps that show where all the fire hydrants are. Then there

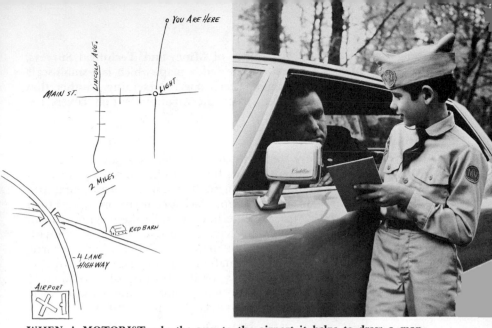

WHEN A MOTORIST asks the way to the airport it helps to draw a map.

are aerial maps and political maps and temperature maps and marine maps—each designed for its special use.

These maps are drawn to scale, with a given distance on the map representing a certain distance on the ground. One inch may represent several miles, or it may be no more than a hundred feet.

Maps for Hiking

These maps are not much good for hiking, which is the thing we are interested in at the moment. For hiking we choose a "topog" (topographic) map, made either by the United States Geological Survey or by the topographical survey of your own State or province. Topographic maps are usually drawn to one of three scales: 1:125,000, which means that one inch on the map is equal to 125,000 inches on the ground, or 1:62,500, or 1:24,000. The most popular is the 1:62,500, for one inch on the map is one mile on the ground. (There are 63,360 inches to a mile.) The more detail you need, the larger scale map you should secure.

Topographic maps for areas east of the Mississippi can be purchased from Map Distribution, U.S. Geological Survey, Washington Distribution Section, 1200 S. Eads St., Arlington, Virginia 22202. West of the Mississippi River write to the Denver Distribution Section, U.S. Geological Survey, Denver Federal Center, Building 21, Denver, Colorado 80225. In Canada write to the Survey and Map-

51

ping Branch of the Department of Mines and Technical Surveys, Ottawa, Ontario. Ask first for the index map, which is a small-scale map divided into quadrangles, each one representing another that is drawn to a larger scale. Order the quadrangle that covers the area you wish to hike in.

Using Your Map

Now that you have the map, the next step is to use it. Begin by "orienting" it. This simply means that you place the map in such a position that north on the map is actually pointing toward the north.

To do this, spread out the map, place a compass on it, and turn the map until the compass needle lines up with the magnetic north arrow on the map. If you do not have a compass, find the north with a watch and the sun, and turn the map until the north arrow corresponds. The top of the map is usually north if there is no arrow.

If you are in familiar territory, or if you can positively identify a road or other landmark on the map, you can orient the map by simply placing it in position to match the surroundings.

A Map Tells a Story

Part of the fun in mapping is knowing how the map tells its story. This is done in part by symbols that represent certain details. They are known as conventional signs, and on the topographic map they are usually printed in three or more colors.

The works of man, such as cities, towns, roads, bridges, railroads, names, boundary lines, et cetera, are indicated in black. Blue indicates water—rivers, lakes, swamps, springs. Contour lines for hills and valleys are in brown. On some maps, woodland areas are in green, and main highways in red. These conventional signs form a picture language that indicates landscape features. They are easy to learn.

Some of the main signs are shown on the opposite page.

Contour Lines

Contour lines are lines that show elevation above sea level. Looking at them, you can picture hills, mountains, valleys, and canyons. Each line represents a given height above sea level, and the difference in height between lines is indicated on the map. It may be 10 feet, 20 feet, 100 feet, depending on the scale. These lines are a very valuable aid when hiking cross country. Where the

CONVENTIONAL SIGNS are an easy way to put a great deal of useful information onto a map so the next person who uses your map can tell where roads, bridges, buildings, and other important objects are located.

Good Motor Road

Poor Motor Road

Pack Trail

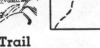
Communication and Power

Spring

Ford (Wading Place)

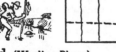
Foot Bridge

Bridge

Lock (Point upstream)

Lake

Railroad — Any kind

Railroad — On fill

 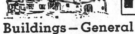
Railroad — In cut

 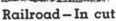
Buildings — General

Schoolhouse

Church

Cemetery

Town

Windmill

Quarry — Mine

Woods — Broad leaves

Woods — Pines, etc.

Grassland

Marsh

Corn and Cultivated Land

Palm and Palmetto

Sand and Sand Dunes

Hill (Shown in hachures)

Fences. (Wire-Stone)

Hedges

To show how **CONTOUR LINES** work, make a model mountain by spreading plaster of Paris over crumpled newspaper. Mark it every half inch from base to peak. Set it in a dish and pour water to the first mark. Carefully draw around at the water line, then add water to the next mark and draw another line. Finally, look straight down and you will see contour lines for every half inch of elevation just as they appear on a map.

lines are far apart you know the ground is flat or only gently sloping. But when the lines are close together there is a hill or cliff where hiking might be very difficult if not impossible.

MAKE A MAP

A traveler asks you the way to the city airport. You tell him to go half a mile till he reaches town, and turn right at the first light, then go three blocks and turn left, and continue two miles to the red barn and turn—but already you see a blank and bewildered look on the traveler's face. "Just a minute," you say. "Let me draw you a map."

You pull out a piece of paper and the stub of a pencil and with a few swift strokes you've made a map that shows the important landmarks on the way to the airport. The traveler takes it gratefully and is soon on his plane. The map was good enough to get him there, yet you would be the first to admit that it was crude.

A good map must be accurate. With a few simple tools and a bit of know-how, it isn't hard to make one that's almost professional.

54

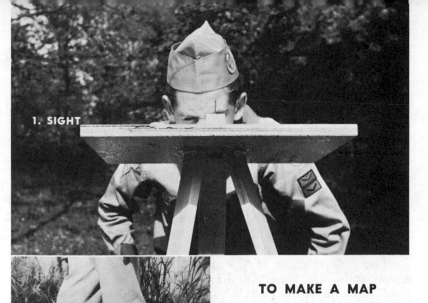

1. SIGHT

2. STEP

TO MAKE A MAP

Fasten paper to table and stick in a pin to mark where you are standing. Place alidade against it and SIGHT to a landmark ahead. Draw line along alidade. STEP off distance to landmark; figure the scale distance and put another pin. Set up table carefully and backsight, then sight ahead to next landmark. Finally, go around boundaries, SKETCH in details. Your map now looks like this:

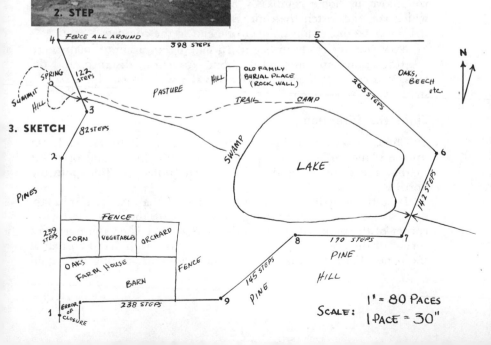

3. SKETCH

FENCE ALL AROUND
398 STEPS
SPRING
122 STEPS
Summit HILL
PASTURE
HILL
OLD FAMILY BURIAL PLACE (ROCK WALL)
OAKS, BEECH etc.
265 STEPS
TRAIL — — CAMP
82 STEPS
SWAMP
LAKE
PINES
142 STEPS
FENCE
239 STEPS
CORN VEGETABLES ORCHARD
OAKS
FARM HOUSE
BARN
FENCE
PINE HILL
190 STEPS
145 STEPS
PINE
ERROR OF CLOSURE
238 STEPS
PINE

N

SCALE: 1" = 80 PACES
1 PACE = 30"

Tools You Will Need

The tools you need can be made or bought very easily. Here they are: a plane table, a sight ruler (called an alidade), a pencil, paper, thumbtacks, a couple of pins, and two good human legs to stride off distances. A compass and two small levels are helpful if you want to be very accurate.

The *plane table* may be made from a piece of three-fourths inch plywood 18 inches square, with three legs 4 feet long, attached with brass hinges near the middle underneath. (Brass does not affect the compass.) If you have a camera tripod made of wood or other nonmagnetic material, you can fasten the plywood top to it. Screw onto the table (with brass screws) two small levels, at right angles, for making the table level every time you use it.

The sight ruler, or *alidade,* is a piece of one-inch lumber cut square and a foot long, with a ruler glued to one side. Hammer a small finishing nail near each end for sights. If you are working in hilly country, make the sights out of metal cut from a tin can. Cut a point on one piece and a notch in the other. These pointers can be bent and will save considerable time when you're sighting up or down hill.

To use these tools, fasten a piece of drawing paper to the plane table with Scotch tape or thumbtacks. Draw a straight line along one edge of the table and put an arrow at the far end, pointing north. Fasten a compass over this line for orienting the table every time you move it. Some compasses have a hole in the base through which you can fasten the compass with a screw. Otherwise screw a strip of brass or aluminum over one end of the compass.

Now you are ready to begin. In making an accurate map there are three points to be careful about—direction, distance, and details. You can call them the *three D's* if you like—or the *three S's,* sight, step, and sketch.

Sight the Direction

Choose a starting point for your map and call it Station 1. Set up the plane table, make it level in both directions, and orient it so that the compass needle lies directly along the line pointing north.

If Station 1 is in the southwest corner of the area you are mapping, be sure to start drawing your map in the lower left-hand corner of the paper. And, of course, if Station 1 is on the northeast corner of the area, start the map in the upper right-hand corner of the paper. Place a pin in the plane table at your starting point and

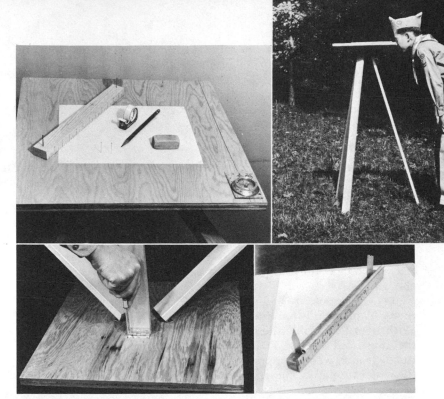

MAP-MAKING TOOLS. Make a plane table from three-quarter-inch plywood or one-inch wood eighteen inches square. Fasten four-foot legs to the bottom with brass hinges and screws. For the alidade, cut wood a foot long, put finish nails in each end. In hilly country use metal from a tin can instead of nails, cut a point on one sight, a notch in the other. On rough ground extendable legs are a help. Cut them three feet long; drill holes every two inches. Fasten three-quarter-inch dowels with pipe clamps. A nail in the holes keeps legs the right length.

then place the alidade on the table, with one edge against this pin.

Pick out the first sighting point (a sharp bend in the road, a large tree, a fence corner, et cetera) and sight over the nails, changing the direction of the alidade until the nails line up with the sighting point. Draw a line along the edge of the alidade. The line may be any length.

Step Off the Distance

Put all the loose things in your pocket, fold up the tripod, and step off the distance from Station 1 to the sighting point. Take a normal walking step and write the distance down in steps. You can convert steps to feet when the map is finished by working out a suitable scale for your particular map.

For right now use a scale such as one inch to 40 steps. (If your step is 30 inches, then 40 steps is 1,200 inches, or 100 feet.) If this scale is too large for your paper, use one inch to 80 steps or whatever else will fit.

Let us suppose it is 80 steps from Station 1 to the first sighting point. Your scale is one inch to 40 steps, so 80 steps is two inches. With the ruler or the side of the alidade measure two inches along the line from Station 1, and make a mark with the pencil. On rough ground where stepping off the distance is not accurate enough, the distance may be measured with a steel tape, a rope, or a light chain.

Set up the plane table at the sighting point and call it Station 2. Level the table both ways and turn it until the compass needle points along the north-south checking line. Then place the alidade alongside the line you drew from Station 1 and backsight through it to Station 1 as an added check for accuracy. The correct orientation of the plane table is most important if an accurate map is to be made, so it must be done carefully.

Stick in a pin at the pencil mark that represents Station 2, and sight through the alidade to get the direction to the next sighting point. Do everything just as you did at Station 1 and continue like this all around the edge of the area. Whenever possible, take long sights, as this saves much time and is more accurate.

Traverse and Error

When you are finished, the outline of your map is made up of the straight lines or *rays* that you have drawn on the plane table and is called a *traverse*. If you end at the starting point, it is a *closed traverse;* otherwise, it is an *open traverse*.

In an open traverse there is no means of checking for accuracy,

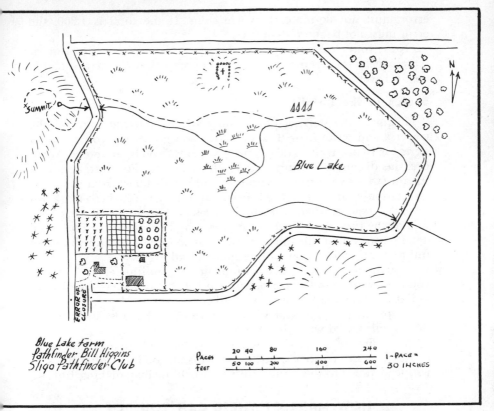

Blue Lake Farm
Pathfinder Bill Higgins
Sligo Pathfinder Club

| Paces | 20 | 40 | 80 | 160 | 240 | 1 - PACE = |
| Feet | 50 | 100 | 200 | 400 | 600 | 30 INCHES |

YOUR FINISHED MAP will look like this. Bill, the Pathfinder who made it, took a fresh piece of paper when he got home and drew up this professional-looking sketch from notes he had made in the field, and which you can examine on page 67. Notice how he showed the error of closure. Then he signed his name and wrote the date and club name.

but for a closed traverse, there is. In drawing a closed traverse you plan to end up at the starting point. If this doesn't happen on your map, don't be alarmed, for it would take extreme accuracy and complicated instruments to be so successful. Leave the starting point and the finishing point the way they come out on the map and write in the gap, "error of closure."

If this error of closure is more than 5 per cent you will have to go over the traverse again and check for mistakes. Is the direction from one station to another wrong? Is the distance between all the stations exactly right? By 5 per cent error is meant 5 per cent of the total steps around the traverse. If the number of steps is 100, the error must not be more than five steps. If the total is 1,000, the error must not be more than fifty.

Now your map outline is complete. Next comes the fun of sketching in the details, of making the map show a picture of the area it covers.

Sketch in the Details

Begin at the starting point and walk around the route of the traverse and write in with a pencil as you go all the conventional signs for roads, trails, grass, fences, streams, woods, et cetera. Measure the distance to things along the traverse. For instance, if a stream crosses your traverse line step off the distance from the nearest station that you sighted from, and make a pencil mark on the map exactly where the stream crosses. For anything on either side of the traverse line, the distances may be estimated. The more details you put in, the more useful your map will be and the more fun and satisfaction you will get out of making it.

You do not need to make contour lines to indicate elevations, but you may want to indicate a prominent hill by *hachures*—small lines radiating from the top of the hill like sun rays.

Letter in the names of streams, forests, and roads, show which side is north, and write down the scale.

Your first really professional map is finished. It may not be as accurate as Livingstone's, but even if it's as good as Columbus's, it will lead you into the wonderful new world of map-making fun.

HOW MANY OF THESE CAN YOU DO?

Check each one when you finish it.

☐ 1. Sketch a map of campsite, school ground, or a farm, using a compass and pacing.

☐ 2. Take a hike, then draw a map to show where you have been.

☐ 3. Divide a city map into territories suitable for the units of your club to use for Ingathering or for collecting food at Halloween.

☐ 4. Earn the MV Honor award in *Orienteering*.

INTERESTING BOOK ON MAPS

Down to Earth: Mapping for Everybody, David Greenhood (Holiday House)

The second part of this book discusses several ways to make maps.

Play **ORIENTEERING.** Have the girls set up a course with five or six stations like this. The stations are marked on maps that are given to the boys. Boys leave by twos five minutes apart. Girls write down the times when boys reach the stations. The two boys finishing the complete course in the shortest time win. On another day, boys change with girls.

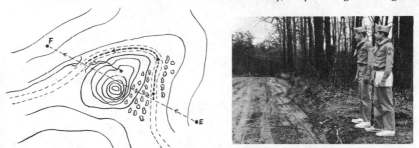

Draw a line on your map from station to station. When it crosses a road, it may be quicker to run on road than cross and go uphill through woods.

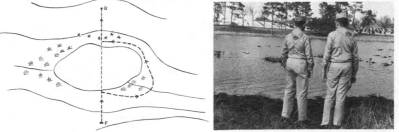

At the edge of a lake or swamp, pick out a landmark like a tall tree on the far edge and run quickly around to it, then continue on your course.

61

how high? how wide?

IN THE cold gray light of the Arctic dawn on the morning of May 24, 1941, the German battleship *Bismark* opened fire on the British battle cruiser *Hood* at a distance of fourteen miles—and sank the *Hood* with the first shot! Someone really must have known how to measure distances!

We hope you will never direct the guns of a battleship against an enemy vessel. But someday you may want to cut down a tree, and you will wonder how much space to allow for it to fall. You may have to replace the rope on a flagpole, and you will wonder how long a rope to buy. You may have to build a bridge, and wonder how wide the river is.

For these and many other reasons you will want to know how to measure heights and distances.

Measure Yourself

First of all, you will need some basic measuring rule. Nowadays we use inches, feet, and yards, based on a very precise measurement of the wave length of light. But it was not always so.

In Germany during the sixteenth century the lawful way to determine the length of a foot was to stand in front of a church on a Sunday morning and stop sixteen men, one after another, as they came out from the service. The men were lined up with each man's left toes touching the next man's left heel. The total distance of the sixteen left feet was called a *rood*. A rood divided by sixteen was the standard *foot*.

During the reign of Edward II in England, around the year 1300, the official inch was the length of "three grains of barley, dry and round, placed end to end lengthwise." Other measurements were based on the width of the king's thumb, or the distance from his nose to the tip of his fingers. Of course, when a new king came along, all the measurements had to be changed.

We smile at these methods—they were very inaccurate. But still, when you are out on a hike you probably won't have a ruler or tape measure with you. The length of your own foot or the distance you go at each step may prove very valuable for measuring.

You probably won't have a yard-stick when you want to measure something, but if you know how long your arms are or how wide are your fingers, you will be able to measure it without any trouble.

So fill in the following table and memorize it:

My height is _____ feet _____ inches.

The height of my eyes above the ground is _____ feet _____ inches.

My reach (on tiptoe, arms stretched up, to tip of middle finger) is _____ feet _____ inches.

My spread (finger tip to finger tip, arms wide) is _____ feet _____ inches.

From my nose to the tip of my middle finger is _____ feet _____ inches.

From my elbow to my wrist is _____ inches.

My span (from thumb tip to tip of little finger) is _____ inches.

The length of my foot is _____ inches.

The length of my shoe is _____ inches.

The length of my pace is _____ feet _____ inches.

An inch on me is _____. (It may be the width of your thumb or perhaps the length of one of your knuckles.)

A foot on me is _____. (It may be from your elbow to the bottom of your thumb.)

A yard on me is _____. (It may be from your waist down, or from nose to finger tip.)

In estimating distances the most important measurements to know are your height, the height of your eyes above the ground, and the length of your pace. Learn these first. You can always convert them into feet and inches.

Measuring by the JUMPING THUMB (left) and FALLING TREE methods.

HOW HIGH?

There are several ways to measure the height of a tree or flag-pole or building.

Jumping Thumb

Measure the height of a Pathfinder. Have him stand against the bottom of the tree you want to measure. Back off a convenient distance and hold a stick upright at arm's length. Sight so that the end of the stick seems to touch the Pathfinder's head. Put your thumb where his feet come. Holding your thumb tight against the stick, jump your thumb up to your buddy's head. Notice where the tip of the stick comes on the tree now, and holding the stick firmly, jump your thumb up again to this point. Find out how many times you can measure off your friend's height on the tree. Multiply this number by your friend's height and you have the height of the tree.

Falling Tree

Hold a stick out at arm's length and stand back far enough so you can sight the entire tree on the stick, the top of the stick at the top of the tree and your thumb at the bottom of the tree. Holding your thumb in line with the bottom of the tree, tip the stick over sideways as if the tree were falling down. Have a friend stand out from the tree in line with the end of the stick. The distance from your friend to the foot of the tree is the height of the tree.

MIRROR ON THE GROUND

Place a mirror FLAT on the ground between you and the tree. Stand back from it the distance of the height of your eyes. Look in the mirror for the reflection of the top of the tree. You may have to move yourself and the mirror several times before you find the right positions. The distance from the mirror to the tree is the height of the tree. Tip: Tie this mirror to ankle with string so mirror is always the correct distance—height of your eyes—in front of you.

Three Tops in a Line

Cut a stick the exact length of the height of your eyes above the ground. Lie flat on the grass with your feet pointing toward the tree. Ask a friend to hold the stick upright against your feet. Sight through the top of the stick to the top of the tree. You may have to move nearer to the tree or farther from it. (Always keep the stick against the bottom of your feet.) When the three tops line up—the top of you, the top of the stick, and the top of the tree—step off the distance from your eyes to the tree. This is the tree's height.

Pinhole Camera

You will need a bright and sunny day for this method. Make a tiny hole in the middle of the bottom of a round oatmeal box. Start the hole with a pin, then enlarge it slightly with a sharp pencil. Over the open end of the box stretch waxed paper. You now have a pinhole camera, and you should be able to see on the waxed paper an upside-down image of anything the camera is pointed at.

Measure the length of the box and divide it by ten. Place two marks near the middle of the waxed paper this distance apart. (That is, if the box is ten inches long, put the marks one inch apart; if the box is 7½ inches long, make the marks three quarters of an inch apart.)

Cover your head with a thick cloth to keep out the light, point the camera at the tree you want to measure, then walk back and forth until the bottom and top of the tree touch your marks. Pace off the distance from where you are standing to the tree and divide by ten. This is the height of the tree.

Have someone hold a stick at your feet for measuring by THREE TOPS IN A LINE.

Use an empty, round cereal box and a blanket for the PINHOLE CAMERA method.

Use a stick you know the length of when estimating the height by COMPARING SHADOWS. Measure the stick's shadow, divide into the tree's shadow, multiply by the length of the stick.

Eleven and One

This method is based on the fact that the number of inches in a foot is twelve—*eleven and one*.

Get a stick about five or six feet long and a friend to hold it. Count off eleven units from the bottom of the tree. A unit may be a foot or a yard or a pace, or it may be two paces or three, whatever happens to be convenient. The important thing is to have eleven units all the same length. Count off the eleven and ask your friend to hold the stick upright where the eleven units end. Then count off one more unit and bend down with your eyes near the ground at this point. (Notice that your eyes are now twelve units from the tree.) Look up to the top of the tree. Ask your buddy to move his finger up and down the stick until it comes in line with the top of the tree. The number of inches from his finger to the ground is the number of *feet* from the top of the tree to the ground.

Comparing Shadows

Put a stick into the ground. Measure its height and the length of its shadow. Pace off the length of the tree's shadow. Then *divide the shadows*. (Divide the length of the stick's shadow into the length of the tree's shadow.) *Multiply by the length of the stick.* The answer is the height of the tree.

HOW DEEP?

You may come across a vertical opening to a cave when you are hiking, or you may find an old abandoned well, and wish to find out how deep it is.

Stone on a String

Tie a stone to a string and drop it down the well. When it strikes bottom or splashes in the water, mark the string, pull it up, and measure. But be careful. One man who used this method said the entrance to a certain cave was half a mile deep when really it was only 150 feet. He didn't notice when the stone reached the bottom.

Falling Stone

This is good for very deep holes or high cliffs. Drop a stone and count the number of seconds it takes to reach the bottom. Multiply the number of seconds by itself, then multiply by sixteen (seconds multiplied by seconds multiplied by 16). The answer is the depth in feet.

SALUTE. Stand on the bank and salute. Hold your hand perfectly still, mouth shut, chin on chest. Rotate the saluting hand until the lower edge of the hand lines up with a rock or other landmark straight across the water. Now hold hand and head rigid. Turn your body and look for something on this side of the river that lines up with your hand. Step off distance to this spot; it is width of river.

TWO RIGHT TRIANGLES (below). Put a stick in ground directly across from a landmark on the other side. Go any distance down river, put in stick B, and go same distance farther and place stick C. Walk back from river till stick B lines up with landmark, put in stick D. From D to C is river's width.

If the cliff slopes a little, throw the rock out level in front of you. It will fall to the ground in exactly the same length of time it would take if you let it drop straight down a vertical cliff of the same height.

HOW FAR AND WIDE?

Sometimes you will want to know the width of a river. Or you may have to measure the distance between two objects that have a building or perhaps a swamp between them, and you may be puzzled how to do it. Here's how.

Double the Middle Line

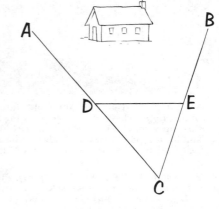

If you have to measure the distance between two objects that have a house or some other obstacle between them, don't give up. Call the two objects A and B. Walk off a convenient distance to one side and put a stick into the ground and call it C. Step off the distance from A to C, and halfway put a stick and call it D. Then step off the distance from B to C and at the halfway point put a stick and call it E. The imaginary line between the sticks D and E is the "middle line." Measure this line, double it, and you have the distance from A to B.

Stick in the Center

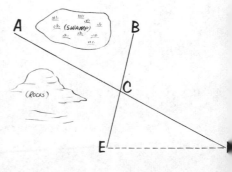

There is another easy way to measure the distance of two objects with an obstacle between them. Call the objects A and B. Walk off to one side any convenient number of steps, counting as you go. Put a stick into the ground and call it C. Keep walking an equal number of steps, put in another stick and call it D. Walk from B to C, counting your steps. After reaching C, continue in the same direction the same number of steps as B to C, then put in another stick and call it E.

Step off the distance from E to D and you have the distance between A and B.

You may have noticed that many of these methods of measuring use triangles. If you are mystified because they work out so precisely, be sure when you get into the ninth and tenth grades to take geometry and learn about the laws of similar triangles. Then you'll understand.

Speed of Sound

Without any doubt, one of the easiest methods for figuring long distances is to use the speed of sound. What we see comes to us practically instantaneously, traveling about 186,300 miles a second. What we hear comes much more slowly, just a little more than 1,100 feet a second. Watch a carpenter nailing on a roof, an axman felling a tree, a car door being slammed down the street. Count the number of seconds between the action and the sound, multiply by 1,100, and you have the distance in feet. Practice counting seconds with a clock in front of you. Say, "One Pathfinder, two Pathfinders, three Pathfinders." Five seconds equals just about a mile.

In a thunderstorm you want to know how close the lightning is striking. Count the number of seconds between a flash of lightning and the beginning of the next peal of thunder, multiply by 1,100, and you'll know.

HOW MANY OF THESE CAN YOU DO?

Check each one when you finish it.

☐ 1. Measure the height of a tree by the jumping-thumb method and check your answer by the falling-tree method.

☐ 2. Measure another tree by the mirror-on-the-ground method and check your answer with the eleven-and-one plan.

☐ 3. Find an old well or a cave entrance and measure the depth by dropping a stone into it. Check results with a string.

☐ 4. Estimate the width of a river with the salute technique and check your answer with two right triangles.

☐ 5. Measure the distance between two objects that have a house between them, using the double-the-middle-line method. Check by using stick-in-the-center method.

☐ 6. Send a Pathfinder across a field and tell him to hammer on a log where you can see him. Estimate his distance by counting the time the sound takes to reach you.

codes and calls

"One if by land, and two if by sea."

THE watcher stood by his horse and gazed impatiently at the steeple tower. The signal should be there any minute now. Ah, there it was! Two lamps.

He leaped onto his steed and galloped into the darkness—and into everlasting fame by awakening the colonists with his thrilling shout, "The British are coming by sea!"

Some Pathfinders had planned a three-day outpost camp. The supply party, with two heavily laden mules, left at daybreak. The rest of the Pathfinders were to leave base camp as soon as camp council was over.

Halfway up the mountain, Bill discovered that the pancake flour had been left behind. To go on without it would upset the well-planned menu; to go back would upset the schedule. Bob glanced at his watch. Camp council was on.

He climbed out onto a bluff that overlooked the council area, whipped off his shirt, and waved it. There was an answering wave from camp. Bob brought the shirt down to the left once, then over to the right three times: B. Down to the left, down to the right, then down to the left again: R—B-R-I-N-G T-H-E P-A-N-C-A-K-E F-L-O-U-R. Well-filled stomachs the next three mornings made the campout all that a Pathfinder dreams of!

Saving a nation from its enemies—saving a campout from hunger. Signaling plays an important part in the affairs of all of us. It pays to know how to do it.

Signaling is usually done by one of two methods—sound and light.

Signaling by Sound

Probably signaling by sound is the older method. Think of the drums of Africa. As someone has described them, "Shuddering down the wind come their voices. . . . Boom-tap-boom! Dumm . . . dum . . . t-rat . . . t-t-r-r-rat! Bo-o-o-om!" Can you hear them? What a sound to be wakened by, throbbing through the darkness on a campout in the Congo! Those drums are very efficient. Some, made

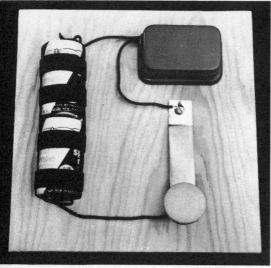

TO LEARN Morse code, make a buzzer outfit. Get a door buzzer from a hardware store; power it with two batteries. Hold them in place with elastic ribbon. Make the key from tin can metal. Then practice sending and receiving messages with your buddy. Be accurate! Go slowly to begin with. Speed will come naturally.

of hollow tree trunks, are twelve feet long and five feet wide, and can be heard for twenty miles. When Queen Victoria died and the news was cabled to West Africa, natives living hundreds of miles from the telegraph lines knew of the death even before some of the government officials did!

Signaling by Light

Light signaling is ancient too. Persian soldiers used their polished shields as heliographs to send messages by reflected sunlight.

Fires on hilltops are another historical method of signaling, and many a city today still has its Beacon Hill.

Flags have long been used for signaling, especially on ships.

Flashlights are probably the easiest instrument for signaling by light. And knowing how to signal in this way can be helpful. Jack and Jim were camped on the far side of an island in a large lake. An unexpected storm in the night drenched Jack, who had not pitched his tent carefully. He was hoarse in the morning, and quite sick by noon. Jim struck both tents by himself and loaded all the equipment into the rowboat. But it was already late, and a head wind made rowing hard. Night overtook the boys far from shore. Jim knew he had to get Jack under medical care quickly. He reached into his duffel bag and got out his flashlight. Dad knew Morse code and might be watching, worried, on the shore. Jim blinked the light several times. There was an answering flash.

A	· —	J	· — — —	S	· · ·
B	— · · ·	K	— · —	T	—
C	— · — ·	L	· — · ·	U	· · —
D	— · ·	M	— —	V	· · · —
E	·	N	— ·	W	· — —
F	· · — ·	O	— — —	X	— · · —
G	— — ·	P	· — — ·	Y	— · — —
H	· · · ·	Q	— — · —	Z	— — · ·
I	· ·	R	· — ·		

Dad *was* watching! Jim sent the message, and in minutes the powerful beam of a Coast Guard searchlight was lighting up the waves. Jim waved the flashlight in wide arcs to help the Guardsmen see him, and soon both boys were snug and warm aboard a Coast Guard cutter.

Mr. Morse's Code

The great drawback to all the ancient attempts to send messages was the lack of a suitable code. Only very limited messages could be sent, often no more than, "Now is the time to carry out the plan we talked over." But this lack was remedied in 1832 by the famous artist, Samuel F. B. Morse, when on board the ship *Sully* he invented the Morse code, a code of dots and dashes that could be adapted to nearly all the old methods of signaling, and to new ones never before thought of. Mr. Morse's code, with some changes, has been accepted around the world. So in all signaling it is wise to start by learning the International Morse Code.

Learning the Code

Learn the code by sound, *not* by memorizing the little dots and lines on a code chart. Make yourself a simple buzzer and get your buddy to do the same; then sit in different rooms and signal to each other.

Take your time. Go slowly. Learn to hear the letters. Make

SIGNALING

ATTENTION!

Before sending a message the sender attracts the receiver's attention by sending a series of A's as one letter. As soon . . .

THE MESSAGE

The sender signals the first word, ending each letter with an upright, each word with a front. He pauses after each word for the receiver to signal E, meaning he understood. If the . . .

SIGNING OFF

At the end of the message, sender waves AR as one letter and waits for the receiver to signal back R. Only . . .

WITH FLAGS

as receiver notices the signal he stands in a position where he can see the signaler easily, sends K, meaning "All is Klear for receiving."

sender makes a mistake, he stops, signals eight E's as one letter, and then repeats the last word. If receiver does not understand, he signals IMI (I Missed It), and the sender repeats.

after this is the message considered officially received. Sender now waits for a reply if one is expected.

The signaler brings the flag to the UPRIGHT POSITION at the end of each letter, makes a FRONT at the end of each word. He waves the flag in clean-cut figures-of-eight to keep it from wrapping itself around the pole.

each dah the length of three dits, pause between dits and dahs the length of a dit, and pause between letters the length of a dah. Get it right the first time. Speed will come with practice.

The following eleven letters can be learned in a few minutes:

E	dit	T	dah	A	di-dah
I	di-dit	M	dah-dah	N	dah-dit
S	di-di-dit	O	dah-dah-dah	R	di-dah-dit
H	di-di-di-dit			K	dah-di-dah

Now practice using them by sending and receiving some of these sentences:

> THE KIT IS A HIT.
> TOM IS NOT HERE.
> HE IS AT HOME.
> THE MEN ARE NEAR.
> RENT A TENT TO HIM.
> THIS TENT HAS A TEAR IN IT.

Make up sentences of your own. You will have a lot of fun sending messages with whatever letters you know. Do not try to learn all the code in one sitting. Add a few letters at a time, and before you realize it you will have learned the whole code and can send and receive with the experts.

Wigwag Signaling

For wigwagging you need two flags each two feet square. One is red with a white eight-inch square in the middle, the other is white with a red eight-inch square in the middle. Each is fastened by ties to a pole four feet long. Taller Pathfinders may want a pole up to six feet long.

78

CHOOSE THE FLAG that stands out clearer against your background. White is better in front of trees; red is usually better against the open sky.

The Morse code is used. The flag is dipped to the right for a *dit* and to the left for a *dah*. (To help you remember, notice that "dit" and "right" sound quite a lot alike.)

For the *upright position,* hold the butt end of the staff in your left hand over your belt buckle. Hold the right hand a foot above the left, with the staff in front of your nose and leaning forward slightly.

To make a *dit,* keep the left hand where it is and swing the staff down level on the right and up again. Move with a figure-of-eight motion, keeping the staff always leading the way so the flag does not tangle.

To make a *dah,* make the same motion but to the left. When *dit* and *dah* come together, make just one long figure-of-eight motion from low on one side to low on the other and up again.

For a *front,* swing the flag down in front of you.

Get the Message Through

The signaling team consists of two Pathfinders: the *signalman* and the *recorder.* In sending, the recorder dictates the message word by word to the signalman, who sends it. When receiving,

79

the signalman receives the message and dictates it to the recorder, who writes it down. When signaling over long distances where binoculars are necessary, add an *observer* as third man with the binoculars.

To establish contact, the sending team take their positions in an exposed place and choose the flag that makes the better contrast with the background. The signalman begins to send a long series of *A's*. When the receiving team notices, they take their position and the receiving signalman waves *K* (klear), meaning he and his recorder are ready to receive.

The sending recorder pronounces the first word, and the signalman sends it. He makes a complete letter, with all its dits and dahs, without stopping. But he comes to the upright position briefly at the end of each letter and makes a front at the end of each word, then stops with the flag down and watches the receiving signalman. If the receivers got the signal clearly, they wave back *E,* and the senders go ahead with the next word.

At the end of a sentence the signalman makes two fronts. At the end of the message he signals *AR* as one letter. This time he waits until the receivers have checked the message through and wave back *R,* meaning that they received the whole message clearly. Now, and only now, do the signalers leave—unless they wish a reply, in which case they had better wait.

The signaler may make a mistake. If so, he immediately drops the flag in a front, then makes eight dits and a front and waits for an answering *E.* Then he starts over on the word he was sending. If the receiver does not understand a word, he signals *IMI* as one letter, and the sender repeats the last word he sent.

In all signaling, accuracy is more important than speed. Speed will come naturally with practice.

Other Ways to Signal

Morse code can be sent with smoke, a car horn, a bugle, even a hammer on steam pipes. When on a hike sometime, get directions on where to go from a heliograph team stationed on a bluff across the river.

If your buddy lives nearby, perhaps you can signal by blinking the bedroom light. Try sending, "M-O-T-H-E-R B-R-O-U-G-H-T I-C-E C-R-E-A-M. C-O-M-E A-T O-N-C-E"—and see what kind of response you get!

Your knowledge of signaling may not change the course of world affairs, but it will change many an ordinary outing into a memorable adventure.

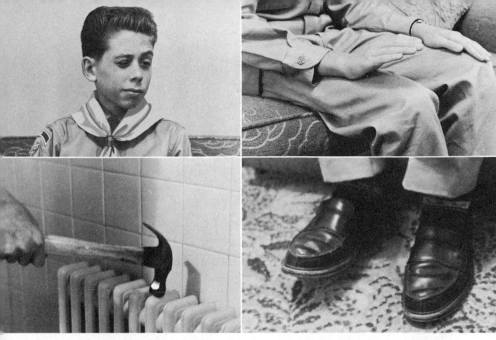

Invent a SECRET CODE for sending messages to other members of your unit. Winking right eye, wiggling right ear can be a dit; the left, a dah.

And in all the learning of signals let's not forget what Jesus said would happen in the last days. Said He, "Great signals shall there be from heaven" (Luke 21:11). No, the Bible says "signs" not "signals," but the meaning is the same. And the signals are flashing all around, announcing, "Christ is coming soon. Get ready to meet Him!" Wave the answer back to heaven, "By Thy grace, we will!"

HOW MANY OF THESE CAN YOU DO?

Check each one when you finish it.

☐ 1. Make a buzzer system for learning Morse code.

☐ 2. Go on a signaling hike, with the directions where to go signaled to you from time to time by a team on a high hill.

☐ 3. On an overnight campout divide the campers, with half camping on one side of a river, half on the other. Signal across with flashlights and fires at night, by wigwag and bugle during the day.

☐ 4. Lay a private telegraph line from your bedroom to the room of a friend your age next door.

☐ 5. Earn the MV Honor award in *Communications*.

stories in footprints

A JACK RABBIT, walking on the freshly fallen snow on the side of a hill, glanced back and saw a coyote on its trail. Immediately it began to run. Suddenly it swerved up the hill. The coyote swerved too, but it skidded on the corner and lost time. The jack rabbit dodged back. The coyote swung round again, but skidded on this corner also, and lost more time. This happened again and again.

Then a second coyote, loping along higher in the hills, saw what was going on and walked down closer. Just as the jack rabbit made one of its turns to escape the first coyote, the second one grabbed it. The first coyote came up in a few moments, and the two went off to dinner, taking the jack rabbit with them.

No human being saw these events take place, yet there is no doubt at all that they happened, for the jack rabbit and the coyotes made records of everything they did, and a man came along soon afterward and read those records.

Footprint Detectives

Olaus Murie saw the tracks of the jack rabbit and the coyotes on a hillside in Wyoming. He knew what animals had been there by the shape of their footprints. He knew the jack rabbit was running desperately fast by the long space covered by each jump. He knew that the second coyote caught the jack rabbit because where the tracks of a second coyote met the tracks of the jack rabbit there were a few drops of blood—and no more jack rabbit tracks. It was obvious that the two coyotes had gone away to share the rabbit because the two coyote tracks went off side by side, and there were no remains of the rabbit at the place where it was killed.

Life-and-death adventure stories like this are taking place in the wilds all the time. A Pathfinder who can read the footprints on the ground outside can tell what the animals have been doing, even though he never sees them, just as accurately as a schoolboy who reads a newspaper can tell what people he has never seen are doing halfway round the world.

It's easy to tell that a squirrel ate here.

HOW TO FOLLOW TRACKS

Have a Track-and-Trail Hike

One of the best ways to start learning how to follow tracks is to go on a track-and-trail hike. Half the unit start off fifteen minutes ahead of the rest, and as they go they lay a trail by making certain signs. When the fifteen minutes is up, the second half of the unit set out to catch up with the first half by following the signs. See pages 86 and 87.

In forests a trail is sometimes blazed by cutting bark off the trees, but don't you do this! It may kill the tree by letting in disease. In national parks the park rangers usually mark trails by fastening strips of colored metal to trees or by painting colored stripes on rocks. All these form permanent markers. Pathfinder trail blazers make only temporary markers, and the trackers remove them as they come to them so they won't confuse other hikers.

Follow Pathfinder Tracks

As soon as possible you'll want to follow real tracks. If there is a beach nearby you're in good fortune. But if there is no beach, clear a piece of land and rake it smooth and it will do almost as well.

Have one Pathfinder walk across the smooth surface, then study his tracks. Sketch pictures of his footprints. Carefully measure the tracks of a boy, a girl, a man, a woman.

Play the "What Did He Do?" game. Rake the ground smooth and have all the Pathfinders turn around while one of them walks across the ground—or runs, or hops, or zigzags, or limps—then have everyone turn around again and study the tracks and try to figure out what the first Pathfinder did.

All this is fun. But it is only the beginning.

Track Wild Animals

The real fun of tracking comes when you get on the trail of a wild animal, when you find out "Who went there?" and really unravel the mysteries of nature. It's something very few people can do nowadays.

Expert trackers keep five simple rules in mind. You'll be wise to practice them.

Rule one: *Study one track carefully.* Successful woodsmen consider this rule so important that they often take the time to draw a sketch of the track they want to follow.

Be sure you know what kind of animal made the track. In learning to recognize tracks, remember that there are four differ-

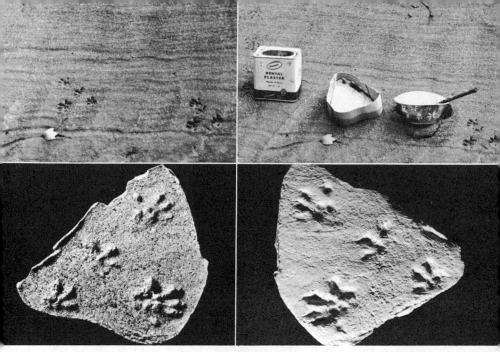

Make a **PLASTER CAST**. Here is the track of an opossum in mud on the bank of a stream the day after the stream flooded. Notice the footprints beside the leaf. A cardboard collar is put around these prints, and plaster of Paris poured on. When this is dry—about thirty minutes later—it is removed. Clean it the next day with water and a toothbrush, making the cast as in the lower left corner. If a thin layer of vaseline is spread over this cast, and more plaster of Paris applied, a print just like the original track in the mud is obtained, as you can see in the lower right.

ent ways animals walk. The *flatfoots* walk on the whole foot, and include bears, raccoons, skunks, muskrats, opossums, and you yourself. The *long hind-leggers* nearly always hop, and they bring their back feet down in front of their forefeet. In this group are squirrels, rabbits, and mice. The *toe walkers* walk only on their toes. The group includes cats and dogs, lynxes, foxes, and wolves. The ones that stalk their prey often bring the back feet down exactly where the front feet were. The *toenail walkers* actually walk on their toenails. These are the deer, cows, moose, sheep, goats, and pigs.

In studying this first track, try to figure out how old it is. If it is old, the animal that made it may be far away. Wind and rain damage tracks. If the track is sharp and clear and you know that the rain stopped at four-thirty this morning and the sun came up at five, and if you know that this animal is a day sleeper, the track must have been made between four-thirty and five. If it is now

No 1 — THE DIRECTION THE TWIG IS BENT

No 2 — THIS WAY / EARTH

No 3 — LONG DISTANCE THIS WAY

No 4 — SHORT DISTANCE THIS WAY

No 5 — FOUR MILES TO

No 6 — THIS WAY

No 7 — THIS IS THE WAY

No 8 — TURN TO THE RIGHT

No 9 — TURN TO THE LEFT

No 10 — GRASS MARKING TRAIL

No 11 — TURN TO THE RIGHT

No 12 — TURN TO THE LEFT

No 13 — (STICKS) THIS WAY

No 14 — (PEBBLES) THIS WAY

No 15 — (BRANCH) THIS WAY

Study the sketches on this page, then see
if you can tell where the photographs lead.

TRAIL SIGNS

These signs are made from whatever natural materials are present. In a field a bunch of grass may be knotted and the top bent over to point the direction. In rocky country one rock placed on a larger one means "This is the trail." If a small rock is placed on the left of these two it means "Turn left"; if the little rock is on the right, "Turn right." Small pebbles may be laid out in the form of an arrow. A straight stick may be placed with one end on the ground and the other supported in the crotch of a forked stick. In this case the upper end of the straight stick points the direction to go.

seven o'clock, the animal is no doubt snoozing somewhere close by.

No two animals ever make the same tracks. For months Ernest Thompson Seton tracked Lobo, wolf king of the Currumpaw. He hardly ever saw the wolf, but he knew practically everything it did, for he had observed that Lobo's pug mark measured five and a half inches long. No other wolf made one so large. Jim Corbett tracked a man-eating leopard in India for ten weeks without ever seeing it except for a brief glimpse once in a while in the dark. Yet he knew almost everywhere that leopard went, for he had observed that the paws of the killer's left hind foot showed the mark of a scar resulting from a bullet fired at the leopard by a soldier five years before Mr. Corbett came on the scene. No other leopard left this mark.

So rule one: *Study one track carefully!*

Rule two: *Look at the trail as a whole.* There may be several places where a footprint is missing, but by looking ahead you can see the trail standing out clearly, especially if the animal went through a field and bent the grass.

Rule three: *Use the sun.* Tracks stand out much more clearly when the sun casts a shadow along one edge. The best time to track is when the sun is low, making longer shadows. So get out early, when the tracks are fresh and the shadows long. No lying in bed for successful trackers! It would be helpful if the tracks always went straight toward the sun. Since they don't, the next best thing is to walk, if possible, on the side of the track away from the sun.

Rule four: *Imagine you are the animal you are tracking.* This helps tremendously, especially where the track is hard to follow. If you are tracking a raccoon, ask yourself, "Where would I go if I were a raccoon?" Of course, you would go along a river, turning over stones looking for crayfish. Presently you would leave the river and find a tree to climb. If you are following a squirrel and lose the tracks at the edge of a wide stretch of gravel, look beyond the gravel. Perhaps there will be an oak tree there down to your left. Twenty yards up to the right there may be a bramble thicket. Now, if you were a squirrel, most likely you would hop over to that oak tree to look for acorns. But if it's a rabbit you're following, say to yourself, "If I were a rabbit I'd head for that bramble thicket." Go first to the oak tree to look for your squirrel's tracks, or to the bramble to seek the rabbit's. Obviously, it pays to find out ahead of time all you can about the habits of the animals you want to track.

Rule five: *If you lose the trail, mark the last track and cast around.* The trail must go somewhere, and it can usually be found. Mark the last track you can see with a stick or a bright piece of

There are five rules for following footprints. Rule 1: STUDY ONE TRACK CAREFULLY. Measure it with a ruler and draw an accurate sketch of it.

Rule 2: LOOK AT THE TRACK AS A WHOLE, rather than hunting single prints. Rule 3: USE THE SUN. The sun makes footprints stand out clearly.

Rule 4: IMAGINE YOU ARE THE ANIMAL. Where would I go if I were this animal? Rule 5: If you lose track, MARK LAST PRINT AND CAST AROUND.

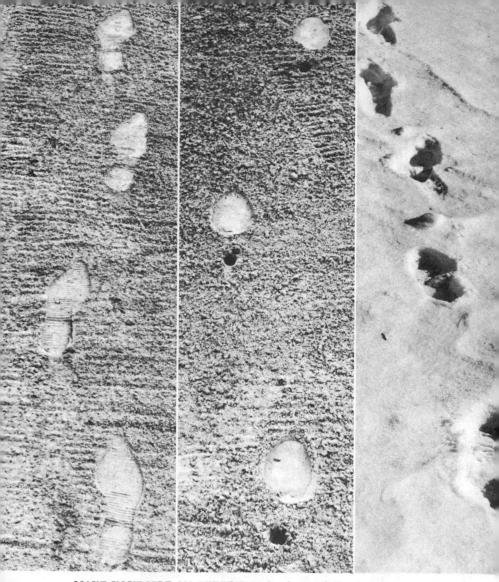

MAKE YOURSELF AN EXPERT tracker by carefully observing as many tracks as possible. Learn what to look for. The first track here was obviously made by a girl—no boy would wear shoes that shape! She was walking normally. The second track shows holes made by high heels—again obviously made by a girl, in her teens or older. But the track in the snow was made by a man. Why has his heel left a long skid mark? He was walking backward. Rake some ground, walk on it, forward, backward, carry a load. Notice how tracks differ—become an expert.

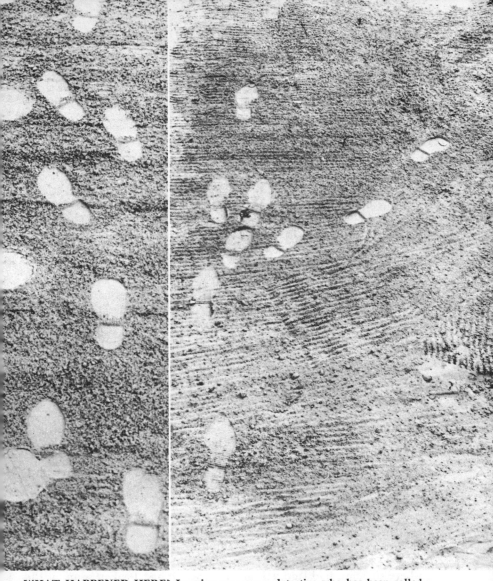

WHAT HAPPENED HERE? Imagine you are a detective who has been called in to explain these tracks. In the first photograph it is obvious that some-one has been walking; but how old? And what caused those round marks? In the second, how old were the people involved? And where did that second track come from? There is no evidence that it came up from the left.

The first picture: A child about six or seven years old (notice the size and shape of the shoe prints) was bouncing a volleyball. The second picture: A Pathfinder girl carrying a little girl piggy-back stopped and let her down.

cloth so you can find it again. Then walk around in circles, first small, then gradually larger. And look at each part of the ground from several different directions so as to get the advantage of shadows. This is a good time to ask yourself, "Where would I go if I were the animal?"

Tracking Tips

The best time to track animals is in the morning following the first warm night after a snowstorm.

Rake a piece of ground near your tent. Animals that walk across it in the night will leave clear tracks.

Practice following the tracks of your *dog* or *cat.* Their pug marks are very much like those of a wolf or lynx.

Never walk on the tracks you are trying to follow. You may need to go back and study them.

Teach yourself to *see.* The difference between an expert tracker and everyone else is largely that the tracker has trained himself to see what he looks at. Patrol Inspector Miles J. Scannell of the U.S. Government trained himself to see. Driving with a friend through the southwestern deserts, he suddenly stopped the car, walked over to a dagger plant, then turned and walked to a grove of trees—and discovered a cache of illegal liquor. The friend couldn't figure out how he knew the liquor was there. Mr. Scannell showed him what he had seen. Among the thousands of dagger plants in that desert Mr. Scannell had seen one with its tip cut off. The tip was lying on a branch, and Mr. Scannell had hiked in the direction the top pointed. Why did he suspect liquor? He knew something of the habits of the "animal" he was stalking!

Know what to look for. Skilled woodsmen look for much more than footprints. The droppings are often helpful. So is a gnawed twig, a scratch on a tree trunk, fur on a fence post, a dropped feather, the scent of a skunk, the "hill" of a mole. One of the aborigines of Australia—the most fantastic of all trackers—amazed a white hunter by following a wounded emu across fifty yards of mossy rock by blowing on the moss. The aborigine figured that where the emu had stepped on the moss he had broken some of the tiny, needlelike moss leaflets. When the aborigine blew in the right places little clouds of broken leaflets flew up. He found his emu!

Get acquainted with the *animals in your area.* Don't start off trying to learn the tracks of all the animals in the world. Most of them you'll never see anyway. Find out from an expert what are the half dozen most common animals near your home, and learn them first.

Play the **WHAT DID HE DO?** game. Pathfinders stand with their backs to a piece of ground that has been raked smooth. Another Pathfinder makes tracks on it by jumping, walking, hopping, running, going backward, et cetera. Pathfinders turn around, study the tracks, and guess what he did.

HOW MANY OF THESE CAN YOU DO?

Check each one when you finish it.

☐ 1. Go on a track-and-trail hike with your unit.

☐ 2. Play the "What Did He Do?" game.

☐ 3. Get your unit to hike half a mile along a stream some morning and figure out from the footprints "who went there" during the night.

☐ 4. If you have a dog or cat, make a plaster cast of one of his footprints.

☐ 5. Make a plaster of Paris collection of ten different animal tracks for your Pathfinder clubhouse.

INTERESTING BOOKS ON TRACKING

A Field Guide to Animal Tracks, Olaus J. Murie (Houghton Mifflin Co.)
Tracks and other "signs" and pictures of all the wild animals in North America. A must for trackers.

Animal Tracks and Hunter Signs, Ernest Thompson Seton (Doubleday & Co., Inc.)
Written by the most famous tracker of them all. Helps you read the stories the tracks tell.

Tracks and Trails, by Bill and Mary V. Hood (Nelson Doubleday, Inc.)

stalking wild animals

NOW that you are a successful tracker, having put into practice all the suggestions in the preceding chapter, you are ready for the greatest thrill known to outdoorsmen—stalking an animal till you find it, then watching what it does when it thinks there is no one around to see.

Wild animals will try to get away from you, for they are sure you are there to harm them. They protect themselves by smelling, hearing, and seeing. If you want to get close, Don't be smelled, Don't be heard, Don't be seen! Put these three simple rules into practice, and you can watch almost any animal you like for as long as you wish.

Don't Be Smelled

Smell travels on the wind. Lick your finger and hold it up. The cold side is the one from which the wind is coming. Drop dust or grass into the air and watch which way the breeze blows it. Then make sure the wind always blows from the animal to you—even if you have to make a wide circle and come at the animal from the far side. When stalking animals in the mountains in the early morning, stay above them, for the air in the valley is warmed before the air higher up, and rises.

Don't Be Heard

A snapping twig, a rolling stone, a crunching leaf, will warn the animal that you are coming. Prevent such noises by wearing shoes with soft soles. The Indians used to wear moccasins for this purpose. Bring your toe down first when walking on rocks, your heel down first on grass. Be sure your foot is firmly planted before putting your weight on it. If possible, move only when the wind rustles the leaves or grass around you. Stay near to a noisy stream when there is one, so its noise will drown yours.

Stop a sneeze by pressing a finger below your nose. Stop a cough by squeezing your throat, and by trying to think about something else.

Of course, *don't talk!*

CAMOUFLAGE yourself by tying some leaves around your head. A small piece of netting is helpful—push the twigs into the netting holes.

Don't Be Seen

Five things make you easy to see: Bright flashes of light, shadows, contrasting colors, contrast with your background, and sudden movements.

Avoid *bright flashes of light* by checking your clothes for bright buckles, watch bands, or brooches that might reflect sunlight. Remove them or cover them so they won't reflect the sun and tell the animal where you are.

Avoid letting *shadows* give you away by remembering that although you may be hidden your shadow may be in plain view. Stay close to your cover, so your shadow will blend with the shadow cast by the tree or bush you are hiding behind. Move when a cloud covers the sun and there are no shadows.

Avoid *contrasting colors* by wearing clothes that blend with the countryside. Jungle soldiers wear suits splashed with dull brown, rust, and green. Commandos on night raids used to make everything black, even their face and teeth. Russian soldiers wear white uniforms in winter. Indians got close to buffaloes by covering themselves in buffalo skins.

The boys' Pathfinder uniform makes a good start for tracking across brown fields. The girls' is better in woods. Or make a simple covering out of camouflage material from an Army surplus store. Splotch up an old pair of pajamas. Put netting on your hat and stick grass and leafy twigs into it. Be sure to cover your face. Don't let white socks betray you!

Avoid *contrast with your background* by keeping low. When the sky is your background you stand out clearly. Going over the crest of a hill, slide on your stomach. Keep yourself hidden. Take advantage of trees, shrubs, boulders. Zigzag when necessary, to

96

DO'S AND DON'TS OF STALKING. DON'T let yourself be silhouetted on the top of a hill. DO keep down low. Can you find the Pathfinder in the grass?

DON'T peer over the top of a rock. DO look around it low down. Better yet, look beneath a projection of the rock, as this Pathfinder is doing. DON'T stand up to look around a tree (below). DO keep down near the ground.

When you are close to your quarry use the THREE C'S: crouch, bending low from your hips; crawl on hands and knees; finally creep forward very carefully on your stomach.

keep out of sight. When looking around trees or boulders, keep your head low. Better yet, when possible look *between* trees or boulders that are close together.

Avoid *sudden movements*. Always move slowly and deliberately. When you are some distance from your quarry you may walk erect. As you come close, however, it's the *three C's* that count—crouch, crawl, creep. *Crouch* with body bent at the hips, eyes on quarry, glancing frequently at the ground to make sure of quiet places to put your feet. *Crawl* as you come near. When you stop, be sure your buttocks are in front of your knees so you can go down flat in one silent movement if necessary. Closer still, *creep* on your stomach, sliding your feet forward, digging in your toes, shoving yourself forward. At all times be ready to *freeze*—come to an instant and complete stop the moment your quarry lifts its head or seems to be the slightest bit nervous—and stay that way until the animal relaxes.

Attracting Animals

There is one exception to the "don't be heard or seen or smelled" rule. Sometimes you can attract an animal closer by making certain sounds or movements.

Hunters regularly lure bull moose closer by imitating the love call of the female. Eric B. Hare tells of hearing a tiger one night in Burma catch a sambar by attracting the sambar to within striking distance by often repeating the come-and-be-friends call

Play the SLEEPING SETTLER game. Pathfinders stand around "settler," who sits blindfolded on a stool with an ax under it. Pathfinders try to get the ax without wakening him. If a slight noise disturbs him, he points where he thinks it came from, and if there is a Pathfinder there, that Pathfinder goes back to the circle. The Pathfinder that gets the ax is the settler for the next game. Dry leaves on the ground make the game more difficult.

that sambars make. Tapping on the side of a canoe may bring beavers out to find what all the noise is about. Imitating the distress call of some of the animals they feed on may bring coyotes closer. And deer, being very curious, often cannot resist coming over to investigate two upside-down feet waving in the air.

Attracting animals is quite a trick and well worth studying.

HOW MANY OF THESE CAN YOU DO?

Check each one when you finish it.

☐ 1. Play "Stalk the Blind Animal." Blindfold a player (the blind animal) and let him choose one player to act as his keeper. The animal and his keeper sit in the center of a clearing strewn with dry branches and dead leaves. The other players form a circle around them, about twenty feet away. They try to stalk the blind animal, crawling up to touch him without being heard. No running is allowed. When the blind animal hears a sound he points to the spot from which he thinks it came. If he's right, the keeper motions that player back and he must go to the outer edge of the circle and try again. If no one succeeds in touching the animal before time is called, the one nearest to him is the blind animal for the next round.

☐ 2. Play the "Sleeping Settler" game.

☐ 3. Stalk a wild animal and take pictures to show how close you came.

99

sharp blades

GEORGE WASHINGTON cut down a cherry tree, or so the story goes. Abraham Lincoln was a champion rail splitter. Both boys were handy with an ax. Both became famous Presidents.

An Indian woman was exiled from her tribe in late November. She escaped into the thick of the forest with no food and little clothing—and a knife. She fared well all through the winter. With the knife she cut firewood, designed traps, skinned animals, made herself blankets and a shawl.

Knowing how to use knives and axes may not make you President or save your life, but it can be most helpful at times.

KNIVES AND AXES

There are knives and axes of many kinds to choose from. Some take their name from the locality where they were first popular. There are the Michigan ax and the Hudson Bay ax, the Yankee and Connecticut, to mention only a few.

Choosing an Ax

A Pathfinder unit should have one large ax for cutting up timber. The single-blade ax is best, with a 28-inch handle and a 2½-pound head.

Sooner or later every Pathfinder wants his own hand ax. Get one that isn't too heavy to carry on a hike. A 13½-inch handle with a 1¼-pound head is good.

Choosing a Knife

A hunting knife can be used for many things, from making kindling to kitchen duty use. Choose one with a thin blade about 4½ inches long, well tempered, and with a leather handle.

Get a pocketknife with a large blade you keep fairly dull for rough work and a small blade you keep sharp for fine work.

Keeping Them Sharp

Every good woodsman keeps his axes and knives sharp at all times. A sharp tool is safer than a dull one, because it will do

AX SAFETY. When carrying an ax, keep the head flat and the blade turned away from your body. Grip a hand ax around the head, with the blade out. On a hike always use a sheath. Pass an ax with the head down, blade turned away.

what you want it to do, whereas a dull one may bounce instead of cut, and seriously injure you.

Set up an ax beside a log and file it with an 8-inch flat mill file, working from the edge of the blade toward the back. Do this every few days when you are camping. Finish up with a round carborundum stone, working with a smooth circular motion. Carry a small carborundum in your pocket.

Sharpen a knife on a flat carborundum. Lay the blade almost flat on the stone, the back raised about an eighth of an inch, and draw it toward you, as if you were cutting into the stone.

WOOD FOR YOUR CAMP

Cutting Logs

To cut up a large log, stand on the log with feet wide apart and chop into the side. Use the large ax. Plan to make a V cut, or "kerf," as wide at the outside as the diameter of the log.

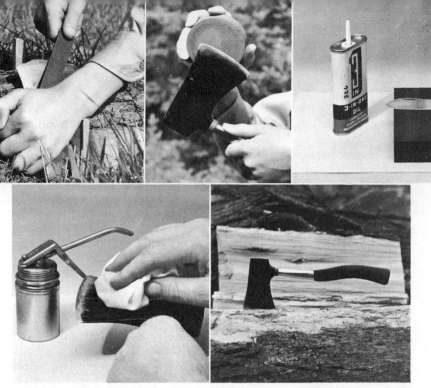

AX CARE. Sharpen an ax against a log with an 8- or 10-inch mill file. Hone with a round carborundum stone. Use a flat stone for a knife. Wipe blade with an oily rag to prevent rust. Sink the blade into a log when you rest.

Always cut at an angle of about 45°. Cutting straight in will get you nowhere. Make three cuts at the right edge of the kerf first, using the *forehand* stroke. Grip the handle firmly with the left hand. Touch the log to get the distance. Raise the ax above your right shoulder, letting the right hand slide up near the head. Keep your eye on the target! Swing the ax easily, your right hand sliding down to your left hand, and let the weight of the ax do the work.

Make the first cut near the top of the log, the second near the bottom, and the third in the middle. Then switch to the *backhand* stroke, gripping the ax with the right hand and letting the left hand slide, and make three cuts at the left edge of the kerf. Repeat this until you have cut halfway through the log, then turn around and finish the cut from the other side.

Smaller logs can be chopped from the top side and turned over when the cut has gone halfway. You'll go through a six-inch log in one minute—after you've had some practice.

Making Firewood

Split logs with the grain. Take advantage of any cracks that may be present. For difficult wood, make an opening with the ax and widen it with wedges cut from hardwood.

Cut up small branches with your hand ax. Use only one hand and always hold the handle near the end to get maximum swing. And always use a chopping block so that when you go through the wood you won't come down on the ground and wreck the blade. Hold the wood so that the point to be cut is resting firmly against the block and bring the ax down onto it. Or hold the ax against the wood high in the air, and bring both down together.

TIMBER-R-R!

Felling a Tree

When you've practiced so you can bring the blade down where you want it every time—with big chips flying clean at every stroke—you'll feel no end pleased with yourself, and you'll have a right to. Also, you'll be ready to start on a tree.

But no Pathfinder ever fells a tree without the owner's permission, and then only if it is absolutely necessary. Trees to be cut for firewood should be dead.

Use the large ax. Decide which way the tree will fall. Notice which side has the heaviest branches. Using the ax as a plumb, determine which way the tree leans. And be sure to notice how the wind is blowing. Wait till another day if there is more than a light breeze.

When you have determined which way the tree will fall, cut into the trunk on that side. The bottom face of the notch should be flat; the upper face should be at a 45° angle. When you have gone about halfway through, make a similar notch in the other side of the tree, two or three inches higher.

Soon the tree will begin to topple. Check to be sure which way it is falling, shout "Timber-r-r!" and *run to the side*. Do not run back, for the tree will probably bounce or kick back when it strikes the ground, and it could kill you.

Logging It Up

When the tree is down, cut off the branches, slicing from the bottom side toward the top. One good swing with a sharp ax will be enough for the smaller ones.

Then climb up onto the trunk and begin cutting it into logs the

FELLING A TREE

Holding the ax by the tip of the handle, **PLUMB THE TREE** to determine which way it will fall.

CLEAR GROUND ALL AROUND so ax won't strike a shrub or a branch, glance off, and hurt you.

Cut a kerf about halfway through the tree on the lower side, and another one three inches above it on the higher side. When the tree begins to fall, shout, "Timber!" **STEP TO ONE SIDE.** Then cut off branches, log up the trunk.

size you want. When you have cut a notch for the first log, do not turn around and finish the cut, but move along the tree and cut a notch for the second log. Continue like this to the end of the trunk, then turn around and work your way back, completing all the cuts as you come.

PLAY IT SAFE

Axes and knives are a doorway to a world of fun and satisfaction. But they can send a fellow from camp to hospital with permanent injuries quicker than anything else. Fortunately, good ax sense is similar to good common sense. Here are a few pointers that you might overlook.

Blades at Rest

Keep all blades masked when not in use. Keep knives and axes in their sheaths. Do not lay an ax down when you rest, but stick the blade into a log. Remove it soon and sheath it, or it may rust. Keep a pocketknife *closed* when you aren't using it.

Carry axes with the blade out, pointing away from you. Grip the handle firmly just below the head. Do not swing your arms widely. Rest a large ax on your shoulder, with the blade on its side pointing out. When hiking, keep ax and knives in a sheath.

Hand an ax to someone else vertically, with blade down, and do not let go until you are sure the other person has a firm grip.

To prevent rust, *rub the blade occasionally with an oily rag.*

Blades in Action

Before cutting, swing the ax gently around you and *make sure there is nothing in the way the ax might hit.* Especially watch for low-hanging twigs and branches.

Keep onlookers at least two ax lengths away, so they won't be hit by flying chips.

Get a firm footing. Falling with a sharp ax could put you "down for the count."

Spread feet apart and keep them out of the way. More than one foot has been cut wide open by an ax that missed the wood.

Stop when you are tired. You cannot control an ax properly when you are weary.

Be sure the head is on tight. A loose head can do more damage than a rifle bullet if it flies off. If the head is loose, it can sometimes be tightened by tapping the end of the handle. Or soak the head in water, and thus swell the wood. Or split the wood in the

106

Gradually you will want to make a collection of knives, for each kind has its own use. With small blades you can whittle many interesting objects. But DON'T use your knee for a table, like this!

eye of the ax and insert a hardwood wedge. If the handle is weak or breaks, and you have trouble removing the wood from the eye of the ax, bury the blade in moist earth and build a fire around the part of the blade that sticks up. A temporary handle can be made from straight-grained hickory, ash, or white oak. A straight handle will be quite satisfactory for a while, until you can get into town and buy a new one. Be sure to split the end in the eye and insert a hardwood wedge. Leave the wedge long for a day or two, then tap it again and cut off flush.

When using a knife, *work away from you.* After you get some practice you will be able to use other methods safely.

Don't cut on your knee! Knees are not worktables! Many a blade has cut through a piece of wood and failed to notice where the knee began.

Keep fingers out of the way. Enough said!

HOW MANY OF THESE CAN YOU DO?

Check each one when you finish it.

- [ ] 1. Cut through a six-inch log in two minutes.
- [ ] 2. With a pocketknife whittle a ball in a cage.
- [ ] 3. Fell a tree that must be cut down, and log it up.
- [ ] 4. Put on a demonstration for your club, showing the correct way to sharpen axes and knives.

tie it right

ALL day long a man had been laying brick near the top of a giant smokestack. As evening approached he began to let himself down by means of a rope that was wound through a series of pulley wheels. But because of a mistake someone had made, this thick rope gave out while he was still a great way from the ground. A crowd gathered. There was plenty of rope lying on the ground, but no one knew how to attach it to the end of a thin piece that dangled from the bricklayer's perch. Finally a boy came to see what the excitement was about and sized up the situation immediately. This was a problem that needed the sheet bend knot, and he knew the sheet bend well. A few months before, his instructor had passed him in a knot test without realizing that he didn't know the sheet bend. The boy had practiced it religiously ever since, so he could feel honest with himself. In a moment he tied the bricklayer's rope and the spare together, and a cheer went up as the stranded workman finally came the rest of the way down.

Margaret's Heart

Margaret had never been a healthy child, and now that she was eleven, the doctors gave her only three or four years to live—"unless," as one doctor said, "she were to have an operation on her heart." A date was set for the delicate surgery—Margaret's heart would actually be cut open. If you had visited the surgeon before the operation you might have seen him busy tying knots. "It's to keep me in practice," he would have explained, "so when I sew up Margaret's heart, I can tie knots in the stitches I must make, for the space is extremely small and I cannot see what I am doing." Margaret is a healthy girl today, thanks in part to the good knots the surgeon tied.

You are helping in your first evangelistic effort. Large crowds fill the huge tent night after night. Suddenly the radio crackles a warning: "High winds and heavy rains due between seven and nine tonight." That's meeting time! Will the tent withstand the gale? Must you cancel the program and send the people home?

You can make your camp surprisingly COMFORTABLE by lashing wood to make tables and fireplaces like these. Many other conveniences are possible too.

Much depends on you and the knots you tied to hold the tent to its stakes.

Knots to tie your shoes with, knots to tie your tie, knots to wrap a package! Knots are not just something to pass a Friend requirement with. Knots are for all the time. In an emergency they may save a life. They may even save a soul! So——

Know Your Knots!

Someone has estimated there are nearly three thousand different kinds of knots. Fortunately, you don't need to learn them all. Six important knots provide for practically every ordinary need: *square, bowline, two half hitches, clove hitch, sheet bend,* and the *timber hitch.* The pictures on the next few pages show how to tie them.

While you're learning the knots, go on and learn the lashings too. There are three simple variations: *square, diagonal,* and *shear.*

Since knots and lashings are for real uses, learn them by practicing on real things. For instance, square knots are often used for bandages, so practice square knots on bandages. The clove hitch is used for tying tents to stakes, so practice on stakes. This way, when you need a knot for a certain purpose, the right knot will come instantly to mind.

Open the Door to a New World

Knowing how to tie knots and lashings will open a whole new door of possibilities to you. Pitching tents on a campout, of course, will be a snap. More than that, camping will become a comfortable experience. You can make chairs and tables, coat hangers and stoves and washstands, and all sorts of other equipment that will make life outdoors more pleasant.

You can begin to plan on sailing, too. Sailors use more knots probably than any other sportsmen.

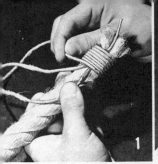 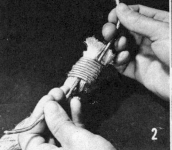 

Rope should be **WHIPPED** so it won't unravel. Cut a three-foot length of twine, place the ends side by side pointing in opposite directions on the end of the rope to be whipped. Wrap twine tightly around rope, starting a quarter inch from rope end (1). When whipping is as wide as rope is thick, pull ends of twine tight, to remove slack (2). Cut ends of twine close (3).

Best of all, you can get the thrill of pioneering. Erect towers twenty-five feet high for a bird's-eye view of the land around camp, and for signaling great distances. Make rustic shelters for real wilderness living. And build bridges across chasms and rivers that have never been bridged before.

HOW MANY OF THESE CAN YOU DO?

Check each one when you finish it.

- ☐ 1. Learn the six basic knots.
- ☐ 2. Practice till you can do them with one hand behind your back.
- ☐ 3. Build a signal tower.
- ☐ 4. Make a monkey bridge.
- ☐ 5. Make a board for your clubroom with fifteen different knots nailed on.
- ☐ 6. Make models (one inch to a foot) of a trestle bridge, a single-lock bridge, a monkey bridge, and a signal tower.
- ☐ 7. Earn the MV Honor in *Pioneering*.

INTERESTING BOOKS ABOUT KNOTS AND LASHING

Lashing, Visual Aids Service (Girl Scouts of America)
  Large pictures, for a teacher to use.

Knots and How to Tie Them, Donald A. Smith (Boy Scouts of America)
  Well-illustrated book showing many knots.

Pioneering Projects, John Thurman (C. Arthur Pearson, Ltd., London)
  Specializes in bridge building, rafts, and towers.

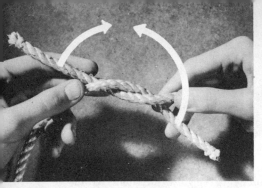 

SQUARE KNOT. Twist the lefthand rope over, behind, under the righthand rope.

BOWLINE. With a twist of the hand make a loop in standing part. Then bring

Then again twist the same end of the rope as before: over, behind, and under.

. . . the end up through the loop, behind the standing part, then down through loop.

The square knot is for tying ropes of equal thickness. Also used in first aid.

The bowline makes a knot that will not slip and that is also quite easily untied.

112

SHEET BEND. Form a bight on the heavier rope of the two, bring light rope . . .

CLOVE HITCH. Bring the end of the rope around pole, then lay it over rope.

through bight, then twist over and under the bight, then bring it in under itself.

Bring the end of the rope around the pole again and carry the end under the rope.

The sheet bend is very good for joining two ropes of different thicknesses.

The clove hitch is frequently used for pitching tents, and all lashings need it.

TWO HALF HITCHES. Pass the rope around the pole, over, under the standing

TIMBER HITCH. Pass the end of the rope around behind timber then under . .

. . . part, through the loop thus formed. Go over, under, and then through it again.

and over the standing part. Then twist it around itself two or three times

Two half hitches provide a very easy way to fasten a rope around a pole.

The timber hitch is good for dragging timber. Use it in diagonal lashing also

SQUARE LASHING. Start with a clove hitch on lower log. Twist the leftover end on standing part (1). Make three turns, going outside rope on the upper log, inside on lower one (2). Frap between the logs, finish with clove hitch.

DIAGONAL LASHING. Start with a timber hitch around both logs (1). Make several turns with the lay of the timber hitch, then do several more the other way (2). Frap three times between the logs; finish with a clove hitch.

SHEAR LASHING. Tie a clove hitch around one log (1). Make several loose turns around both of the logs, then frap with three turns around rope between the logs, tie with a clove hitch (2). The logs now "shear" like scissors.

115

swimming and boating

L ET'S go swimming!"
What is better than a cool refreshing swim on a hot summer day?

How many are going? Where are they going? Who is going? Is it a safe place? And do you know the safety rules?

By the way, how well do *you* swim? Do you really know how? or do you only splash? Can you hit the water with a good racing dive, and hold your own in the dash to the raft?

What did you say? You have an Honor in swimming! Fine! Then you must already know:

The Swimming Safety Rules

1. Swim only where there are proper lifeguards. If there are none, ask a qualified adult to go along.

2. Know your swimming area. Go only where you know the water is safe. A regular, proven swimming pier or pool is best. Never dive or swim in unexplored waters.

3. Maintain the safety water depth at all times: Nonswimmers, waist deep; beginners, shoulder deep; swimmers, over-the-head.

4. Never swim alone.

5. Follow the buddy system. Every swimmer must have a buddy, and it is best to have a buddy who swims about as well as you do. Know where your buddy is at all times. You are your buddy's keeper! When the lifeguard says, "Buddy up!" buddy up, and *fast,* or out you go!

6. Never go swimming right after a meal. Wait at least an hour and a half.

7. Never swim a long distance without someone to accompany you in a boat.

"Now! Come on in. The water's fine!"

And it is, too, when all is right! There's the whistle! In you go! Johnny hit the water first with a racing dive. He's streaking toward the raft, leading the pack! He's doing the American crawl; that's why he's out ahead. And no wonder! He earned the Advanced Swimming Honor last year at MV camp!

117

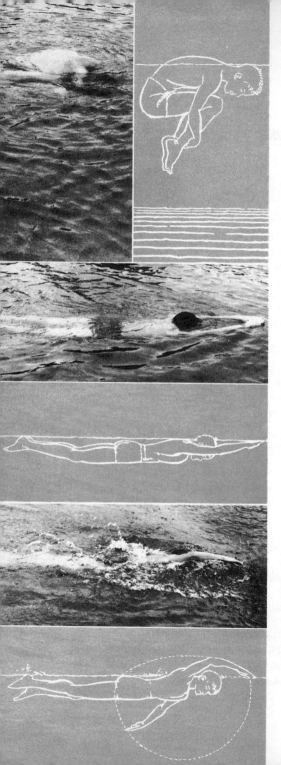

1. CONFIDENCE. First, become confident in the water, sure that the water will keep you up. Wade out into waist-deep water. Bend down, grip your ankles, drop your head on your chest, and let go. You will not sink. You will float like a ball on top of the water. To return to standing position, just let go of your ankles.

3. PLUNGE. Now you are ready for your first plunge. Stand in waist-deep water and stretch your arms out in front of you in the water, head down between them. Push off from the bottom, toward the shore, arms and legs extended, head low. Practice several times. See how far you go without swimming. You will be surprised. Always start in waist-deep water and then head for the shore.

5. ARM STROKE. Try the arm stroke first on land, perhaps on a piano stool. Extend right arm directly ahead from shoulder. Bring arm straight down to hip. Turning palm outward, raise elbow upward and carry hand straight forward again to first position. Now do the same with your left hand. Then do both hands alternately. Go into chest-deep water, face shore, plunge forward, and pull yourself toward shore using the arm stroke; keep feet idle.

THE CRAWL STROKE

2. BREATHING. Swimming-breathing is different from ordinary breathing. You breathe in through the mouth, out through the nose. In waist-deep water, put hands on your knees. Take a deep breath through your mouth, get down under the water, blow out slowly through your nose, making bubbles. Practice it.

4. KICK. Get into water deep enough for you to place your hands on the bottom with your legs straight back. Move feet slowly up and down past each other, each foot moving about twelve inches; hold your legs straight, ankles relaxed, the toes turned in. Speed up gradually. Practice till kicks are rapid and even. Go out waist-deep, plunge toward the shore, then start kicking slowly and powerfully.

6. CRAWL STROKE. Legs and arms work together this time. In chest-deep water, plunge forward, toward shore. Get the feet into action, then the arms. Use easy, slow movements of the arms. Beat legs six times for each full movement of the arms. Fit your breathing to your stroke. Turn head sideways for a quick intake of air instead of raising your head to the front. Take one breath for each full stroke. Breathe out slowly through nose with face under water.

STAY BY THE SHIP! Do not leave a swamped boat unless you KNOW you can reach shore. The picture shows a swamped boat supporting twenty-one people.

How Do You Swim?

Do you swim with sure certain strokes, or do you splash, roll, and flounder? You can learn to swim expertly if you follow instructions, stick to it, and practice! You will be surprised how easy it is.

First, you learn to hold your face under water, then how to breathe out under water. Next comes the prone float and the jellyfish float—and all of a sudden you're well on your way to learning almost any stroke!

The *crawl* is the easiest stroke to learn. It is also the fastest.

The *trudgen* is also a speed stroke, though not so fast as the crawl. It is easy to learn and is not so tiring.

The *breast stroke* and the *side stroke* are both very useful. They are quiet, less tiring, and necessary for lifesaving. They are fun to master.

The *back float* is easy unless you happen to be one of the few people who have very little body buoyancy. Even then, you can still learn. It's simply a bigger challenge! The back float is a good way to rest in deep water and helps you learn some of the back strokes. It's fun to roll over on your back, look up at the blue sky laced with clouds, and just *float*.

There are several Swimming Honors Pathfinders can earn: *Beginner's Swimming, Intermediate Swimming,* and *Advanced Swimming.* Then try for the Honor in *Junior Lifesaving,* and perhaps next year you can be an assistant lifeguard at **camp!**

Two canoers can easily be supported by a SWAMPED CANOE. If you are ever tipped out, crawl back in, lie low, and flip the water out with your hands.

Diving Is Fun

Don't you like to see a graceful dive? Swimming would not be complete unless you could do at least a few dives.

Learn the *surface dive* first. It is done in the water, and takes you under the surface whenever you choose. Next, learn the *front dive* and the *racing dive*.

Did you know that you can actually open your eyes and see under water? Try it sometime! It may feel strange at first, but it works and it won't hurt you. It adds so much to the fun!

After you have learned the surface dive, front dive, and racing dive it's just a step to the springboard and the *jackknife,* the *swan,* the *back dive,* and the *back jackknife.*

ROWING

Rowing is a skill, and to master it is a thrill! You can be justly proud if you earn the MV Honor in *Rowing.*

Rowing is not as easy as it looks. The usual basic course takes fifteen hours of practice and instruction. But it's more than worth the time and effort.

The Rowing Stroke

The complete rowing stroke contains four parts: *catch, pull, feather,* and *recovery.* The four-part stroke will become natural to you with practice. Once you have it, it will serve you well and bring you much satisfaction.

As a rower you will learn to pivot, row stern first, row a straight course, "scull," "trim" your craft, land and launch, "ship" your oars, sink and recover, besides making the agreeable discovery that a swamped boat will support several persons even though it is full of water! You will learn how to empty the water out of your rowboat, and how to hand paddle it to shore. All of these things and more you will learn in rowing, and they all spell one word—F U N!

CANOEING

Canoeing is a great sport, and it is beautiful and graceful when done by an expert. It is best to learn rowing before you learn canoeing. You *row* a boat, but you *paddle* a canoe, and of the two, canoeing is the more challenging. The Indian chose the canoe, and he was extremely skillful in his lightweight birchbark vessel. It is remarkable what can be done with a paddle and a canoe!

You can be an expert in a canoe also! Why not? Earn your MV Honor in *Canoeing* and you will be well on your way toward being a master of this exciting art.

The Canoe

A canoe is a delicate, beautiful craft, and should be given proper care. When out of the water it should always be carried. Never drag it on the ground. Never run it aground when coming in to shore. Either anchor it in the water, or lift it out of the water and place it on a rack, or rest it on the ground upside down. When launching a canoe put it into the water without dragging. If launching from a dock or pier, be sure you know the right way, or "oops"—one second you're in the canoe and the next you're in the water!

Position

Learn to paddle a canoe that does not have seats. Many canoers believe that the kneeling position is the only proper one. It is safer than sitting, for it keeps the center of gravity low, which helps prevent tipping. Use knee pads and lean back against the thwart. Other expert canoers, however, point out that kneeling on both knees for long periods is so tiring as to become dangerous. These experts recommend the use of canoes with seats. Sit comfortably in the seat, or for speed, on the front edge of the seat, with one knee on the kneeling pad and one foot flat on the floor. Learn all ways, so you'll be at home in all types of canoes.

CATCH. Lean forward, back straight, arms extended, dip blades into water.

PULL. Bring arms to chest, back upright, pulling oars through the water.

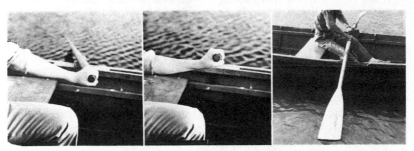

FEATHER. Turn knuckles back, twisting oars flat to reduce wind resistance.

RECOVERY. Lean forward, back straight, arms out, oars above the water.

When **LAUNCHING** your canoe, carry it into the water with a Pathfinder on each side holding it.

ENTER a canoe carefully, holding onto the thwarts. Put your first foot beyond the center line.

Paddling

In rowing there are two oars fixed into position with oarlocks. In canoeing, however, *you* are the oarlocks, and you use one paddle, not two oars.

There are more than twenty different paddling strokes, and they are fun to learn, every one of them! Each stroke has a specific purpose, and a good canoeist will blend several strokes into one as the need arises. A canoe responds very quickly to the different strokes.

Learn to master the canoe! You and practice can do it! Learn to paddle first with a partner, then learn solo paddling—paddling alone. When you can paddle a canoe alone, on either side, and send it any way you wish, wind or no wind, *you can paddle a canoe!* Congratulations!

Trim

Trim is adjusting weight and balance in your canoe with the wind and the passengers in mind. It is just one of the many fascinating features in canoeing.

With twenty paddles and more, canoes like these really speed across the waves!

CUP END of paddle in one hand, dip blade two thirds into water, and pull back close to the canoe.

WHEN ALONE at back, make J-stroke by turning paddle like the letter J; keeps canoe on course.

FEATHER PADDLE on return stroke by dropping the handle and twisting blade flat to cut down the resistance of the wind.

PULL CANOE toward the dock by reaching out, dipping paddle into the water, then pulling the paddle blade toward the canoe.

125

Someday when canoeing alone try the RUT-STRAM STROKE instead of the J-stroke. Turn blade at an angle to canoe and pull it straight back. The secret of success is to find the right angle. This stroke is much faster than the regular J-stroke, and you will not zigzag as before.

Rescue Skills

What would you do if your canoe turned over in the middle of a five-mile lake? What would you do if you lost your paddle a mile from shore? What if your canoe should become swamped with water? These questions are excitingly answered in the MV Honor course in *Canoeing!*

SAILING

"Land ho!" is what Columbus said.

"Sail ho!" must be what the Indians said.

Sailing was new to the Indians when Columbus discovered America, but it had been a science for centuries before that. Empires were born on the wings of the sail. Other empires died for lack of them.

Today sailing is done mostly for pleasure and sport, not business. But the science and art and thrill and fun are still there! Especially when you can obtain a small sailboat for one or two persons and run merrily with the wind, then go merrily against the wind. But to go either way requires SKILL!

When you talk about the mast, the boom, the sail, the battens, the rudder, lee boards, or centerboard, you are talking about sailing and adventure! It is as exciting as it sounds. Let's go sailing!

126

WHEN THERE IS a breeze blowing, hoist a sail above your canoe and skim effortlessly over the waves. There is no sport that can quite compare with it!

You can't! Why not? It doesn't take a large lake. And you can use the same canoe for both canoeing and sailing. All you need is a sailing rig for your canoe and you're all set!

"Sail ho! Let's go!"

HOW MANY OF THESE CAN YOU DO?

Check each one when you finish it.

☐ 1. Play a game of follow-the-leader in the water, each player copying the strokes used by the leader.

☐ 2. Examine a likely looking swimming hole by joining hands with your friends in a line and wading into the water slowly. Check for hidden boulders and tree stumps and unseen holes. Wear sandals.

☐ 3. Rig up a sail for a canoe.

☐ 4. Get your unit to go on a fifteen-mile canoe trip, using three or four canoes.

☐ 5. Get some swimming races going—each swimmer holding an umbrella, or keeping both thumbs out of the water, or doing three laps, each lap a different stroke. Let your imagination go, and think up others.

☐ 6. Earn the MV Honor in *Sailing*.

INTERESTING BOOKS ABOUT WATER SPORTS

Swimming and Diving, American Red Cross (Blakiston Co., Philadelphia)
How to swim and dive, illustrated with many pictures.

Way of the Wilderness, Calvin Rutstrum (Burgess Publishing Co., Minneapolis)
An excellent chapter on canoeing.

warm fires

TRY to imagine camping without a fire.

Impossible, isn't it? Like swimming without water.

Then let's get a fire started.

But hold on! What are we going to use for fuel? Right here's where the pre-Pathfinder shows how much he needs to learn. He rushes around starry-eyed, gathering everything he sees that looks like wood—green or dry, sound or rotten. He doesn't care, he scarcely knows the difference.

But you don't run a high-compression automobile engine on kerosene, and you can't build a good campfire out of just anything that's lying about. A Pathfinder with experience chooses his firewood with the same care that a rocketeer fuels up for a shoot at the moon.

So what do the "pros" pick for their fires?

Tinder for Starting

First, they think about *tinder*. They want it dry—that is, if they can't find a fallen birch tree. If they can find that they strip off some of the bark, and they don't care how wet it is; they know it will burn anyway. They never strip bark off a living tree, of course. And if they can't find a down birch they look for dead cedar. The inner bark makes excellent tinder.

Barring these, they look for almost anything that's small and flammable and dry. Fluffy weed seeds are great, especially goldenrod. Next, they'll settle for tiny twigs the size of straw. They choose dead leaves and brown grass only as a last resort. Under the best of conditions these may give a quick flame, but they usually go out before they get the fire started. Leaves usually smolder, making a lot of smoke and nothing more.

Even after a heavy rain experienced fire builders can find dry tinder. They look under leaning trees, or they split a log and whittle fine slivers from the dry heartwood.

Wise campers who know they may be in for prolonged wet spells take trench candles with them. They roll up a sheet of newspaper before they leave home, tie string around it every two inches,

Before lighting a fire, first CLEAR THE GROUND TEN FEET AROUND.
Remove all the grass and leaves in a ten-foot circle. This is an absolute must!

cut between the strings, and dip each section into paraffin wax. Or
they cut waxed cardboard milk cartons into narrow strips and tuck
them in their duffel.

They take good care of their matches too. They use only the
wooden, strike-anywhere type, and they keep them in waterproof
holders with screw tops. They have a reserve supply painted with
nail polish or dipped in paraffin.

It doesn't take much tinder if it's the right kind. A handful or
two is sufficient.

Kindling Next

With the tinder taken care of, the experts next think of *kin-dling*. And what they want in kindling is softwood that is small and
very dry. They look high up on a softwood tree for twigs that are
dry enough to *snap*. If they won't snap, they leave them alone.

Kindling should be about the size of a pencil; some can be as
large around as your thumb, and about a foot long.

And it should be softwood. All the evergreens are soft—fir
and spruce and cedar and pine. So are some of the broadleafed
trees, especially basswood, sumac, box elder, and tulip. They are all
good for kindling, because softwoods burn quickly with a hot flame,
and that's what kindling should do.

NEVER LEAVE A FIRE UNATTENDED. Before you go, be SURE it is out. Sprinkle water on it, drown it, stir it up, and drown it again so it is OUT!

Then Comes the Firewood

Choosing the *firewood* is really what separates the experts from the beginners. The experts select their firewood with the greatest of care. They want red-hot coals that will last till the dinner's cooked, and they know they can't get that from softwood. Oh, sure, if all they want is to boil some water, they may use softwood. The hot flame will boil water quicker than anything else, and they don't care to have coals left over. And for baking in a reflector oven they use softwood too. But for a good steady cooking fire they look for hardwood always.

And hickory is what they like best. There's nothing else quite so good. It gives off the most heat and leaves the longest lasting coals.

Next after hickory comes oak. Almost any oak will do, but there is a best here too, and it's white oak. Then there are beech, white ash, sugar maple, and birch, especially white birch. All make satisfactory fires. And once you've used them you'll see why the experts pass up the ordinary stuff and pick only the best.

And be sure to split your firewood. It will burn much better split than round. In rainy weather stack it crisscross so air can get to it. Spread a tarp over it or, if you have room, take some into your tent.

131

When CUTTTING FIREWOOD always use a chopping block. Lay the stick on the block; bring the ax down on it. But the wood may split easier if you bring the ax and the stick down together. Kneeling gives you better control.

The "Song of the Firebuilders" may help you remember what it takes to make a good fire:

"Collect a pile of tinder that is very, very dry,
Then snap a lot of kindling from evergreens up high—
The smallest like a pencil, the largest like your thumb—
Then feed the flames with hardwood and hear your kettle hum."

So you've got your tinder, your kindling, and your firewood gathered. Let's get the fire going.

Lighting the Fire

Hold up a minute! Where did you say you were going to light the fire? Out there in the open away from the trees? Good! And your best buddy has already cleared an area ten feet in diameter, right down to the solid earth? Great! You say he removed the turf with the trenching shovel first, and laid it to one side so he could put it back when you're ready to leave? Tremendous! Only far-sighted campers think of that.

With the fire space now thoroughly cleared we can start the fire. Pile the tinder in the center, then place the kindling around

In a **TEPEE** fire the firewood is arranged like a wigwam around the tinder. Light it on the windward side; add more fuel on the lee side. Start a **CRISSCROSS** fire with a small tepee. Use larger logs to make a campfire.

it like a wigwam—not too close together, for a fire needs lots of air. Around the wigwam place the split firewood—first, two large pieces to make a foundation, then smaller pieces, layer on layer, till you have a cube twelve or eighteen inches on a side. Face the pile with your back to the wind, strike a match, hold it a moment cupped in your hands till the flame has caught in the wood, then place it against the tinder. In a few minutes you have a roaring, blazing masterpiece, and the cooks can move in with the food.

Fixin' for Cookin'

You may be planning to cook with aluminum foil, in which case you'll do nothing more with your fire till the wood is all turned to coals. But more about that in the chapter on cooking.

Chances are you'll want to cook your food above the fire, and you'll need something to hold up the pots.

The simplest thing is a dingle stick. Get a stout stick about an inch in diameter and five or six feet long. Knotch one end to hold the bail of the pot, support the stick a foot or two from the other end with a forked stick or a stone, and weight the far end down with a rock or bury it in the earth.

133

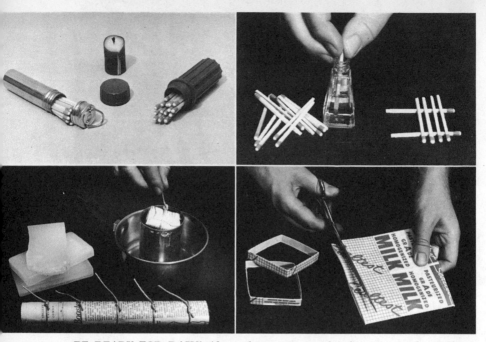

BE READY FOR RAIN! Always keep your matches in waterproof containers and carry a candle stub in your duffel. Or dip the matches in nail polish. When dry tinder is hard to find, you'll be glad for a trench candle made out of newspaper dipped in melted paraffin. Or cut milk cartons into strips.

The experts use different kinds of fire depending on what and how they wish to cook. You will find several types described on page 137.

Make cooking as comfortable as possible. Nothing can be so sore as a back that has been bent for hours over a reluctant fire. Build an "altar" and set your fire on top of it. Make a simple mound of earth, if the ground is soft, or pile up some rocks. Even wood can be used. Lash poles together to make a table and put sod on top for insulation. At all events, make your cookin' fixin's as convenient as possible.

Fires for Sitting By

Most Pathfinders feel that sitting around the campfire in the evening is the best part of camp. So make sure the fire's right for sitting by.

Again, hardwood makes the best fuel, for it keeps a pleasant fire going all through the program. If at some time extra light is

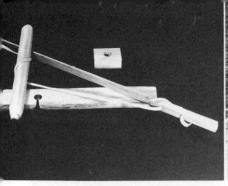

To make **FIRE BY FRICTION** you need (1) a fire board of yucca, basswood, or elm; (2) a spindle of the same wood; (3) a bow with (4) a leather shoelace; (5) a "thunderbird," which is a small piece of hardwood with a hollow for the top of the spindle; and (6) tinder of inner cedar bark. Cut a notch and a hollow in the fire board, and place some tinder on the ground. Hold the fire board on it with your left foot, with the notch and the hollow above the tinder. Put one twist of the leather thong around the spindle. Set the spindle vertically in the fire board, with the thunderbird cupped in your left hand, and the spindle pressed firmly against your left knee. Make long strokes with the bow. When a spark forms, knock it into the tinder, gather the tinder into your hands, blow the spark gently into a flame.

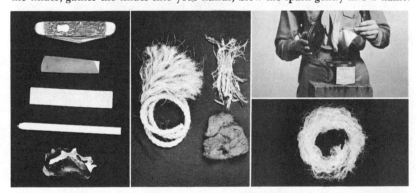

FIRE BY FLINT AND STEEL. Get flint, steel (pocketknife or file), tinder (inner cedar bark or frayed rope), and punk. Make punk by smothering a burning wick in a closed can. Place the punk in the tinder to form a nest, strike flint downward with the edge of steel. When a spark falls in nest, **BLOW.**

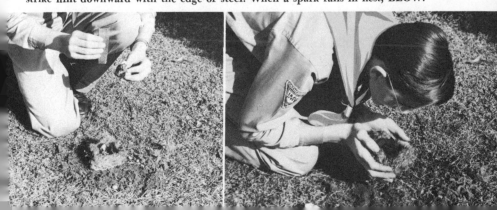

For fun, try a **BALLOON-BURSTING** contest, as at this Pathfinder fair. Put poles in the ground with a string across the top and dangle balloons from it. Light fires under the balloons, and see whose balloon bursts first.

needed, put on some softwood, especially pine and fir branches, to make a big blaze.

Where only one unit is camping, try a star fire. Make a wigwam fire with the tinder and kindling, then lay five or six long logs with their points feeding the fire and their outer ends arranged like a star. As the center points burn, push the logs into the blaze. This is especially good, too, for all-night fires in cold weather.

Putting Out the Fire

No Pathfinder ever leaves a fire without first making sure it is out. And out means OUT! More than one camper has lost his tent when a sudden breeze whipped an overlooked spark into a flame while he was hiking. And many a square mile of forest has been destroyed because a fire that was thought to be out wasn't. It is a crime to leave a fire unattended.

At all times there should be tools within easy reach for putting out the fire if it should begin to spread. Every time you leave a fire, put it out. Soak it in water, stir, and soak again. Do not pour water onto it. Put your hand into the bucket and splash the water onto the fire. When you think it is out, stir the ashes with your hand. Then splash on more water.

On your last day smash the ashes small and scatter them. Take down everything you have built around the fire. Sprinkle earth on the fire place, or replace the sod your buddy took off at the beginning. Step off a few paces and look back. Can you see where the fire was? No? Then you've cleaned up well. Stop by at the property owner's house on the way home and thank him for letting you use his land—and rest assured that he will give you permission to come again because he likes the way you left your campsite so tidy.

TYPES OF COOKING FIRES

BACKLOG FIRE. Good if you want to boil, fry, and bake at the same time. There are two fires, one is under the boiling pot on the crane against the backlog and the second is under the frying pan. The baking is done by means of the heat reflected from the frying fire.

HUNTER'S FIRE. Drive into the ground two forked sticks and set a green stick across the forks to hold up your boiling pot. Build the fire between two green logs that have been placed close enough together to support the frying pan.

BAKING FIRE. Place two green logs in a V with ends touching. Build a fire where these ends meet, and when you have a good bed of hot coals put a roof of logs over them to reflect the heat for baking. Prop your baking pan in front of the fire at an appropriate distance away; then get set to enjoy some well-baked food.

TRENCH FIRE. Use this one when the weather is hot or windy. Dig a trench twice the length of the space the pans will occupy, and in the direction the wind blows. Slope the bottom, making it shallowest on the windward end, deeper at the other. If soil is sandy, line trench with rocks.

REFLECTOR FIRE. This is good for cold weather, when you want to throw heat into a tent. It can also be used for baking in a reflector oven. Make the back wall of green logs and fill the spaces with mud so there will be no draft. You can also erect a crane at the side of the fire for boiling, or you can bring one in over the middle of the back logs.

camp cookery

COME 'n' get it!"

What's better than sitting down to a well-cooked meal at camp? Nothing. Absolutely nothing! All that fresh air and exercise do something to mealtime that's simply grand and glorious.

The cook is likely to be the most popular fellow around. Certainly he's the most indispensable.

And of course, the best cook is the best because he's planned and practiced. Here's how he plans—and some of the tricks he practices.

MAKE IT BALANCED

A good cook knows that a well-balanced meal will put pep into you, just as good balancing puts life into a baseball bat, so he balances his meals.

You can balance your menus too. Divide your food into the basic groups, then make sure you eat some food from each group every day.

God's Three Groups

God divided food into three basic groups. Adam and Eve were given two of them to eat in the Garden of Eden—fruits formed one and nuts and grains the other. After Adam and Eve were put out of the Garden, God added vegetables.

America's Seven

About 4,400 years later, the United States Government paid some food experts to study many different kinds of foods, and as a result the experts divided food into seven groups.

Here they are: Group 1: Green and yellow vegetables. Group 2: Citrus fruit, tomatoes, salad greens, berries, melons. Group 3: All other vegetables and fruits. Group 4: Milk, cottage cheese, buttermilk. Group 5: Eggs, beans, peas, lentils. Group 6: Bread and cereals. Group 7: Butter and margarine. Of course, the U.S. Government put meat and fish in there, too, but Pathfinders know that meat is not necessary in the diet.

TAKE THE TEMPERATURE. Place one hand where the food will go and count the seconds you can hold it there comfortably. One second, very hot (over 500°); 2-3, hot (400-500°); 4-5, medium (325-400°); 6-8, slow (250-325°).

When you plan the menu for your next campout put down the foods you would like to eat in a column, and beside them write the number of the basic group each one belongs to. Is there something from each of the seven? If so, go ahead and add any good food you happen to like. You'll know you're getting well-balanced meals with all the essentials.

And that is *intelligent* meal planning.

THE CHEF'S LIST

Here are some good ideas for your first campout. Later, as you get more experience, you will want to branch out and experiment.

Breakfast

Make this a large meal. You're hungry, and you'll need fuel for the day's events.

Cereals are great. For an overnight, you could take along prepared cereals, especially in individual packages. For more primitive camping you'll want to cook your own, and chances are they'll be better for you, especially if you pick oatmeal and Farina and corn meal. Just follow the easy directions on the box. Cooked cereals stick to your ribs as no others do.

Then, there are *pancakes*. Mix according to the directions on the box, making the batter about the thickness of melted ice cream. Put a little cooking oil or margarine in the pan and heat till a drop of water sizzles when dropped in. Pour in enough bat-

To **BOIL WATER** get a big blaze going with softwood. Cut notches in the stick that holds the pot so you can move the pot down closer to the fire or up farther from it and so control the temperature when boiling a camp stew.

ter to cover about two thirds of the pan, heat till there are burst bubbles all over and the edges of the pancake are slightly brown. Turn with a knife or a pancake turner if you must, but it's much more fun to flip. Just be sure the pancake is completely loose before you try to toss it!

Fruit is a natural for breakfast. An orange, apple, or banana pack easily for an overnight outing. For lighter packs take dried fruit—raisins, apricots, prunes, apples, peaches. Eat them as they come from the package, or soak them all night then cook slowly in the morning fifteen to thirty minutes, till they are tender.

A few drops of lemon juice added to the prunes, a dash of cinnamon and a lump of butter added to the apples, and sugar in all of them will improve the flavor. But for the good of your teeth, go easy on the sugar!

Fresh *milk* will be no problem if you're camping close to a store. But in remote areas it's too heavy and bulky, and too liable to sour. So take powdered milk. It's for sale in every food store. It's no problem to mix the powder with water, and it tastes just like milk. Well, almost! For variety, mix with Ovaltine.

Some mornings you'll want *eggs*. Cook them gently in boiling water for twenty minutes for hard boiled. As you climb higher in the mountains, increase the time. The temperature of boiling water goes down one degree for each thousand feet of elevation, and cooking takes longer.

Fry eggs in a hot greased pan. Break the shell and pour the

141

egg into the pan. Leave it as is for "sunny side up," otherwise stir with a knife or fork. Be sure to add salt.

For *poached* eggs begin by boiling water about an inch deep in a pan. Break an egg and pour the contents into a bowl (to be sure it's good), then pour gently into the boiling water. The egg's done when the white is white. Some cooks add salt to the water, others wait till the eggs are dished up. Serve on buttered toast.

For *scrambled* eggs break eggs into a bowl, add a few tablespoons of milk, then stir with a fork. Cook on a hot frying pan.

Lunch

Make lunch a light meal. Nobody wants to spend all morning cooking, and a heavy meal slows you down the rest of the day. Besides, if this is only an overnight hike, you'll be home for supper.

Soup's ideal, especially on cool days. Both canned and powdered take almost no time at all to prepare.

Then have some sandwiches. Thick slices of homemade wholewheat bread have the most staying power. For filling use sliced cheese, cream cheese, peanut butter, lettuce and tomato, mashed egg, a vegemeat steak, or a slice of nutmeat.

Finish with nuts and raisins, carrot sticks, celery, milk, and a couple of oatmeal or date cookies.

Supper

You'll want this to be another large meal. Eat early so the digesting will be finished before bedtime. You'll sleep better.

Potatoes are a mainstay. To *boil* them, peel, cut in quarters, put in pot, and add enough water to come up about halfway. Put on the lid, bring to a boil, then simmer. After twenty minutes, test with a fork. Potatoes can be boiled with the skin on too. They peel very easily after they're cooked.

Serve as they are, or (after peeling) add a little milk and margarine to the pot and mash with a potato masher or a fork.

Frying is quicker, but no one wants too many fried foods— too much grease. Slice the potatoes and cook them in a hot greased pan till brown. Or steam-fry them by keeping the lid on the pan while you're frying. Salt and onions improve the flavor.

To *bake* potatoes, three methods used to be popular and are handy to know. Wrap the potato in mud, then wrap the mud in paper that has been thoroughly soaked. The final product is twice the size of the original potato and is placed on the coals.

Or put the potato in a can and fill with sand, being sure that the sand completely surrounds the potato. Put on the lid to keep the

BEAN-HOLE BEANS

Bean-hole beans are a treat you will want to enjoy often. Get 1½ pounds of white navy beans, ½ pound of vegemeat, 10 tablespoons of brown sugar, an onion, and some salt. Soak beans overnight and in the morning boil until the skin cracks when you blow on it.

Early in the morning dig a hole several inches deeper and wider than the bean pot. Line it with rocks, build a crisscross fire over it, let the fire burn till red-hot coals fill the hole.

Mix all the other ingredients with the beans and then cover the pot with aluminum foil.

Dig the coals out of the hole, set the filled bean pot in it, then shovel the coals back, and cover them with earth.

Leave until suppertime, then uncover the pot and eat the beans with vast satisfaction.

143

sand in, then place on the coals. Or rake back the coals, dig a hole about three inches deep, put the potato into it, cover with earth, and replace the coals. In any case, the potato should be ready in about forty-five minutes to an hour. A much simpler method is to use aluminum foil. (See page 147.)

Most *other vegetables* should be washed, peeled if necessary, and boiled gently in salted water until tender. These are the cooking times for some common vegetables:

Carrots	25 minutes	Corn on the cob	7-10 minutes
Peas	15 minutes	Spinach	8-10 minutes
Cabbage	10 minutes	String beans	30 minutes
Cauliflower	20 minutes	Potatoes	20 minutes

Bean-hole beans are a sure-fire good meal, and easy to prepare. Soak a pound and a half of white navy beans overnight in a pot (a No. 10 can will do). Immediately after breakfast dig a hole a foot and a half wider and a foot deeper than the pot. Line it with flat stones to keep the heat in and the temperature steady. Build a crisscross fire above it of good hardwood, and when the coals have fallen into the hole, add more wood till the hole is full of glowing coals.

While the fire is burning, boil the beans till the skins crack when you blow on them. Drain off the water, but save it. Add half a pound of vegemeat that has been cut in one-inch squares, a chopped onion, ten tablespoons of brown sugar, and a teaspoon or two of salt. Pour in enough of the boiling water to cover, and put on the lid. Then take to the fire.

Remove the coals from the hole quickly with a shovel, set the pot in place, fill the hole around and above with the coals and cover everything with earth. Go off and play. Return six to eight hours later for the best beans you ever ate.

A *one-pot camp stew* is a complete dinner in itself. Get half a cup of water boiling in a pot and add one potato, one turnip, one small onion, one carrot, three sticks of celery, butter, and salt. All the vegetables are finely cut in small cubes. Keep the water simmering. After fifteen minutes add several lumps of VegeMeat, one *peeled* tomato (cut up), and a cube of Vegex. Simmer continuously for thirty or forty minutes longer, and that's all there is to it. But is it good!

Most of the cookbooks you read say you have to have meat to get enough protein. Pathfinders know better. Several Adventist food factories are now producing foods to take the place of meat. There is a tremendous variety available—and they provide more and better protein than meat does and do so without the dangerous

144

Learn to MEASURE with your fingers. Between one finger and thumb equals 1/8 teaspoon; two fingers and thumb, 1/3 teaspoon; three fingers and thumb, 1 teaspoon; and handful, 1/4 cup. But it may be different for you. Experiment!

poisons and disease-causing organisms that all meats contain. Most come in cans, and this is the best way to take them to camp.

Bread

Of course, you'll want some kind of *bread,* and you'll want it fresh. Bake it yourself. Take to camp a plastic bag about half full of prepared biscuit mix. When you want bread, pour in about a quarter cup of water and stir with a stick until a thick dough comes out with the stick. Pat this gently—with dry flour on your hands— till it is about a half inch thick, cut it with a cooky cutter or tin can, and place on the greased cooking shelf of your reflector oven. Put enough softwood on the fire so it will flame steadily for fifteen minutes. Test the biscuits by pushing a grass straw or tiny stick into them. When it comes out clean, the baking's done.

Bread on a stick is even easier. Peel the bark off a stick about three feet long and an inch thick. Dry it over the fire and grease the middle portion lightly. Mix dough, roll it between your hands till it looks like a long sausage, then twist it around the middle of the stick. Push one end of the stick into the ground so the dough is over the coals. Turn occasionally, and push the other end of the stick into the ground after a while. Test with a straw.

145

FOLD THE FOIL so as to keep in all the moisture. Use a piece that is large enough to cover the food and allow sufficient for crimping. Put the food near the center, bring the foil over it, then roll the edges on the three open sides and pinch them tightly. Place the wrapped food on glowing coals.

You can make real *stone-baked bread* too. Build your fire on a flat rock. Brush aside the coals, lay on the dough (about an inch thick), and cover with ashes, then coals. After ten minutes test with a straw, remove the bread, and eat. Dirty? Not a bit of it. Satisfying? Like no bread you ever ate!

COOKING TIPS

Practice at Home

It's wise to practice cooking at home. Make up your camp menu, then ask mother to let you feed the family for a day.

How Hot?

The stove at home has a thermometer, the oven at camp does not. Find out the temperature of your campfire by holding your hand where the food will go. Count, "One Pathfinder, two Pathfinder," et cetera, slowly, until you have to snatch your hand away to keep it from burning. If you can count up to six or eight, the fire is slow (250°-325°), four or five means medium (325°-400°), two or three means hot (400°-500°), and if you can scarcely get to one, it's very hot (over 500°).

How Much?

Chances are you won't want to bog yourself down with a great assortment of measuring devices. Use your fingers!

146

COOKING WITH FOIL

There are no pots to scrape when you have cooked in aluminum foil, and the foil is much lighter than pots and pans to carry in a pack. It comes in two weights, single and double. Use one thickness of double weight, or two thicknesses of single weight for best results.

CORN. Remove husks and silk, rub with butter, wrap, and cook for six to ten minutes, turning once.

APPLE. Cut out core, sprinkle on a little sugar, wrap with foil. Cook ten to twenty minutes, depending on the type of apple.

POTATOES take 45-60 minutes if whole, 10-15 minutes if sliced. Allow 15-20 minutes for CARROTS.

A BANANA cooked in its skin is a rare treat in eight minutes.

A WHOLE MEAL of nut meat, potato, and carrots can be cooked at one time. Cook the length of time needed for the slowest item.

Remember to turn the food over halfway through the cooking time.

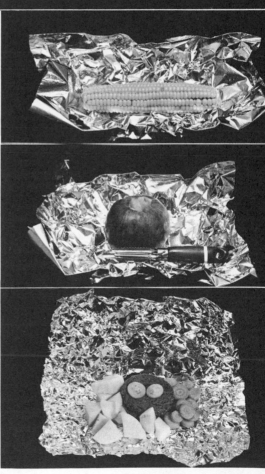

A pinch between the thumb and finger is $\frac{1}{8}$ teaspoon; between thumb and two fingers, $\frac{1}{3}$ teaspoon; a thumb and three fingers, 1 teaspoon. A fistful is a quarter cup. A gob of margarine on the end of a finger is about $\frac{1}{2}$ teaspoon.

Try these measurements. You may have to adjust them for the size of your hand. Then memorize them so they'll be right where you need them when you are far from home.

Measure Before You Go

One trick that saves no end of fuss and muss is to measure the exact quantities of food you will need before you leave and wrap them in cloth or plastic bags or tinfoil. It is an especially good idea for short trips.

By the way, stay away from paper sacks! They have a distressing habit of tearing and getting the flour mixed up with the salt and the sugar!

Cook in Aluminum Foil

Smart camp cooks nowadays use aluminum foil. Wrap the food, lay it on the coals, take it off, open up and eat. No dishes, no dish-washing, no dirty pots!

It is important to have enough coals to keep hot till the cooking is done. And the next important thing is to see that the foil is on right. All the moisture must be kept inside.

To wrap, place the food on the foil, bring one side over and crimp it tightly to the other side. Then fold the other two sides on themselves and crimp tightly.

Turn the food at least once, about halfway through the cooking time, using a stick. When the cooking is finished, rake the packages off, open, and eat.

Double-thickness foil is recommended. When using the standard weight, wrap with at least two layers.

Corn, cleaned and buttered, cooks in six to ten minutes on the cob. An apple, cored and sprinkled with sugar, tastes delicious after five to ten minutes. Good for dessert! Whole potatoes are ready to eat in forty-five minutes or a bit longer, but if sliced they are ready in ten to fifteen minutes. A banana's done in ten minutes, and carrots in less than twenty. Biscuits, wrapped loosely to allow for rising, take about eight.

And if you think bananas are a strange food to cook, that proves you've never eaten any that were!

Plan how much foil you need to take with you and wrap it around a dowel. Folding often makes holes.

Make BREAD in various ways. Carry the mixed flour in a plastic bag, open the bag, make a cuplike depression in the top, and pour in sufficient water to make the amount of dough you need, mixing it in the bag. Put dough for CAMP BREAD on the end of a stick. Bake BUNS in a reflector oven, TWIST around the middle of a stick, or ASH BREAD on a flat stone under the ashes.

STORING FOOD AT CAMP

Keeping It Cool

There are no refrigerators in the woods, but the pioneers kept their food cool, and Pathfinders can too.

If there is a stream near camp, there's no problem. Put the food that needs to be kept cool in a large pot with a strong lid. Set it firmly in the stream with a heavy rock on top to keep curious animals out. If the water is too deep, suspend the pot from an overhanging tree branch.

For large camps, make a box at home with sturdy wooden sides and lid and a wire mesh bottom. Set this in the river, and it will keep things as cool as the old-time spring box did.

If there is no stream handy, food can still be kept cool. Put water in a pan. Suspend a can below this pan and put the food into it. Wrap burlap around the whole thing, with the ends of the burlap in the water. Soon the burlap will be wet, and evaporation will keep it cool. Refill the water pan as often as necessary.

For larger camps dig a hole and line it with rocks, place the food in it, and cover with a strong lid insulated with wet burlap or a thick mat of grass or leaves.

Keeping It Safe

All the time you are in camp you are being watched. Hundreds of animals from ants, to mice, to coons, to skunks, have their eyes on you, waiting their chance to invade your camp and share your food. They'll get it, too, if you don't watch out!

At some times and places it may be safe enough merely to build a simple platform of poles high in a tree and store the food there.

But the safest way is to suspend dried or canned food by a wire or a rope from a tree branch. Throw the rope over the branch and tie the end where you can reach it, so you can raise and lower the pantry as needed. Where there are squirrels, put a tin can around the rope just above the pantry.

Canned food can fool you! Cans are not as safe as they seem! Animals have been known to carry them off, then puncture them with their teeth and eat the contents.

WASHING UP

After eating comes— right! Dishes!

Can't get away from them anywhere. And no self-respecting Pathfinder shirks his duty. But it's no crime to learn a few tricks to make the ordeal easier.

Have some detergent along and a tea towel, a metal pot scraper, and some scouring powder. (There's that planning again!) Smear soap or shaving cream all over the outside of the pots and pans before use, and they will be easier to wash.

As soon as the food is cooked and you begin to eat, fill your largest pot with water and set it on to boil. Fill the frying pan too, and put it beside the pot if the fire area is wide enough. The hot water will remove most of the grease.

By the time you are through eating, the pot will be boiling. Wipe the plate refuse into the fire, especially if greasy. Pour half the boiling water into a basin and add detergent. Keep the rest hot on the fire. Wash the cups first, then the silverware, finally the dishes. Dip everything into the boiling water if the pot is large. If not, scoop the water up with a cup and pour it over the dishes, letting the excess fall back into the pot. Lay the dishes and silverware in a clean place to dry, then store them in a net bag suspended from a tree branch where the sun can get at them.

Pots and pans should be scraped. Then pour the soapy water into them and back into the basin and rinse. Do not try to clean the outside. Leave it black until you get home. Then give the pots a real cleaning and set them away for the next trip.

Cooking will be much easier done on an ALTAR FIRE. Pile up rocks, make a big heap of earth, or lay logs on each other, as in this picture. When using wood, put a layer of earth on top so fire won't burn it. Use a crane and some stones to support your pots and pans.

On the first day of camp a hole is dug for the dishwater. Put a strainer on top made of sticks and grass. Pour the dishwater through this strainer into the hole, then put the strainer—after each meal— onto the fire. Fill the hole with earth when camp is over.

If you don't have a pot scraper, try using sand. If you don't have wash basins, dig holes and lay a waterproof cloth in them.

Well, dishwashing wasn't so bad after all! We may even be able to show mom a trick or two when we get home!

HOW MANY OF THESE CAN YOU DO?

Check each one when you finish it.

- ☐ 1. Make a cooking kit with necessary pots and pans, pot holders, and cleaning equipment.
- ☐ 2. Go on a unit cookout and prepare a one-pot camp stew.
- ☐ 3. Find "God's Three Basic Food Groups." Look up Gen. 1:29 (fruits; nuts, and grains), Gen. 3:18 (vegetables).
- ☐ 4. Cook all the meals at home for a day, using a menu good for camp.
- ☐ 5. Earn the MV Honor awards in *Baking* and *Cooking*.

INTERESTING BOOKS ABOUT CAMP COOKING

The Golden Book of Camping and Camp Crafts, Gordon Lynn (Golden Press)
   Beautifully illustrated suggestions for simple cooking.
Cooks and Chefs (Esda Sales and Service, Washington 12, D.C.)
   Tells how to earn the important award in *Cooking.*

outpost camping

WOLVES were gathering in a circle around him, but Ernest couldn't get away. That afternoon he had gone out to inspect his traps and had accidentally stepped backward into one he had just set. It now held his leg in its relentless grip, and the tool he needed to open it with lay inches beyond his reach. The wolves sat on their haunches, staring at him, licking their chops. And now one of the largest of the beasts came over and sniffed at his face . . ."

You are sitting on a gentle slope beside a mountain lake. It's been a rugged day, full of fun and action. You've hiked three miles through the woods from the nearest gravel road. You've pitched tents, swum in the lake, cooked your food over glowing coals; and now it's evening and time for campfire.

The counselor's telling a story. You gaze over the leaping flames to the lake. There's a mist rising off the water, and your eyes travel upward, up the tall trees that stand beside the lake, up to where the sky shows in patches through the branches then stretches, full of stars, across the opening above the water. The counselor pauses, and in the silence you hear the chorus of a thousand frogs at the water's edge, the gentle plip-plop of a trout rising to catch a fly, the lapping of waves along the shore.

You look closer at the firelit faces of your friends, your very best friends, gathered here close beside you in God's great outdoors, and you know this is a night you will always remember.

You are on a Pathfinder campout, and there is no experience in the world to compare with it. Pathfinders who go outpost camping once want to go and go and go again.

CHOOSING A CAMPSITE

Most people begin planning for a campout by dreaming of the place they want to go. It's a logical beginning. But perfect campsites are not easy to find. You'll want to keep your eyes open for likely spots whenever your unit is hiking. And keep your ears open when you hear people talking of places they have been. Jot down the information where you'll be able to find it quickly when you need it.

The ideal campsite checks positive on the *Six W's*—water, weather, wind, wild things, wood, and willingness. (Some people say the ideal campsite has never been found. They are probably right, but it's good to keep the Six W's in mind, and insist on as many of them as possible.)

THE SIX W's

Water

The ideal site has an abundance of pure drinking water. Of course, if your chosen spot doesn't, then you can purify the available water with Halazone tablets or drops of iodine, or by boiling. See the chapter on Hiking. And of course everyone will be glad if there is safe water for swimming.

Weather

What will the weather do to your camp? Will hot summer sun find you without shade? Will rain send streams of water under your tents, or make the ground around them swampy? Will a flash flood wash everything away? Will lightning be attracted by tall trees and electrocute you all?

The ideal location for tents is a flat place part way up a gentle slope, with gravelly, loamy, or sandy soil topped by short, coarse grass. It is bathed by the morning sun that wakens campers bright and early, but shaded from the hot sun of the afternoon that makes folks dull and lazy.

Stay away from clay soil, for it quickly becomes muddy in rain, and avoid sand, for it gets into everything. Don't camp on the top of a ridge, for there is danger of lightning, and keep far enough back from streams and gullies—especially in the western desert country—so that sudden floods will not destroy your tents.

On the ideal site you won't need to ditch. But if your site is less than ideal, it may be necessary. Pitch the tent so the entrance is slightly lower than the back. Dig the trench the width of the shovel and three or four inches deep. Be sure the water flows from the back to the front, then away from the tent. The wall of the tent should overlap the trench on the inside. Cut the sod neatly and lay it along the outside of the trench, where it will form a wall against water running downhill, and where it will be available to fill the trench when you leave. Always fill in your ditches when you take your tent down. Only ditch when necessary.

154

WILD THINGS, like this box turtle, add a lot of interest to your camping trip.

Careless ditching has often started erosion that has resulted in serious damage months after the campers had left.

Wind

What will wind do to your camp? Wind can rip canvas to shreds, it can pull up stakes and carry tents away. And it can blow down trees. So you need shelter—a line of trees or a large rock—to protect you from stormy winds. But you must be enough in the open to get early morning breezes that can put freshness into your tents. So pitch away from trees that might blow over onto you. And stay away from trees anyway, for dead limbs may fall on your tent even on a calm night. More than one camper has been crushed that way.

Wind can blow swarms of insects into your campsite—or away from it. It is better to have the wind blowing from behind your camp toward a lake, rather than from the lake toward your camp.

Wild Things

Ants, mosquitoes, midges, no-see-'ums, gnats, ticks—you name them. They are wild things all set to ruin your campout. But they can be avoided. Here's another good reason for pitching your tents in the open and at least ten to fifteen feet above a stream or lake. Most flying insects swarm down close to the water's surface. Those that venture higher will be blown away if there is a breeze. Ticks love thick grass and bushes—so stay away from them.

Poison oak, poison ivy, and poison sumac are wild things too that can ruin a campout, especially for those who are sensitive to them. Include them on your check list.

There are other wild things that can add a lot of interest, or a lot of trouble, depending on how you prepare for them. Raccoons can spoil a whole week's supply of food if you aren't careful. But they are very interesting animals when you get to know them! Generally speaking, the more wild things there are near your campsite—wild animals, wild flowers, wild birds, wild trees—the more interesting your campout will be.

Wood

You'll want to be sure there is plenty of wood nearby, not only for fuel but also for making camp gadgets. It's no fun having to haul wood a long way.

More and more, however, wood is becoming hard to find in the popular camping areas. You can take wood with you, or use Sterno, Heatabs, charcoal, or gasoline stoves for cooking.

Willingness

Don't overlook the sixth W—willingness. Be sure that the owner of the property is willing to let you camp there. Get his permission, then live up to whatever restrictions he imposes. On Government land, find out first if you need camp or fire permits, and get them in plenty of time.

WHAT TO TAKE

What you take with you depends on the type of camping you are going to do—outpost, wilderness, pack—as well as the time of the year and how long you will be gone. In this chapter we're talking about overnight camping on sites that don't require too much walking to get to them. It is the simplest kind, but it is basic to all the others. Master it, and the others will come easily.

It's not hard to make up a list of what you'll need if you think through the various activities of the campout.

Part of the time you'll be *sleeping,* so you'll need a bed, a pillow, mattress, pajamas, tent, stakes, ground cloth, Bible, and *Guide* or lesson quarterly.

You'll *get up* in the morning, so you'll need toothbrush (in a container), toothpaste or powder, comb, mirror, soap, towel, wash basin, toilet paper, and shovel.

You'll eat and drink, so you'll have to have food and cooking

156

Pathfinders always love INSPECTION on a camporee, for that's the way the conference MV secretary finds out how well their club keeps their tents.

utensils and water purification tablets. You'll want a spoon, fork, knife, cup, plate, bowl; and soap, scouring pad, dishcloth, and tea towel.

And of course, you'll want *clothes*—Pathfinder uniform, T-shirts or blouses, jacket or sweater, poncho or raincoat, change of underwear, socks, a second pair of shoes, handkerchiefs, bathing suit.

And there will be *miscellaneous* items such as watch, purse with money, first-aid kit, flashlight, notebook, mending kit (with needles, thread, buttons, pins) a few feet of cord and copper wire, an ax, Chapstick, sunburn lotion, insect repellent, and a sharpening stone.

And you may want to add a camera, film, binoculars, compass, maps, game equipment, magnifying glass, and nature books, depending on the activities you are planning.

Some of these items are discussed in the rest of this chapter. For fires and cooking see chapters 12 and 13, "Warm Fires" and "Camp Cookery."

SLEEPING EQUIPMENT

Beds

The purpose of your bedding is to keep the cold of the night out and the heat of your body in.

On a summer night in the eastern part of the country a couple of cotton blankets may be enough. But wool blankets are

Check as you pack
Sleeping equipment

..... Tent
..... Groundcloth
..... Sleeping bag
..... Mattress
..... Packsack
..... Pajamas
..... *Guide*
..... Bible

Toilet equipment

..... Plastic bowl
..... Towel
..... Face cloth
..... Soap in container
..... Comb
..... Mirror
..... Tooth paste
..... Toothbrush in container
..... Toilet paper
..... Trench shovel
(not shown)

Clothes

..... Pathfinder shirt
or blouse
..... Pathfinder pants
or skirt
..... Tie for boys
..... Belt and buckle
..... Neckerchief
..... Underwear
..... T-shirts
..... Socks
..... Shoes
..... Raincoat
..... Sweater
..... Swim suit

SHOULD TAKE

Eating equipment

...... Pot with lid
...... Frying pan
...... Plate
...... Cup
...... Knife, fork, spoon
...... Collapsible cup
...... Soap
...... Scouring pad
...... Dishcloth
...... Tea towel
...... Matches

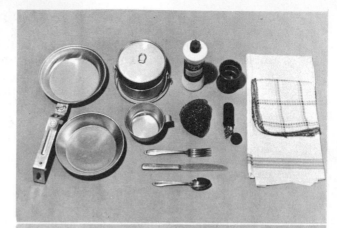

Miscellaneous equipment

...... Rope
...... Wire
...... Chapstick
...... First-aid kit
...... Snake-bite kit
...... Watch
...... Insect repellant
...... Sunburn lotion
...... Ax
...... Sharpening stone
...... Notebook, pencil
...... Scissors
...... Sewing kit, buttons, pins, thread, needles
...... Purse with money

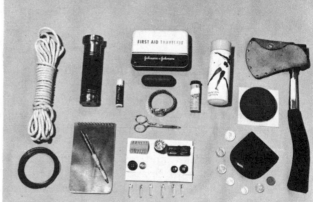

Optional equipment

...... Camera
...... Flash bulbs
...... Film
...... Map
...... Compass
...... Magnifying glass
...... Binoculars
...... Bird book
...... *MV Handbook*
...... Other outdoor books

much better. What keeps you warm are the pockets and layers of air in the bedding. Cotton mats up, leaving very few air pockets. Wool will not mat. It remains fluffy and warm.

Two or three thin blankets are warmer than one thick one of the same total weight, because layers of air are trapped between the blankets. Study the pictures to see how the blankets should be folded so as to keep you covered. Be sure you have plenty of blanket beneath you.

Better than blankets are sleeping bags. They come in various shapes with different fillings. Choose one that has the greatest amount of warmth for the least weight at a price you can afford. Kapok filling is popular and good. Wool is good too. Dacron Polyester Fiberfill is probably better, and down is the best—and also the most expensive!

You can make your own sleeping bag by folding a wool blanket in the middle and sewing across the bottom and about a third of the way up the open side.

Mattresses

It's no fun to sleep on the bare ground. The earth gets harder with every passing hour, and every little stone digging into your flesh grows to the size of a boulder by morning. Besides, the ground turns out to be very cold and damp before the sun comes up, no matter how warm and dry it seemed when the sun went down.

A rubber air mattress folds small. Blow it up, then kneel on it, letting the air escape until you feel the ground with your knees. Then plug the air hole. A mattress with too much air in it makes you feel you are rolling off all night long.

If you can't afford to buy a mattress, take a cotton *tick*. A tick is a cloth bag something like a pillow case, three feet wide and six feet long. Fill it full of straw, grass, or leaves, and fasten the opening with large safety pins or ribbons. It is surprisingly comfortable and very light and compact for packing.

To save weight, remember that the mattress needs only to reach from head to hips. Backpackers like foam rubber in a waterproof cover. Ensolite is a special product that is good for mattresses because it is waterproof, soft and light, and needs no cover.

You'll probably sleep better with a pillow. Jacob was able to sleep well with only a stone, but you may not. So take a small pillow with you. At least roll up a sweater and put that under your head. There's a good way to tell the experienced Pathfinder from the rest—the experienced Pathfinder sleeps comfortably.

160

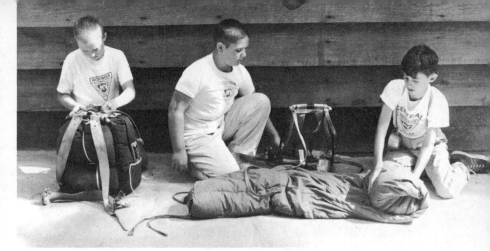

Rolling a sleeping bag before an outpost trip at summer camp. Much of the fun of a campout depends on a **GOOD BED**. Study the styles pictured here.

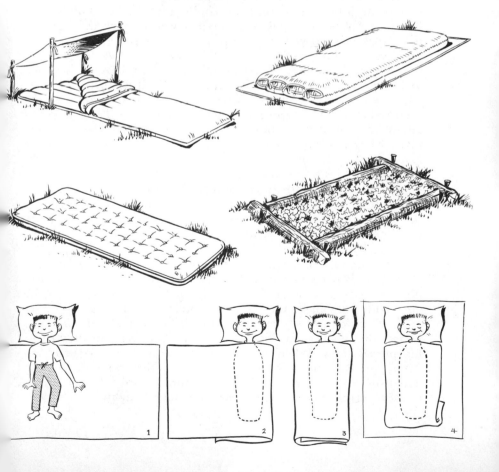

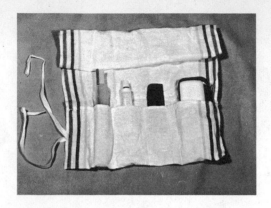

A handy **TOILET KIT** can be made by sewing pockets in an old tea towel and attaching tapes to tie it with.

And So to Sleep

Wise campers are very careful about how they get ready for the night. John was so tired he couldn't be bothered fixing his bed properly. The weather was terribly warm, so he didn't think he'd need many covers. He flopped down on the grass, pulled a blanket over him, and was asleep in seconds. But long before morning he was awake, shivering. There was an ache in his back and a pain in his side where a stone was drilling in.

He wanted to get up and make his bed all over again, but the other fellows were sleeping soundly, and he knew if he wakened any of them he'd be in trouble for sure, so he just lay there. He managed to cat nap once or twice, but morning found him groggy and weary and wondering why the other Pathfinders thought sleeping out was so much fun.

Allan did differently. First, he stretched himself on the ground and noticed where his hips and shoulders came. He scooped out the earth three or four inches deep at these places. Then he examined the ground carefully and made sure not one stone or twig or bump remained.

Next, he placed a waterproof ground cloth over the earth, and on this he laid his mattress, then the bedroll. He fluffed the bedding to make sure he got as much air into it as possible, and he also made sure there was nearly as much covering beneath him as there was on top. He put his pillow in place, and only then did he feel that his bed was set for the night. Yet even this didn't end his preparations. When bedtime came he put his pajamas on. "Only pre-Pathfinders sleep with their clothes on," he remembered his counselor saying. "The perspiration soaked up by your clothes during the day will freeze you out at night."

162

You can get ready for the great day of your first camp-out by making a model camp-site in your club meetings. Notice all the details that our Hawaiian Pathfinders have put into this model, even to the Bibles on the suitcases in each of the tents.

And one other thing. When taps sounded, Allan stopped talking. He knew jabbering after taps was another sign of the inexperienced camper. It's no wonder Allan slept well, or that he woke up rarin' to go when reveille sounded.

Allan aired his bedding in the morning. He had slept so warm that the bedding was damp from perspiration. He knew the dampness would make him cold the next night. So he hung the bedding in the sun for a couple of hours, then rolled it up and placed it in the back of his tent where it would stay dry and also leave him room to do things in the tent without trampling all over the sleeping equipment.

TENTS AND SHELTER

Some kind of shelter is needed on almost any camping trip. It may be possible to make a shelter of native materials, but on most campsites this will not be permitted.

Simple Shelters

A shelter may be made by placing poles across boulders and covering them with a blanket, tarpaulin, or poncho. A rope may be tied between two trees and a poncho laid over it to form a simple pup tent. Poles can be lashed together and a poncho laid on them like one side of a low roof. If this is on the windward side and there is a campfire on the open side, you will be very comfortable.

Tents

But it is best to plan for tents. Tents come in many shapes and sizes that are modifications of three basic types, *cone, pyramid,* and *prism*. The Indians' tepee was a cone-type tent, the umbrella tent belongs to the pyramid type, and the popular pup tents and wall tents are of the prism type. Each has its good points. You should examine several tents and choose the one that's best for you, considering how much money you can spend, how much weight you can carry, and how often you'll be camping.

It's a good idea to make your own. Choose the style you want. **Plan it large enough so there will be fifteen square feet of floor** space for each sleeper and at least four feet of height (six feet is much better, as it lets you stand up). Make a paper model with a scale of one inch to the foot. Then with poles and string make a full-size model. Measure all dimensions carefully. Buy enough **cloth. Parachute or rip-stop nylon is best, but unbleached muslin** with a *tight* weave is all right. Cut it out carefully, allowing extra size for seams. Sew it together with French seams. (Mothers are wonderful at times like these!) Sew on grommets and tapes. Then waterproof.

For waterproofing dissolve one pound of laundry soap in two gallons of hot water and soak your tent in it for one hour, being certain that every part is thoroughly wet. Then squeeze (do not wring) and hang on a line till completely dry. Dissolve a half pound of alum in two gallons of water and soak the tent in this for four hours. Finally squeeze again and hang up till dry—and there you are. But remember that no waterproofing job is infallible. In a rainstorm give your tent a break. Don't touch the cloth **or bump it with your head. It may start leaking at that spot. Better yet, don't waterproof. Use a fly of 6-mil polyethylene. Suspend it from a rope tied between two poles 4 inches above the tent.**

KEEP CLEAN!

Almost the first thing to do when you reach camp is to build the latrine. Choose a spot about 150 feet from the tents and at least 200 hundred feet from your water supply and sheltered by bushes. (If there are no bushes, set up a canvas screen.) Dig a trench the width of the shovel and about eighteen inches deep and long enough to allow about nine inches for each camper. Pile the earth in a ridge at one side. Lash poles together to form a seat if the camp is to last more than a day or two, otherwise the ditch can be straddled by placing a foot on each side. Toilet paper should be placed near, protected by a tin can. Hang a candle lantern at nightfall so the latrine can be found easily in the dark. Put a shovel or paddle in the pile of dirt.

Choose a TENT to fit your needs. Pup tents are easy to carry, but may be too small for long camping trips. Another type may be better for you. Study these. Perhaps the club can raise money to buy several. Or make your own.

Every time the latrine is used, some of the earth is shoveled back into the hole. At the end of the campout shovel in the rest of the earth, piling it a few inches above the ditch. The loose earth will soon settle level with the ground. The correct use of a latrine is sufficiently important that you will find directions in the Bible. Look up Deuteronomy 23:13.

Of course, when boys and girls camp together, two latrines will be dug. As soon as they are finished their location should be announced to the campers.

Wash Your Hands

Clean hands are a *must* at camp! Always wash your hands after going to the latrine and before meals. Use enough soap and water to form a lather. Remember that germs like camping too, and their ideal campsite is unwashed hands.

For convenience, put wash water in a No. 10 can. Punch a hole in the side near the bottom. Whittle a bit of wood and use it to plug the hole.

CAMP COMFORT

Some people think that camping has to be uncomfortable. Nothing could be further from the truth. With a little ingenuity you can rig up a hundred gadgets that will give you all the comforts of home and all the satisfaction of being a second Edison.

A rope stretched between two trees makes a clothesline. Three sticks lashed together in the middle, then spread apart, make a stand for your wash basin. A short forked stick lashed at right angles to a curved stick makes a clothes hanger. Trenches dug on the four sides of a square with a cloth spread over the center part of the square make a table everyone can sit down to. Read the chapter on knots and lashings for other ideas.

LET'S GO CAMPING

Sooner or later every Pathfinder says, "Let's go camping!" It's what every Pathfinder likes best.

So let's go camping! But remember that successful camping is well planned.

Getting Ready

Start getting ready as soon as possible. Begin gathering your equipment together. Buy or make a tent. Practice cooking. Then as the day approaches, figure out the costs, collect money from each camper, and get written permission from all the parents.

Give each camper a definite job and make sure he knows exactly what will be expected of him.

Away You Go

Announce exactly when you will leave and exactly when you will be back. Have all the campers meet in the clubhouse. Lay out neatly everything that is to be taken and check it carefully to be sure that nothing is left behind. Divide up tents and cooking equipment so each person has about the same weight to carry.

Then pack it onto pack frames or into cars and hit the trail.

At Camp

First thing when you reach the campsite, lay out all the equipment and food in a neat line. Then everyone to his duties!

Let us suppose there are eight boys. Four form the tenting crew, four make up the cooking crew.

Two boys in the tenting crew go off to build the latrine. The other two dig a hole for disposing of wash water. Then they erect all the tents, two boys to a tent. They stretch out the ground cloths in the tents and unroll the beds. This done, they prepare the wood for the campfire.

While this is going on, the cooking crew is taking care of the food. Two of the boys prepare a place for the cooks' fire, and

THE PANTHERS GO CAMPING

The Panthers met in the home of our captain, Ray, to lay plans for the trip. Larry, our photographer, got the picture when Ray had his mouth shut.

Here is the chow
master (and me) in the store,
laying in supplies.

When we reached the
campsite, the tenting crew go
busy with tents.

And the food crew
got busy with the food.
We selected for cook a
fellow who really likes to eat!

Two fellows from the tent
crew went off and dug a latrine and fixed up this
comfortable bench.

The food crew started, digging this dandy table. The
tent crew helped finish it;
we were hungry!

It was getting dark after
supper. We dug two holes,
put a plastic cloth over th
and washed up.

Here's Alan, our song master, leading the singing around the campfire. Our counselor turned on the lights of his car to help Larry take the picture.

Before we turned in we studied our Sabbath school lesson by flashlight and knelt on our beds and prayed.

In the morning, brrr! Cold! But nothing like that stops the Panthers from washing!

I mentioned our counselor. Here he is. Dear Mr. James, We could not get on without all his help.

And here's Ray, helping me make out the record of our trip. We can't wait till we can go again.

gather plenty of wood and get it burning. Then they prepare a place for eating, possibly digging trenches to make the "table and bench" arrangement shown on page 168. The other two members of the cooking crew look after the food, getting supper ready.

When anyone completes his assigned duties, he pitches in to help the others finish their jobs. Soon the cook calls, "Come and get it!" and everyone sits down, just as at home, and eats a well-cooked meal served in the proper order.

After supper comes—you can't get away from it!—dishwashing. And then—at last!—games and campfire. And bed.

The campers undress and get into their pajamas. There is a whistle or bugle call—time for devotions. Out come Bibles and Sabbath school lessons. Then each camper kneels on his bed for his private prayers, then snuggles down between the covers. Taps floats in the darkness, and all is still and quiet. Not a whisper from anyone, only the night sounds of the forest.

And then it's morning!

Morning

Out of bed, and a quick dip in the lake. Then comb that hair and brush those teeth. Morning devotions, and breakfast. The tent crew swap off with the cooking crew for this meal.

All morning there are games, preferably Pathfinder games such as signaling and stalking and other activities that develop outdoor skills.

Lunch is a simple meal, because no one wants to take too much time to cook. There are a couple more hours of fun, and before you know it, it's time to take the tents down.

Striking Camp

The tent crew rolls up the beds, folds up the ground cloths, takes down the tents, fills in the latrine and wash-water holes, and covers the campfire so it won't show. The cooking crew packs all the food, stacks the unused firewood, and makes sure the cooking fire is out.

There is a quick but thorough check to be sure the campsite is cleaner than when you arrived, then you leave.

You meet at the clubhouse. The equipment is carefully inspected. What belongs to the club is cleaned and carefully put away. Personal equipment that may have been borrowed is returned. The scribe enters a brief report in the club record book. And right on schedule the boys head for home, saying as they go, "That was fun! Let's camp out again soon!"

Make a HAND-WASHING CAN. Drill a hole near the bottom of a No. 10 can, make a valve with a three-inch bolt, nut, and eraser. Place the bolt through one end of a piece of wood that moves on a fulcrum and is held in place with a rubber band. When you press the wood, the water pours out. When you release the pressure, the water stops. Can is good for drinking water too.

HOW MANY OF THESE CAN YOU DO?

Check each one when you finish it.

☐ 1. Find three possible campsites and check them against the Six W's. Choose the best.

☐ 2. Make a homemade tent.

☐ 3. Waterproof it.

☐ 4. Show that you can make a bed with two wool blankets.

☐ 5. Go outpost camping one night with your Pathfinder unit at the campsite you have chosen.

☐ 6. If you want to know what happened to Ernest and the wolves read the story of Bingo in the book *Wild Animals I Have Known,* by Ernest Thompson Seton.

☐ 7. Earn the MV Honor award in *Campcraft.*

INTERESTING BOOKS ABOUT CAMPING

The Golden Book of Camping and Camp Crafts, Gordon Lynn (Golden Press)
Everything is illustrated with color pictures. Packed full of helpful information.

The Junior Book of Camping and Woodcraft, Bernard S. Mason (Ronald Press Co.)
Much good information.

Camping and Woodcraft, Horace Kephart (Macmillan Co.)
Goes into a lot of detail. Many interesting experiences woven in.

Your Own Book of Campcraft, Catherine T. Hammett (Pocket Books, Inc.)
A smaller book. Sometimes disagrees with the others listed here.

pack camping

FOR the real thrill of camping go pack camping!

In pack camping you go wherever you feel the urge. With your clothes and your equipment and your food wrapped up in a pack on your back you are completely independent. You need no cars or roads or grocery stores or houses. Wherever the trail leads, through forest or stream or over mountain, there you may go, and when night falls you set up your camp where darkness finds you, and in the morning you go on again.

HOW TO GO ABOUT IT

The best way to get ready for pack camping is to take part in several outpost campouts. And for two reasons. First, outpost camping will sharpen your ability in cooking and tent pitching and other campcraft skills. Second, outpost camping will help you to know what you need to take and what you don't.

When you are pack camping it is most important that you take exactly what you need, and no less and no more. For when it's tied to your back, a pound in the morning weighs a ton at night. You should aim to keep your pack less than twenty pounds. Certainly don't go over twenty-five, and go even that high only after you've toughened up. Only by camping several times will you learn what you must take and what you can safely leave behind.

For the most part you should take the things that are listed in the chapter on outpost camping. But make everything as light as possible!

Clothing

Your shoes and your socks are your most important clothes on a pack campout. Read again the chapter "Hiking Along Together." Of course, you'll want a change of underwear, a sweater for evenings, and a raincoat or poncho in case of rain. If you're going through woods, both boys and girls should wear strong trousers or slacks and long sleeves to protect against thorns and brambles and poison ivy. Even out in the open protect your skin,

173

especially early in the summer, for you can get a painful sunburn hiking, just as well as when you're swimming.

Sleeping and Shelter

Bedding must be light. Here's where a very light sleeping bag pays off. If you don't have one, take wool blankets. (You'll know how many you need after you've been outpost camping a few times.) An Army surplus mummy bag is good. Take pajamas along.

For a tent, you can share with your buddy the two halves of a pup tent (if you have the kind that is made in two pieces). But probably even this will be too heavy. Use your poncho for a tent and a plastic tablecloth as a ground cloth. Or take along a rubberized nylon tarpaulin, 8 by 10 feet, to use as a tent, and use your poncho as a ground cloth. Be sure to pack several feet of nylon rope. It's lighter than ordinary rope.

You'll need some kind of mattress. An Army air mattress of rubberized nylon is light and strong. Plastic ones are light too, but don't last as long. A cotton tick is light and easy to pack. One no bigger than 2½ by 4 feet will do. Foam rubber is the favorite of many backpackers. Use rolled-up sweater as pillow.

Food and Cooking

Before making a trip through the forest, the Indians used to parch corn by drying it in the ashes of their campfires. They would grind the kernels in a mortar and fill a small sack with the powder. At mealtime they would mix a few spoonfuls of the powder in a cup of cold water, or they would put the dry powder in their mouths, and swallow it quickly with the help of water. It would swell slowly in their stomach and give them a pleasant "full" feeling and plenty of energy for many hours. Added to the wild food they found in the wilderness, a small sack of this parched corn would last them for months.

So the Indians knew the value of dehydrated foods on pack trips.

You'll be wise to use them as much as possible. And fortunately you have a wide selection to choose from. You can find many different kinds at the supermarket—ready-mixed pancake flour, oatmeal, powdered milk, instant potatoes, dried eggs, soup powders, dried fruit, and so forth. Stores that sell sporting supplies often have an even greater variety. Several weeks before your trip write to the companies listed on page 178, and ask for catalogs.

Before you leave, measure out the exact quantities of food you expect to use and wrap them in aluminum foil or plastic bags.

A PACK FRAME helps a lot. Put the heavy things high. Cross the ropes so they can't spread apart and let the load slip through.

This way you'll cut down on the weight and save the bother of measuring outdoors. Mix together as many ingredients as possible before leaving home too. For instance, blend milk powder and dried egg powder with your pancake flour before packing it. Then all you'll have to do is add water and butter for breakfast pancakes. Do the same, as far as possible, with other items on the menu. Be sure you wrap them well enough so they will stay dry.

You'll want a cup, plate, fork, and spoon to eat with. Use your pocket knife for cutting things and you won't need to take a table knife. A frying pan and a small pot may be unavoidable, but you can avoid anything heavier if you've become an expert at aluminum foil cookery.

You'll need a heavy knife or light hand ax to cut firewood, and waterproof matches to start a fire with. If you're in an area where open fires are forbidden you may be allowed to take a gasoline stove. There is one that weighs only two pounds. Be sure to wrap it well in cellophane or plastic before putting it into your pack so the gasoline smell won't get into the food. For short trips there is a very light aluminum stove that uses Heatabs.

Take a plastic bag to use as a water pail.

YOUR PACK

Choosing a Pack

When you go out to buy a pack, remember that there are two basic types of equipment used for carrying camping gear on a person's back. The first type is the *packsack*, sometimes called a *day bag* by backpackers and a *summit pack* by mountain climbers.

175

It is a cloth bag and comes in many styles and sizes. It is used to carry lunch, flashlight, parka, rope, et cetera, on a short trip out from camp. The *pack frame* is the second basic type. It is especially useful in hot weather, for it keeps the pack from resting on the back and thus reduces perspiration. Generally speaking, it makes heavy loads easier to carry.

Before choosing your pack, examine several different kinds. Be sure the one for which you pay your money is *strong, light, waterproof,* and *large enough* to carry what you need. Be sure the *straps are wide,* so they will not cut into you. Leather straps are better than woven ones, because in rain the web curls, making the straps narrow. Padding under the straps where they cross the shoulders is desirable. And the straps must not cross on the chest, for this makes breathing difficult. They should start at least two or three inches apart at the top of the pack, for if they are closer together the pack will not hang straight. Finally, be sure the pack *fits you.* It should touch your shoulders and rest lightly on your hips and nowhere else. It should be fairly high on your back. Many experienced hikers in America like to buy the Kelty type aluminum contoured frame with fitted waterproof packbag and waist belt with quick-release buckle. If you do not live in the United States, check on locally made gear. Europeans especially have developed some lightweight equipment that is amazingly strong.

If you can, check on some European packsacks and pack racks. Europeans do a great deal of pack camping and have developed some extremely lightweight equipment that is amazingly strong.

In an emergency you can make an improvised pack out of a *pillow case, flour sack,* or pair of *trousers.*

If using a pillow case or flour sack, first put a stone in each of the bottom corners, then tie a 30-inch cord to each corner. (The stones keep the cords from slipping off.) Fill up the sack, then tie the other ends of the cords around the mouth of the sack. The cords now form two large loops. Put your arms through these loops.

Tighten up the cords by adjusting the knots at the bottom of the sacks, until the weight rests comfortably on your back. Put a handkerchief or bunches of grass under the cords where they cross your shoulders, for padding.

To use the trousers, put your things into the upper part of the trousers and tie them in securely with rope. Turn the trousers upside down and bring the legs over your shoulders. Tie rope from the bottom of the legs to the belt and that's all there is to it.

A DAY BAG is light and it makes carrying lunch and a flashlight and a first-aid kit quite simple. Straps must be wide or they will bite your shoulders.

Packing the Pack

A well-packed pack is *organized*. There are "bags within bags." Divide your equipment into departments, then put each department into a separate bag.

Thus, the comb, mirror, tooth paste, toothbrush, et cetera, will go together in the "toilet bag." Your cup, plate, fork, and spoon will go into the "mess bag." Needle, thread, pins, and buttons go into the "mending bag." Your second pair of shoes go into the "shoe bag." Be sure all the small items have their bags. And if possible, make the bags of different colored cloth or clear plastic so they are easier to recognize. If you pack this way, when it comes time to eat, all you have to do is haul out the mess bag and you have all the equipment you need, instead of searching all through your things to find a missing fork or a lost spoon.

When all the items are in their little bags, pack them into the big bag, the packsack. Be sure to put the blankets or bedroll on the side of the pack that rests against your back. This will keep it soft and comfortable. Then place at the bottom of the pack the items you probably will not need till the day is over, and put the items you may need in an emergency—first-aid kit, flashlight, poncho—in the side pockets or on top.

Packing your pack correctly for outpost campouts will get you set for the day the fellows say, "Let's hit the long trail."

BICYCLE CAMPING

Instead of tying your pack to your back, tie it to a *bicycle*. You can travel much farther. When you back-pack you should

YOU CAN GO so much farther so much easier when you tie your duffel to a bicycle and ride. Put heavier articles at the back; only light stuff up front.

plan on not more than about eight or ten miles a day; but on a bicycle you can go forty miles on good roads if you are in condition.

Keep the weight down! Take about the same things you would on a back-packing trip, but in addition take a tire-repair kit.

Use saddlebags. Fasten them securely and as close to the rider as possible, to reduce sway.

Plan your route so as to go in a circle and return on different roads from the ones you started out on.

If you are going to use a pack frame, you should pack your pack differently from this. You won't need to put your sleeping bag into the pack, you will roll it up and tie it directly to the frame.

Now, if you are going to be hiking along a smooth, level trail, you should put the heaviest items inside the pack near the top, at the front of the pack, so they will lie against the frame. But if you are going to be climbing rocks or hiking through snow, where you might stumble or slip—put the heaviest things in the bottom of the pack against the frame. On a level walk, tie the sleeping bag to the frame below the pack; for rocks or snow, tie the sleeping bag above the pack.

178

DEHYDRATED FOODS will help keep your pack light. Get them from camping supply stores or order them from the reputable companies listed here.

WHERE TO ORDER DEHYDRATED FOODS

1. "Trail Packets"

A. D. Seidel & Son, Inc.
2323 Pratt Boulevard
Elk Grove Village, Illinois 60007

2. "Kamp Pack"

Bernard Food Industries, Inc.
P.O. Box 1497
1125 Hartrey Avenue
Evanston, Illinois 60204

P. O. Box 487
222 S. 24th Street
San Jose, California 95103

3. Other good brands

Chuck Wagon Foods
P.O. Box 1269
Woburn, Massachusetts 01801

DriLite
11333 Atlantic Avenue
Lynwood, California 90262

Galley Slave Foods
13237 Saticoy Street
North Hollywood, California
91605

NOTE: These companies sometimes change their address. Some go out of business. It is wise to write for an order blank several weeks before your planned camping trip.

HOW MANY OF THESE CAN YOU DO?

Check each one when you finish it.

- [ ] 1. Make a pack frame.
- [ ] 2. Make a bag to fit this pack frame.
- [ ] 3. Pack your equipment into a pair of trousers or a flour sack, and fasten it properly to your back.

snow camping

CAMP in the snow?
Sure! Why not?
It's *cold!*
Of course it's cold. But you know before you go that it's going to be cold, so you can prepare for it. You will be warmer on a well-planned snow trip than on some summer outings. And that's the truth!

There are many good reasons for camping in the snow. For one thing, most people think snow camping is impossible—so you get the satisfaction of showing them you can do it. And second, there is so much fun in it. You can imagine you're on the trail of Peary and Scott on the way to the Poles. You can learn so many secrets about the animals, for they are much easier to track over the snow than over the hard-packed earth of summer. And there is nothing to match the beauty of a campfire on the snow.

In that case, *let's* go camping in the snow.

But the snow's cold!

What of it!

CAMPING IN THE SNOW

Proper Clothing

Wearing the right clothing is very important. Loose-fitting woolen garments are the secret of keeping warm. Your winter list should include several pairs of heavy woolen socks, wool or flannel shirts, wool coat, woolen pants, a pair of mittens, and a winter cap to protect your ears. Thermal or insulated underwear is very satisfactory.

For your feet you should have water-resistant boots with room enough to permit plenty of freedom after putting on two pairs of wool socks. Tight shoes produce cold feet.

The greatest winter enemy is dampness. Dry clothes both day and night are important. Sleeping in daytime clothing is dangerous. It is damp from perspiration. You should have dry sleeping clothes for night use as part of your sleeping-bag equipment, and

A SLED is the natural way to transport your equipment on a snow campout.

always change into them when you go to bed. The clothes you wear during the day should be aired and dried by the fire at night, and your night clothes and sleeping bag aired and dried by day.

Watch out for sunburn. You can burn quicker in the winter than in the summertime. Take some sunburn preventive in your pack.

And be sure to include sunglasses. Snow blindness—from the glare of the sun on the snow—is a very real danger. Charcoal rubbed around the eyes will give some relief.

Sleeping Gear

If your sleeping bag is not warm enough, you can improve it. Use a wool blanket or a wool Army mummy liner inside it, and cover the outside with a heavy cotton cloth or Army cover. Two Army surplus feather mummy bags, one inside the other, are adequate for most winter camping. A mummy bag is much warmer than the square bag because there is less space to heat, and you can zip it up until your head is covered by the hood, with only your nose exposed. You can cover your nose with a wool scarf to warm the air you breathe. Because it is important to keep your head warm, wear a wool cap to bed also. If you must use a rectangular bag, wear your parka with hood to bed to keep your head and shoulders warm.

You can heat a rock, if available, and cover it with a cloth to put down in the bottom of the sleeping bag. At bedtime, warm yourself by the campfire, then run to your tent and dive into your sleeping bag. Cover your head, zip the bag quickly, and you will be snug and warm all night.

182

BUILDING A FIRE ON SNOW

It is no problem to build a fire on snow—if you do it right. Cut half a dozen or more small logs about two feet long and lay them beside one another like a raft.

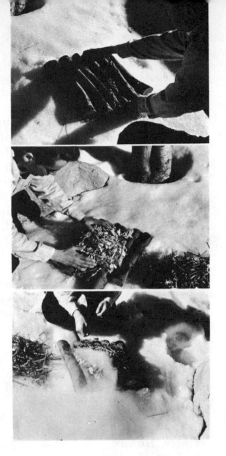

Gather tinder and kindling. It may be easier to find dry wood after a long cold spell in the winter than in the middle of a rainy summer. If you have difficulty, split a log; make shavings of the wood in the center.

Arrange the tinder, kindling, and firewood in the usual way and then put a match to it. You will have a nice warm fire going in no time.

Winter Foods

Next to sleeping well, food of the right sort is the most important item in winter camping. Foods with extra heat-producing fats and sugars are needed. Make your food list as simple as possible, and use some dehydrated foods, for they will lighten your load and they won't freeze. If possible use the corner of your tent to store food that might freeze. Plan your menu with a very active program in mind.

Be sure to drink enough water. Melt clean snow if there is no better supply. Add fruit-juice powder to improve the flavor.

Winter Shelter

Use a tent with a waterproof floor that comes up about a foot on the sides. Double-wall tents are warmest, such as a nylon tent that breathes (not waterproof) covered with a fitted waterproof fly with three or four inches of air space between. Aluminum tent pegs hold solidly in hard snow and ice. You may need to bury them and stamp snow down over them. Rocks or logs can also be used to weight tent edges down.

To guard against dampness, use a waterproof ground cloth or plastic sheet under the tent if it does not have a waterproof floor. Sweep snow out of the tent with a whisk broom or sock. Leave the small vents in the ends of the tent open to let moisture out. Do not heat the tent unless absolutely necessary, for this causes moisture to collect. If a small stove is used provide ventilation to prevent carbon monoxide poisoning. Sleep with head by entrance.

Fire Building

If the snow is deep, lay some logs side by side to make a platform on top of the snow, and then build the fire on top of the platform. However, if there isn't much snow, just brush it away.

To find dry fuel when everything seems wet, look for dead limbs on standing trees. The inner wood will generally be dry, and so will small twigs hanging in the air. Many stumps or dead trees lying on the ground have dry wood inside them or dry leaves underneath them, where rain or snow have not reached. Caves and ledges in rocks are a catchall for leaves and bits of wood. Don't neglect the shredded bark of such trees as cedar and birch. It is good tinder. It is wise to lay in a supply of wood under canvas if you are going to camp any length of time.

Winter Nature

The white world is full of stories for Pathfinders who can read them. The combat, failure, and success of animals and birds are evident everywhere. Every track of a wild creature tells its own story—a rabbit escaping an enemy, a squirrel looking for food, a deer mouse wandering in all directions taking his exercise, and the trail of a grouse ending in flight.

Many birds inhabit the winter woodlands. You may see the blue jay, screech owl, redheaded woodpecker, crow, ruffed grouse, and many others. Danger lurks in the winter woods. Hawks are ready to make a meal of a woodpecker, chickadee, or nuthatch. Owls are waiting for mice, and foxes are hunting rabbits.

Have you ever heard of collecting insects in winter? Well, just go to the woods and turn over a few rocks or dig a log open. You will find beetles and insects of many kinds. If you are observant you may see the mourning cloak butterfly fluttering about on almost any mild day. Be sure to examine insect galls. There are a

You'll find new surprises in even the most familiar woods on a SNOW HIKE.

large variety of them, and they will prove to be interesting. On the snow you will find tree seeds that have blown down. Examine them and determine which trees they came from. It is a much greater challenge to know the woodland in winter than it is in summer.

HOW MANY OF THESE CAN YOU DO?

Check each one when you finish it.

☐ 1. Light a fire on deep snow.
☐ 2. Follow an animal track in snow and tell what the animal did.
☐ 3. Camp overnight in the snow.

INTERESTING BOOKS ON SNOW CAMPING

Field Book of Animals in Winter, Ann H. Morgan (G. P. Putnam's Sons)
All about what happens to insects, birds, and mammals during the cold weather.
Also read the books listed at the end of the other chapters on camping. Many of them discuss snow camping.

185

survival camping

EVERY kind of camping has its thrills, but none come up to the thrills of wilderness-survival camping. Here is adventure at its peak. You walk out of your house into the forest or mountain wilderness with nothing but the clothes on your back—no ax or knife or matches, no food or bedding or shelter, nothing but the clothes you happen to be wearing—and you stay out there for a day or a week or a month, and come home like Daniel, "fairer and fatter in flesh" than you were when you left. Wilderness camping is the ultimate challenge.

Get Ready!

It would be foolish to go into it without adequate preparation. Begin by camping often. On hikes look for edible wild plants and bring home samples, press the leaves, and put them in a scrapbook.

In Pathfinder meetings learn to make fire by friction or with flint and steel. Gather tree bark and wood in your locality and make your own fire-by-friction set. Look for stones that produce sparks when struck together.

Gather bark and weed stems and make rope. Learn to make knives and ax heads from flint as the Indians did.

On a hike sample the wild plants you find. On a campout be sure one meal is made up entirely of wild food. On another campout eat a meal that has been cooked without any store-bought utensils. Sleep in shelters made of poles and brush.

Thus, gradually, prepare yourself step by step for the big day when you can walk into the wilderness just as you are and stay as long as you want.

Since there is hardly anyone in the world who can do that today, we can't tell you exactly what to do. But here are some suggestions to get you started.

Clothing

It is basic to the whole idea that you wear "just the clothes you have on." Good sense says that these should be strong and sturdy and sufficient to protect you against cold and rain.

A poncho can be made out of bark of the paper birch. Take a strip as wide as you are and nearly twice as long as you are tall. Make a hole in the middle and put your head through it. Roll another piece of bark like a dunce cap and put it on your head. Later try making clothes by weaving the fibers of bark or Indian hemp.

Knife

Begin to make a knife as soon as possible.

The Indians made knives out of flint. Jasper, obsidian, or agate —any hard stone that flakes—will work. The Indians sometimes used part of a deer antler as the flaking tool to shape the stone.

They would file a chisellike point on one end of the antler, then push this point into the end of the stone and pull down. When they did it right, a flake of the stone fell off. They would continue this process around and around the stone, always working on the underside, till the stone was the shape they wanted.

You can do the same, and when you've made a knife you can make many other things that require cutting.

Shelter

The opening to a cave makes the best shelter. Check for snakes. If there are no caves—and there probably won't be—look for a high rock that will shield you from the wind. Build a fire a few feet from the rock and sleep between the fire and the rock. But watch out for landslides and falling stones.

As soon as you have made a stone ax, you can start work on a lean-to. Cut saplings, lash them together with bark rope, and thatch them with evergreen boughs or grass.

With your ax, whittle a wooden paddle and make a sod house. The early pioneers on the plains lived in sod houses for years. Sods are pieces of grass and earth about four inches deep and a foot by a foot and a half wide. Pile several of them like bricks to form the walls of your shelter. Place saplings across the top like rafters, being sure the roof slants as a roof should. Then thatch it. Many homes in Europe are still thatched with straw and have been roofed this way for hundreds of years. Put the thatch on at least six inches thick and tie it down with straw ropes. Heat rocks in your campfire and bring them into the house at bedtime and you'll be warm and cozy till morning.

If there is not much danger of rain, dig yourself a simple trench. Soldiers in World War I lived in trenches for many months, even in the worst of weather. In World War II men lived in foxholes. Some of these holes were deep enough to stand up in without being seen

THE CHALLENGE of wilderness camping is to go out as you are and to stay for as long as you wish, using native materials to keep well fed and clothed.

and wide enough to stretch out a sleeping bag. Yours won't need to be so deep.

And of course, you won't have a sleeping bag. Lay spruce or balsam bows two feet thick beneath you, and more on top.

Since you won't have a ground cloth, dry out the ground by burning a fire for about an hour over an area the size of a bed. Scrape the ashes away carefully. Be absolutely sure no sparks are left behind, then lay evergreen branches and dry leaves on the place. Heated rocks placed in the right spots add to the comfort.

Rope

Make rope from pawpaw bark, hickory shoots, or the inner bark of slippery elm, winged elm, hickory, white oak, buckeye, red cedar, or yellow locust. Or you can use the stems of Indian hemp, nettle, and swamp milkweed, or the leaves of yucca.

Pull the bark apart into long strips then boil the strips in a mixture of ashes and water till they are soft and pliable. Dry them, then lay them on a smooth rock and pound them with a rounded stone until the fibers separate into threads. Take two threads and twist them together. Take two other threads and twist them together. Then twist these two double threads around each other, twisting in the opposite direction from the first twist. Study carefully the pictures on page 193.

Utensils

With your stone knife whittle yourself a spoon and fork. Or make a fork by splitting the end of a silver maple twig and inserting a wedge to keep the two parts separated. The buds on the end of the twig will help to pierce the food.

189

Cups—and pots for boiling water—can be made from soft bark, especially paper birch.

For a cup take a square piece of bark about seven inches on a side and fold it cornerwise to make a triangle. Fold the two lower points up to touch the opposite sides. There are two layers of bark at the top point. Fold one layer forward and the other back. Open up the space between the two layers, fill your cup, and drink.

For a water pot take a strip of bark with square sides. Fold up each of the four sides about four inches. At the corners some of the bark will extend outward. Crease this and bring it around and pin it to the sides with a thorn or small twig. In this pot you can boil water if you have a fire.

Fires

Of course, you won't have any matches. You must start a fire with what you can find. If there are iron pyrites around, you are in good fortune. Struck together, they will send off sparks. If there aren't any iron pyrites, experiment with any other hard stones you can find. Sooner or later you are sure to find some that will make sparks.

Or you can use friction. You must get a fireboard, bow, thong, spindle, and "thunderbird." If you are in the Southwestern desert, cut a piece of yucca for your fireboard and another for the spindle. It's the best wood there is for the purpose. If you are somewhere else, look for wood that is *absolutely dry* and *free of resin*. Dead branches of elm, poplar, alder, cedar, and larch will do. Having practiced friction fire making frequently at Pathfinder meetings, you know what size to make the fireboard and spindle. For the bow use any small strong branch. The thunderbird can be any piece of wood of a comfortable size to hold in your hand. Hollow out the underside and insert a flat stone or shell to reduce friction. For the thong use a piece of the rope you have made.

Now to start the cooking.

Cooking

You can *boil* water in that bark pot by one of two methods. Heat stones in your fire and drop them into the water in the pot. When you add new hot stones, take out the cold ones. Or place the pot directly over the coals. Birch bark will burn quicker than almost anything else, but you can set it over your cooking fire safely if you do it right. Be sure there is water in the pot at all times. See to it that no flames reach the bark *above the waterline*. Wait till there are only glowing coals. Suspend the pot above these coals, then cover ashes

YOUR WILDERNESS HOME

Bind STICKS and BRANCHES with vines, strips of bark, or grass rope to form uprights and cross pieces; cover them with a thatch of DRY GRASS. You will have a sturdy shelter big enough for the whole Pathfinder unit, and snug and cozy too.

over the coals that are beyond the edge of the pot. You may be surprised, but the bark won't burn. (Experiment with a piece of heavy paper folded to hold water and held over a lighted match.)

Fry on a flat stone, first burning a fire over the stone for half an hour, then brushing the coals away and immediately putting on food you want to cook. The Indians used to grind a thin stone into shape, then prop it up with four stones at the corners, and light a fire under it.

You can *bake* by wrapping certain foods in leaves and burying them in the ashes, or by making a fire hole, as for "bean-hole beans."

WILD FOOD

The key to your success in surviving in the wilderness will be finding enough of the right kinds of food. Here is where knowledge can make the difference between life and death. The ignorant starve in the midst of plenty.

Some foods can be found almost anywhere. Others grow abundantly only in certain parts of the country.

Generally speaking, most nuts and berries are good for food. So are a large number of leaves and roots. Learn the ones to avoid and avoid them.

191

Some Wild Foods Found Almost Everywhere

Arrowroot. Common in swamps. Dig up the roots and take off the tubers, which look like potatoes. Serve them like potatoes—boiled, or roasted in hot ashes. The Indians called them wapatoo, and they formed a very important part of their diet. The roots must be cooked. Eaten raw, they are bitter.

Dandelion. Boil the young leaves, then pour off the water, add more, and boil again, to remove the bitterness. Dandelion leaves are a favorite in some parts of Europe. Boil buds three minutes.

Wild mustard, chickweed, stinging nettles, violets, curled and *sour dock.* Boil the young leaves and serve like cabbage.

Clover. Eat young plants raw, before the flowers bloom. Some people prefer them dipped in salt water.

Milkweed. In spring cut the young shoots and boil them. In the fall the young seed pods are good.

Cattail. Common in swamps. The root may be eaten raw. The Indians dug it up, dried it, and ground it into a meal. Do the same, or boil and roast the root like a potato. Boil the blooming spike and eat like corn on the cob. The spring shoots and white inner stems are good boiled or raw.

Wild leek and *wild garlic.* Treat much the same as onions.

Groundnut. These plants have a string of swellings called tubers on their roots, much like potatoes. Boil or roast the tubers. The Pilgrim Fathers ate thousands of groundnuts during their first winter.

Pine nuts. These are found in pine cones. *Piñon nuts* are the most common. Eat them raw like other nuts, or grind into meal and cook in water to make a gruel. The easiest way to gather them is the way the Indians do—find a pack rat nest. There may be as much as a quart of nuts stored there!

Strawberry, blackberry, raspberry. Eat the fruits. Excellent in season.

Acorns. Unlike most other nuts, acorns cannot be eaten raw. They are full of tannin and very bitter. But they make an excellent food when prepared correctly. Dry them in the sun, then grind them into a meal. Soak wood ashes in water to produce lye.

Pour the lye water into another container, making sure no ashes spill over, and put the acorn meal into it and let soak for several hours. Finally, put the meal in a cloth and run fresh water through it until all the lye is washed out. This may take several hours more. The dough that remains can be fried in patties, baked in cakes, or boiled as a breakfast food.

TO MAKE GRASS ROPE

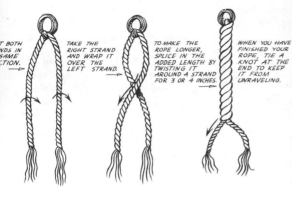

You can make good rope by twisting reeds or vines, grass, or strips of bark.

Some Wild Foods in the East

Chicory. Eat the young leaves raw or boiled like cabbage.

Grapevine. Eat the young shoots raw. The grapes may be boiled into a jelly.

Sumac. Eat the young shoots raw. (Beware of poison sumac, however. Leave it alone!)

Jerusalem artichoke. Dig up the roots and take the tubers and eat them like potatoes. They are at their largest in the autumn but may be dug up all winter.

Indian cucumber. Has a white, thick tuberous root stock, two or three inches long and about a half inch thick. They taste like ordinary cucumbers and can be eaten raw.

May apples. These smell bad to some people, but they taste good. They are best when the plant is dying and falling to the ground. Eat them raw—not too many lest they upset the stomach!

True Solomon's-seal. Boil the young shoots in the spring and serve like asparagus. The Indians used to boil the root, too.

Burdock. Peel the tender leafstalks and eat them raw or in a salad, or cook them like asparagus. Peel and boil the root.

Purslane. Eat the young stems and leaves raw or boiled.

Day lily. Roast or boil the tubers. Eat shoots and inner stems raw or cooked. Buds are delicious cooked like string beans.

Poke berry. Young leaves are good. The berries are poisonous.

MAKING ARROWHEADS

Stone arrowheads, knives, and ax-heads are all made in much the same way. Select a stone somewhat larger than you want the finished product to be. It may be flint, chert, agate, obsidian, jasper, or any other stone that flakes easily. Use a piece of an antler for the flaking tool; it's the best. If you are at home, use a large nail. Press the antler tip against a notch in the stone and then press down. All flakes should be pressed off the underside. Turn the chip repeatedly, flaking it evenly on both sides. Resting the stone against a leather pad will give you much greater control.

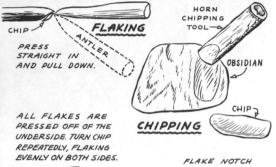

Some Wild Foods in the Southwest

Miner's lettuce. Eat the leaves like lettuce. The name comes from the fact that the miners in the California gold rush got sick from the lack of vegetables until they began eating these plants.

Mesquite. Eat the seed pods. They look like yellow string beans and taste sweet and lemonlike. They may also be pounded into a meal.

Yucca. Peel the tough rind off the stalk and roast the stalk in hot ashes. Boil the flower buds.

Cactus. Several cacti have edible fruits. Slice the leaves and boil them. Cut off the needles first!

Bracken. The fiddleheads of young bracken fern just pushing out of the ground are tender and good. Boil and eat like asparagus.

Wild peas. Boil and serve like ordinary peas.

Manzanita. The berry is red and tastes like green apples. But it's good.

Joshua tree. Roast the buds on hot coals.

PREPARING ACORN DOUGH

Acorns are a good source of food, but they contain tannin, which makes them bitter and must be removed. Gather what you need and lay them in the sun till they are dry. Grind the kernels into a fine meal, using two flat stones. Soak wood ashes in water to produce a lye solution. Soak the acorn meal in the lye water for a few hours to leach out the tannin. Finally put the flour in a cloth bag and set it in a stream or other pure running water to wash out the lye. The doughy mass can then be used in patties or made into a breakfast mush or even baked in a cake.

Ready for Anything

It is not likely that you will ever have to go out into the wilderness "just as you are." Nevertheless, the more camping you do and the more knowledge you can acquire about the ways of the wilderness the better. You never know but what in some unexpected emergency you may be called on to use your skill. A forced landing in a plane, an accident far from civilization—and your life and the lives of others may depend on your knowledge. Or you may get lost on a hike and have to spend days or nights in the woods before you are found. In the time of trouble so soon to come upon the world, the ability to get along in the wilderness will be of great value. While it is true that "bread and water shall be sure," it is also true that those who have prepared will get along better than those who have not.

There is much more to wilderness survival than could be included in this chapter. Get some of the books listed on the next page and read them. They are full of good ideas.

The new shoots of **FERN** are delicious, and certain kinds of **CACTUS** are nourishing and help to quench thirst. Learn the wild foods in your area.

HOW MANY OF THESE CAN YOU DO?

Check each one when you finish it.

☐ 1. Make ten feet of ¼-inch rope out of tree bark or Indian hemp.

☐ 2. Make a cup out of birch bark. (Practice first with aluminum foil.)

☐ 3. Make a bark pot and boil water in it.

☐ 4. Make a knife or Indian arrowhead from flint or other rock.

☐ 5. Collect leaves and flowers of ten edible wild flowers, press, and mount them in a scrapbook.

☐ 6. Process one pound of acorns, cook mush, and eat it.

☐ 7. Eat a complete meal of wild food you have collected.

INTERESTING BOOKS ON WILDERNESS SURVIVAL

Wildwood Wisdom and *Woodsmoke,* Ellsworth Jaeger (Macmillan Co.)

Two excellent books on wilderness living. *Wisdom* has a long chapter on making things from bark, and another on edible plants.

Camping and Woodcraft, Horace Kephart (Macmillan Co.)

The old standby for life in the wilderness. Entertainingly written.

Edible Wild Plants, Oliver Perry Medsger (Macmillan Co.)

Goes into the subject thoroughly. Contains many interesting personal experiences.

Survival, United States Air Force (U.S. Government Printing Office)

Prepared for Air Force men who might be forced down far from help. Very practical and well illustrated.

the great
outdoors

PART THREE

the ground under your feet

WEDNESDAY evening, May 7, 1902.

It had been an exciting week for Paul Cazalé, living in St. Pierre on the island of Martinique. Ashes had been falling like a snowstorm from the Mount Pelée volcano just two miles away. They had piled up so high already that horses and carriages ran silently over the cobblestone streets. Even at noon the day was as dark as evening.

To add to the excitement, it was sugar crop time, and the harbor was full of ships being loaded with the tasty harvest.

Paul's home was several miles away, at Morne Vert. He was staying in St. Pierre so he could go to school—and with so much going on, the teachers had omitted all homework for the last few days.

Then on Wednesday night the family coachman suddenly arrived and told Paul he must come home. What a time to leave!

Thursday morning, May 8, 1902. Ten minutes before eight.

Paul was suddenly jerked awake by an earsplitting, rumbling, booming roar. Mount Pelée had exploded! Rocks of a thousand tons' weight were hurtling through the air.

Worse yet, the southwest wall of the volcano had blown out. A vast sheet of flame engulfed St. Pierre, followed by a great black cloud of deadly gas that poured from the volcano's gaping mouth like an immense inky stream, folded along its edges like the borders of a curtain, glowing with incandescent dust, and lighted up with bright flashes like strokes of lightning.

In three minutes the 30,000 inhabitants of St. Pierre were dead. Only one is known to have survived, Auguste Ciparis, a prisoner at the time in a thick-walled cell of the city's jail.

Paul was safe too, at home.

When the volcano subsided, a lake in its crater, which had been full of water before the eruption, was gone, and the mountain peak stood nearly a thousand feet higher than before.

December, 1955. Winds shrieked across northern California at

"The mountain burned with fire unto the midst of heaven" (Deuteronomy 4:11).

110 miles an hour, bringing nearly forty inches of rain in nine days. The Yuba and Feather rivers crested at eighty-three feet, washing away bridges, destroying homes, spreading boulders and mud over vast areas of farmland.

August 17, 1959. An unexpected earthquake in Montana wrenched the Rocky Mountains, threw 80 million tons of rock into a river, formed a new lake, and sent the geysers of Yellowstone Park into violent eruptions.

Tremendous Power at Work

Volcanoes, floods, earthquakes. What tremendous power they have to change this old earth we live on! And there have been in the past far greater floods and earthquakes and volcanic eruptions than anything we see today. Discovering evidences of these upheavals makes geology fascinating, for geology is the study of the earth—where it came from, and what has been happening to it, subjects every Pathfinder wants to know about.

Where Did the Earth Come From?

Many people have tried to guess how the earth originated. They have talked about whirling gases out in space that slowed down millions of years ago and became solid; and of substances that shot out from the sun and became the earth when a star sailed by too close. But there is no proof for these ideas.

The only statement that is really helpful is the one made in the Bible: "In the beginning God created the heaven and the earth" (Gen. 1:1). How God did it we do not know. But the Bible says, "He spake, and it was done" (Ps. 33:9); and "in six days the Lord made heaven and earth" (Ex. 20:11). The first chapter of Genesis gives a simple story of the days of Creation and is familiar to every Seventh-day Adventist Pathfinder.

In the beginning the earth was beautiful. What a place to hike! There were lofty hills and mountains, but they were not bare and ragged as many are today. They were clothed with majestic trees, and the open spaces were covered with grass and flowers. There were no dismal swamps or gloomy jungles. The whole earth was more beautiful than the grounds of a lovely palace.

After the earth had stood for about 1,600 years, people became so wicked that God had to destroy them and the earth by a flood. This changed the whole surface of the earth, burying trees, plants, men, and animals and throwing up huge mountains. How the Flood was caused we do not know, but we can study its effects in the rocks. This study is called *geology*. When correctly studied,

WATER is a powerful force, changing the earth. Pounding waves alter shore lines, and the Flood brought the greatest upheaval this world has known.

geology reveals the mighty power of God as it was manifested in the destruction of the world that lived before the Flood.

The Earth Is Always Changing

Take a good look at the world around you next time you go on a hike. It will never be the same again. Many forces are constantly at work changing the surface. For instance:

Rain softens the soil and washes it away. *Water* soaks into rocks. *Frost* and *snow* freeze this water, forming ice inside the rocks. As the weather grows colder the ice expands, cracking the rocks into small fragments, sometimes silently, sometimes bursting with a noise that can be heard long distances away.

Running water washes away soil, cuts down hillsides, changes the course of streams. It is one of the most important agencies changing the surface of the earth. *Ground water* is water found in caves and underground streams or filling porous rocks. When it contains carbonic acid it may dissolve away rock, forming caverns. Sometimes it breaks through the surface in springs or geysers.

Waves occur on the ocean, on lakes, or even on large rivers. They cut down the shore line and carry sand to be deposited on beaches or sand bars. *Wind* carries sand and piles it into dunes. It may cut away rocks, using the sand as an abrasive. It may carry dust great distances, and it is the cause of waves in water.

Volcanoes produce flows of lava or clouds of dust that sometimes bury fruitful land or cities. Associated with volcanoes are hot springs and boiling mud pots. *Earthquakes* are sometimes caused by volcanoes. They also occur because there are great cracks hundreds of miles long—called faults—in the surface of the earth. If the rock layers along these cracks slip, there is an earthquake. Earthquakes destroy buildings, cause landslides, and change the course of streams above and under the ground.

201

IGNEOUS ROCKS. BASALT (left) is lava from a volcano. It is dark gray with a fine texture. DIORITE (right) is dark and has a coarse grain.

SEDIMENTARY ROCKS. SANDSTONE (left) is sand grains cemented together. CONGLOMERATE (right) or "puddingstone" is pebbles and rocks.

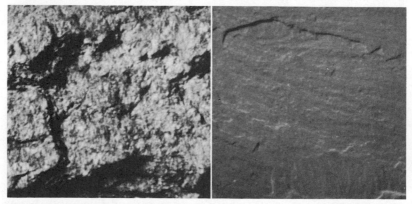

METAMORPHIC ROCKS. SCHIST (left) has a fine texture, with thin scales that crumble readily. SLATE (right) splits easily into large thin sheets.

GRANITE (left) has a coarse grain, and is a mixture of quartz and feldspar. OBSIDIAN (right) is glassy and can be flaked off readily to make axheads.

LIMESTONE (left) is almost entirely calcium carbonate and frequently contains fossil shells from the Flood. SHALE (right) usually comes from mud.

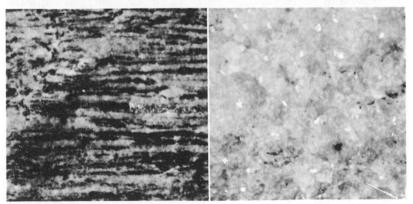

GNEISS (left) may look like granite at first, but it has many dark bands in it that granite does not have. MARBLE (right) comes in several attractive colors.

203

As a result of faulty farming, **EROSION** washed away the topsoil. The underlying ground was unproductive, and the farmer had to abandon his home.

Rock Formations

The rocks of the earth are usually classified in three groups—igneous, sedimentary, and metamorphic.

Igneous rocks are formed by heat. They may consist of *magmas,* molten material poured out on the surface through volcanic craters or through fissures; or they may be in the form of *scoria,* small fragments; or *tufa,* a kind of rock formed by volcanic ash. Sometimes the ash is mingled with water and makes a mud flow that hardens into tufa.

Sedimentary rocks were formed by tiny particles that settled to the bottom of water. As these particles, or sediment, piled up, the pressure near the bottom became greater and greater, squeezing the particles together. Fine grains of sand became sandstone, sea shells and similar calcium-containing materials became limestone, mixtures of pebbles and rock became conglomerate, and clay turned into shale.

Metamorphic rocks are sedimentary or igneous rocks that have been changed by heat, pressure, or chemicals. Thus gneiss (pronounced *nice*) is changed granite, marble is changed limestone, and slate is changed shale.

Rocks Are Mixtures

Rocks are mixtures of minerals, and minerals are fairly definite in their physical properties and chemical composition.

Granite, for example, is a mixture of minerals—quartz, feldspar, and mica or other dark minerals.

204

With wise **SOIL MANAGEMENT** the same land can be made to produce rich crops year after year. Good farmers use contour plowing to prevent erosion.

Quartz is silicon dioxide and consists of one part silicon and two parts oxygen. It is the most common of the solid minerals.

Common *feldspar* contains potassium, aluminum, sodium, calcium, and silicon.

Common *mica* contains potassium, magnesium, iron, aluminum, silicon, and oxygen.

How to Identify Rocks and Minerals

First, get a good rock book. You'll find some listed at the end of this chapter. Then begin collecting. A good magnifying glass is helpful, and so are a file and a hammer. But you don't need them to get started.

Rocks are identified by several features: *Structure*—whether layered, solid, foamy, or frothy; *texture*—coarse or fine-grained, solid, or glassy; *hardness*—there is a regular graded scale of hardness; *fracture*—the way the rock splits, whether in thin sheets, irregularly, in curves, et cetera.

Minerals are identified by color, hardness, luster, and crystal.

SOIL AND SOIL MANAGEMENT

Soil is formed when rain and snow, sun, wind, and frost act on rocks or masses of sand and clay. Good soil consists of sand, clay, and humus. *Sand* is small grains of quartz. *Clay* is very small grains of feldspar, mica, or shale. *Humus* is vegetable matter that is produced when roots, stems, and leaves decay. It loosens the soil and helps it to hold water.

A well-balanced proportion of these three ingredients makes a good soil. Sand is porous, and if there is too much of it in the soil it will not hold water readily. It will quickly absorb a large amount, but will also lose it quickly. Clay is compact and tends to make the soil hard and to bake in dry weather. Soils with too much clay do not hold much water, and they dry out quickly. Humus helps counteract the effects of these other ingredients. Thus a properly balanced soil will be loose because of the sand and humus, will be firm because of the clay, and will retain water well because of the humus.

In addition to these ingredients a number of chemicals are required by plants for good growth. The most important are nitrogen, potassium, and phosphorus, and they can be added to the soil in the form of commercial fertilizers, which are made from rocks rich in the desired chemicals, or from industrial products, or from meat, bone, and fish scraps. Humus is worked into the soil by using manure or by planting crops that are later plowed under. Peat moss is often used for humus in greenhouses. It is the decayed stems of a moss that grows in Canada and other parts of the northern hemisphere.

Soil management today is a highly scientific procedure that takes into account the nature of the soil, the slope of the land, the available moisture, and the climate. It is closely tied in with the sciences of botany (plant study) and chemistry. For fascinating reading ask your Pathfinder director or school teacher for some good books on conservation and soil management.

Erosion

One of the most terrible things that happen to soil is *erosion*. Heavy rain (and often wind) carries away thousands of tons of good topsoil every year. In dry, windy areas wise farmers plant their crops in strips in order to prevent this loss. The crops cannot be grown more often than once in two or three years, for the soil has to lie fallow to gather moisture. If this fallow soil is left in large patches, the wind may carry off much of the top. To prevent this crops are planted in strips, with the bare, fallow soil in narrow strips between. This way the wind is prevented from gaining sufficient force to carry off the soil. To prevent erosion by rain, farmers follow the contour of the hills, planting around hills instead of up and down them. Rows of corn or other crops thus placed check the run-off, and stop the washing. Mulching—placing vegetable material over soil—prevents the fine particles from being washed or blown away.

Get an expert **ROCK HOUND** to go with you on your next hike. He will point out many interesting things in stones you would never notice otherwise.

In areas of heavy rainfall the soil may become so saturated that it washes away very easily. Campsites on which the grass has been destroyed may erode badly. Pastures may be grazed too closely and trodden by the feet of animals until the soil washes. Sometimes it is necessary to dig ditches in these fields to turn the water. A gully that starts in a pasture may be filled with rocks or brush, which will check the stream and catch the fine material and prevent it from being carried away.

Pathfinders do all they can to stop erosion, because the soil that washes away is the soil that's needed to grow our country's food.

HOW MANY OF THESE CAN YOU DO?

Check each one when you finish it.

☐ 1. Go with your unit on a hike. See how many different rocks and minerals you can find.

☐ 2. Start a rock collection.

☐ 3. Collect a bottleful of water from a flooded river. See how much soil settles to the bottom.

☐ 4. Earn the MV Honor award in *Mineralogy*.

INTERESTING BOOKS ABOUT ROCKS AND MINERALS

Field Book of Common Rocks and Minerals, F. B. Loomis (G. B. Putnam's Sons)

A Field Guide to Rocks and Minerals, Frederick H. Pough (Houghton Mifflin Co.)

Rocks and Minerals and Fossils (MV Honor booklet)

stars in the sky

A MISSION launch is plowing through high water in the South Seas, taking a missionary to an island of head-hunting savages. The island is a tiny speck fifty miles away. The least error in direction, and the ship will never even see the island. The captain, a Seventh-day Adventist missionary, peers carefully through his sextant at the stars, glances at the clock, and pinpoints his position on the chart. Next morning the island is square ahead of the ship's bow.

A Pathfinder is talking to a group of neighborhood boys. "Aw, how can you prove the world's coming to an end?" one of the boys sneers. The Pathfinder racks his brain for a moment, then tells of the night of November 13, 1833, when falling stars fulfilled prophecy.

You are lying in your sleeping bag beside a mountain lake gazing up at the stars. Perhaps you are thinking about the future, what you will be doing when you are older. Will you be using the stars to navigate a mission launch? Will you be preaching about the stars in an evangelistic meeting? At all events, if you are true to God someday you know you will be traveling up past those stars toward the home of God. Exciting thing to dream about! A Pathfinder outing to beat all Pathfinder outings! And with stars so important in your future, you begin to wish you knew more about them. Fortunately, it isn't hard to learn some basic facts.

Stars Go in Groups

When you see an older Pathfinder point to the stars and say, "That's Deneb; that's Arcturus," you may suspect that he is making things up to sound impressive. But it is easy to learn the names of the brightest stars.

First, learn the names of the star groups, for stars go in groups, called constellations. (*Con* means "with," *stella* means "stars." A constellation is a group of *stars* that seem to stay *with* one another.) Remember the first time you went to the Pathfinder Club? All the

"The heavens declare the glory of God" (Psalm 19:1).

COMETS, like Arend-Roland comet (left), follow orbits; their return can be predicted. Sun reflecting off the earth makes EARTHLIT MOON (right).

Pathfinders were running here and there, and you couldn't tell one from another. Then the director shouted "Fall IN!" and in a moment the Pathfinders formed orderly units. After a while, as you got better acquainted, you noticed that John was always with Richard, Ellen was always with Diane. It is the same way with the stars.

At first the stars seem all mixed up. But ask a friend to point out some of the constellations to you, and suddenly you will see the sky falling into definite "units." Soon you will know that that blue-white star *must* be Rigel because it isn't far from bright, yellow Betelgeuse, and Rigel and Betelgeuse are always close together.

Begin With the Dipper

Probably the easiest constellation to pick out, especially in the summer, is the Big Dipper, which is part of the constellation *Ursa Major,* the Great Bear. The two stars at the end of the bowl are called pointers, because they point to *Polaris,* the polestar. Hanging off Polaris, like a kettle on a hook, is the Little Dipper, part of *Ursa Minor,* the Little Bear. A little way off you can see a clear zig-zag of five stars looking like a W or an M and called *Cassiopeia.*

If it is a summer evening, imagine a curved line running off

210

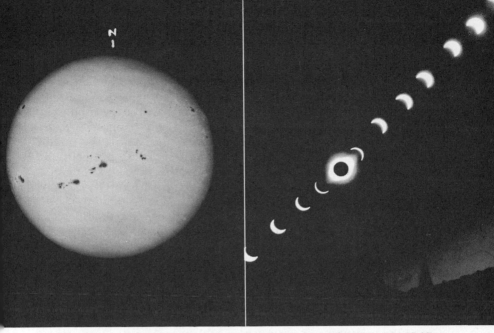

SUNSPOTS (left) are dark areas on sun; they affect our radios, TV. In SOLAR ECLIPSE moon slowly hides sun, making black circle in bright glow (right).

the handle of the Big Dipper. A little farther on you will come to a bright star at the point of six stars arranged like a kite. The bright star is *Arcturus,* the constellation is *Boötes.* Stretch the curved line farther, and you come to another bright star, *Spica* in the constellation *Virgo,* the virgin. (Remember that a curved line is called an arc; so, from the Big Dipper "make an arc to Arcturus, and speak to Spica.")

On the east side of Boötes find a circlet of fairly bright stars. This is *Corona Borealis,* the Northern Crown. Its brightest star is *Gemma.*

Over to the east look for five stars that make an almost perfect cross. On a summer evening the cross will be lying on its side. On Christmas Eve it will be standing upright just above where the sun goes down. The cross is called *Cygnus,* the Swan. The bright star at the head is *Deneb.* On one side of the cross is *Vega,* the brightest star in the summer sky, in the constellation *Lyra,* the Lyre. On the other side of the cross is another bright star, *Altair,* in *Aquila,* the Eagle. These three bright stars, Deneb, Vega, and Altair, make a perfect triangle.

Low in the southern sky, with its tail curling down to the horizon, is *Scorpius,* the Scorpion. The bright star that forms its eye is

Antares. Just to the east of Scorpius, and looking much like a five-pointed star, is *Sagittarius.* Astronomers have calculated that the center of our Milky Way is straight through this constellation.

If you begin your star study in the winter, the easiest constellation to start with is *Orion.* Four very bright stars form a simple rectangle. The bottom right-hand star is brilliant blue-white *Rigel.* The star in the upper left corner is *Betelgeuse.* Across the middle are three bright stars making a straight line called the *belt,* and hanging from them are three faint stars called the *sword.* The middle star of the sword marks the famous open space in Orion. Look at it with field glasses. It is pale green.

Back to the belt. These three stars point upward to *Aldebaran* in the V-shaped constellation *Taurus,* the Bull. (The V marks the horns of the bull.) Stretch the line a little farther and you come to the *Pleiades,* which are part of the Taurus constellation. Job mentioned them, in Job 38:31. (Don't confuse the Pleiades with the Little Dipper!)

Back to Orion's belt again! A straight line downward from the belt leads to *Sirius* in the Big Dog constellation, *Canis Major.* Sirius is the brightest and nearest star in the northern sky.

There are eighty-eight constellations. When you have learned to recognize a few of them you will be amazed how quickly you can learn new ones from studying the star maps.

The Stars Aren't What They Seem

At first glance all the stars look pretty much alike. But in reality they are all different. Sirius is two stars close together. Polaris is three, Theta in Orion is four, Castor is six.

The colors differ too. Some are red, others yellow, blue, or green. The star at the foot of the northern cross, called Beta Cygni, turns out to be two stars in the telescope, one a brilliant blue, the other a golden orange.

The stars vary greatly in size. Our sun is a rather small star, only about 864,000 miles in diameter. Antares, the "eye" of the Scorpion, is 400 million miles in diameter, and Betelgeuse is 460 million miles across. On the other hand, the star that keeps Sirius company has a diameter only three times as great as the earth's diameter, but the star has 250,000 times the earth's mass. Gravity is so strong there that if you weigh 100 pounds here you would weigh 3,000 tons there.

The stars are hurtling through space at tremendous speeds. Relative to the stars around it, our sun travels 12 miles a second, or more than a million miles a day—and takes us with it! Other stars are

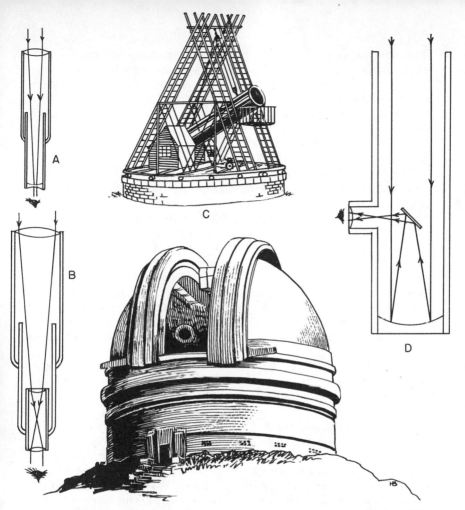

Galileo used a **TELESCOPE** like A, with concave lens at the eyepiece. B is a modern type of refracting telescope. C is the reflecting telescope Herschel made in his back yard in 1796, with a 48-inch mirror. D shows the famous Mount Palomar telescope with its 200-inch mirror housed in the large dome.

known to be traveling at 180 miles per second, or fifteen million miles a day. Many probably go even faster.

The Sun's Family

Our *sun* is a star large enough to hold 1,300,000 earths. Flames shoot out from it as far as 800,000 miles. Tremendous whirlwinds sweep across it and can be seen as sunspots. They affect our weather and the Northern Lights, and interfere with radio and telegraphy.

The sun burns up 700 million tons of fuel every second, but has enough left to last for billions of years at the present rate.

Mercury is the planet nearest the sun and is hard to see, for it never comes very high above the horizon in the farther northern latitudes. It takes 88 days to go around the sun, traveling at almost 30 miles per second. It has no air or water. One side always faces the sun and probably has a temperature of about 900° F. The other side is about minus 450° F.

The next planet is *Venus,* about the same size as the earth but surrounded with clouds so thick that even the largest telescopes cannot see what its surface is like.

The *earth* is the first planet with a *moon.* When the moon gets between the sun and the earth there is an eclipse of the sun, and it is possible to see the sun's flames shooting into space. When the earth gets between the sun and the moon there is an eclipse of the moon, and the earth's shadow can be seen on the moon. The moon is approximately 240,000 miles away. It has no air or water, but it does have 28 mountain peaks higher than Everest, and many canyons, one of which is 24,000 feet deep. The moon causes tides in our seas. A man on the moon would be so light he could jump over a barn.

After the earth comes *Mars,* a little more than half the diameter of the earth and with two tiny moons probably not more than ten miles in diameter. One moon goes around Mars once in a day; the other, three times a day.

In the next space beyond the sun where a planet should be, there are thousands of large chunks of rock instead. They vary from a mile or so to approximately five hundred miles in diameter, each with its own orbit, and are called *asteroids.*

Beyond the asteroids lies *Jupiter,* larger than all the other planets combined, with twelve moons, four of which you can see with a field glass.

Saturn glows next with a pale yellow light and is easily recognized in a telescope by its rings. It has nine moons. *Uranus* and *Neptune* are green. Uranus was discovered in 1781 by Sir William Herschel when he was scanning the sky with the 48-inch telescope he had built in his back yard. Neptune was seen for the first time only after Adams and Leverrier had solved a series of very complicated mathematical problems and told the astronomers exactly where to look. When the astronomers turned their telescopes to the place the mathematicians indicated, there was the planet! But Leverrier never did see Neptune for himself.

Pluto, the most distant of the planets, was discovered only a few

PLUTO 3,550

NEPTUNE 30,900

URANUS 32,400

SATURN 74,200

JUPITER 88,770

MARS 4,220

EARTH 7,927

VENUS 7,700

MERCURY 3,100

DIAMETER OF PLANETS GIVEN IN MILES

HB

Big telescopes reveal many interesting sights, such as the CRAB (left) in Taurus, and the HORSEHEAD (center) and ORION NEBULA (right) in Orion.

years ago after Percival Lowell solved some even more complicated mathematical problems, but he died before there was a telescope good enough to see the planet. When it was first seen, in 1930, it was exactly where Lowell had said it would be. Pluto is so cold that if there is any air on it, it is frozen solid. Its year is as long as 248 of ours.

Besides the planets and moons, the sun's family includes meteors and comets. *Comets* are easily identified by their tails. They move around the sun and may reappear at intervals many years apart. The tails probably do not contain as much material as there is in an automobile, though some of them are millions of miles long!

Meteors generally are tiny particles the size of a pebble or a grain of sand. When they strike our atmosphere they get hot and burn up quickly. Several millions can be seen every night, twice as many after midnight as before, and they add a thousand tons to the weight of the earth every day. Certain large star showers come regularly and can be predicted. Look for remnants of the famous falling stars of 1833 in the constellation Leo around November 15 each year. Large meteors that get through the atmosphere and strike the earth are called *meteorites*.

Everything Circling in Space

For many years everyone thought the earth was in the center of the universe and that the stars and planets went around it. Then in 1543 Copernicus announced that he believed the planets went around the sun. But he couldn't prove it.

After he died, a student of his, Tycho Brahe, studied Mars very

216

carefully and managed to prove Copernicus was right. Tycho never saw a telescope, but he considered astronomy such a sacred subject that he always wore his finest clothes in the observatory, and God blessed him. In 1610, after Tycho died, Galileo looked through a telescope at the stars for the first time and saw four moons going around Jupiter. This proved that moons go around planets, and helped people believe that the planets go around the sun.

So the planets, including our earth, are going in circles around the sun. The sun is one of approximately 100 billion stars in our Milky Way, or galaxy, as it is sometimes called. The sun is taking us in a circle around the center of our galaxy. Our galaxy is just one of more than half a billion galaxies spread out through four billion light years of space.

HOW MANY OF THESE CAN YOU DO?

Check each one when you finish it.

☐ 1. Put a pin outside and another one inside a window and line up the pin heads exactly with a bright star at precisely nine o'clock. Next night note the exact time when the pins line up with the same star. (Should be 3 minutes and 56 seconds earlier.)

☐ 2. Make a star map showing eight major constellations.

☐ 3. Put a long stick in the ground, notice the angle and length of the sun's shadow at noon on various days, especially near midsummer and before Christmas.

☐ 4. Go on a star hike, observing at least seven constellations and five well-known stars.

☐ 5. Earn the MV Honor award in *Stars*.

INTERESTING BOOKS ON STARS

The Golden Book of Astronomy, Rose Wyler and Gerald Ames (Simon and Schuster)
Beautifully illustrated book, ideal for Pathfinders.

Field Book of the Skies, William Tyler Olcott and R. Newton Mayall (G. P. Putnam's Sons)
Excellent for telling exactly what to look for and where.

The Glory of the Stars, Merlin L. Neff (Pacific Press)
Contains many interesting facts about stars.

An Introduction to Astronomy, Robert H. Baker (D. Van Nostrand Company)
Standard book for those who are really serious about astronomy.

sunshine and storm

THE Pathfinders were camped by a lake. The morning was sunny and hot. The afternoon seemed almost ideal for a swim, but the Pathfinders stayed close to their tents, making them ready for a storm. Sure enough, about three-thirty a wind came up suddenly and blew a gale. Black clouds shut out the sun. Lightning leaped to the hills. Rain fell like a waterfall. The Pathfinders sat in their tents, calm and dry, till the fury was past and the sun came out again.

"The campout was a lot of fun," they said when they returned home. "And that storm was the most exciting part of all. But if we hadn't known it was coming it could have wrecked the whole weekend."

How did those Pathfinders know a storm was on its way? Simply because weather follows definite rules and can usually be predicted with a good degree of accuracy.

In making weather forecasts it helps to know what makes weather. So let's see what causes it. Perhaps you can make sure *your* next camping trip won't be rained out!

AIR AND EARTH AND SUN

Three major considerations are involved in the making of the weather—the air, the earth, and the sun.

Air

There is no air on the moon and there is no weather. There are only heat and cold there, 200° F. in the daytime and —250° F. at night. If there were no air on the earth, we would suffer from the same extremes here. We would be frozen stiff every night and fried crisp every morning (even if we could exist without air for breathing).

Air is made up of several different kinds of gases, chiefly nitrogen (78 per cent) and oxygen (21 per cent). It's a good thing there is all that nitrogen. If the air were all oxygen, the first time you

"He it is who makes the clouds rise" (Psalm 135:7, R.S.V.).

tried to light a campfire, the whole world would catch fire. Even the iron and steel would burn!

Air is light, but still it has weight, and it extends up into space 750 to 1,000 miles. If we could make a pipe one inch square and extend it up as high as the air goes, the air in the pipe would weigh nearly 15 pounds. All the air on the earth weighs about 5 quadrillion tons!

About half of the air is within the first 3½ miles above sea level, and it is within these three and a half miles that most of our weather occurs.

When air is compressed it heats up. When it expands it cools. Pumping up a bicycle tire heats the air. But put your finger in front of the valve and feel the air escape from the tire—it is expanding quickly and is quite cool.

Hot air rises, cold air sinks. As the hot air rises its pressure goes down, for the air pressure high up is lower than that at sea level. Therefore, the temperature of the air goes down too, at the rate of about 5° F. for every thousand feet of rise.

Lastly, the air contains not only oxygen and nitrogen but a great deal of water. This is usually in the form of invisible water vapor. The hotter the air, the more water vapor it can hold. For instance, one hundred cubic yards of air at 68° F. can hold 46 ounces of water vapor. But at 61° F. the same amount of air can hold only 36 ounces. When air is holding all the water vapor it can hold at a certain temperature it is said to be saturated. When saturated air is cooled, some of the water must fall out. More of this later.

Earth and Sun

If the world were perfectly motionless and there were no sun shining, the air would be absolutely still. But the sun does shine and the earth is heated, more at the equator than at the poles. The air at the equator becomes warm, the air at the poles remains cold. Therefore, the warm air at the equator rises, leaving a partial vacuum. The cold air of the poles tends to rush in to fill this space. Such movement of the air we call wind.

If the earth did not rotate, there might be only one wind. In the northern hemisphere it would be a north wind blowing always from the cold polar regions to the equator. In the southern hemisphere it would be a south wind.

But the earth does rotate. And because it goes always toward the east, some winds seem to come from the east, just as when you put your arm out of the car window, the wind always seems to come from the place the car is going to.

A **TORNADO** is the most violent of all types of weather. Air in the funnel spins at hundreds of miles an hour. Passing over a house, it causes the house to explode, but may lift people and set them down unharmed.

There are other factors that affect the wind. It sweeps rapidly across the open prairies but is slowed by forests and is deflected by mountains. And because the land heats more quickly in the daytime and cools more quickly at night than does the sea, air rises from the land by day, and "onshore" winds sweep in from the sea, bringing air to take its place; at night the air rises from the warmer sea and "offshore" winds from the cold land blow out over the water.

All these factors—and others—combine to produce regular "trade winds" that blow from the east just north of the equator and "westerlies" that blow from the west, in a belt farther north, across the United States. As a result, weather in the United States comes almost entirely from the west, but local conditions plus the intrusion of cold or warm air masses from polar or tropical regions vary the pattern and occasionally upset the weather bureau's predictions.

HOW THE WEATHER BUREAU PREDICTS WEATHER

In 1851 Dr. Merryweather urged the British Government to establish weather stations along the coast where the activities of captive leaches could be watched, for it was believed that the wiggling and crawling of a leach in a glass of water foretold the weather. Fortunately, his idea came to nothing. Today almost all countries have elaborate systems of weather stations where weather conditions are scientifically observed.

Every day the United States National Meteorological Center receives at least 20,000 items of information on the weather from hundreds of weather observing stations around the world.

Balloons are sent aloft and watched by telescopes to determine the speed and direction of the wind at high altitudes. Other balloons go up with radios that transmit information as they ascend. Radarscopes constantly turn, watching for storms. Planes and ships regularly report conditions in their areas. Satellites telecast photographs of cloud formations.

The direction of the wind near the ground is indicated by a *weather vane*. Its speed is measured by the four twirling cups of an *anemometer*. The pressure of the air is measured by a *barometer;* the temperature by a *thermometer;* and the humidity by a *hygrometer* (air that is saturated by water vapor has a humidity of 100 per cent; air that contains only half the vapor it could hold has a humidity of 50 per cent).

All the information gathered by use of these instruments is sent at frequent intervals to the weather bureau, where it is studied by weather experts and fed into computers. A weather map is drawn, and the forecast is made. In spite of the fun people make of the weather bureau, its predictions are correct most of the time.

HOW YOU CAN PREDICT THE WEATHER

Of course, when you are in camp you won't have any computers or weather maps to aid you. But you can get considerable help from the winds and clouds.

Watch the Winds

If there is going to be a change in the weather, there will often be a change in the wind first, for the winds bring the weather. The kind of weather they bring depends on where they come from.

If the wind comes from a large body of water, it will probably bring rain. Air that moves long distances over land will be dry; from the poles, it will be cold and probably dry; from the equator, warm and usually moist. Thus, if you are camping in the eastern part of the United States, a north wind will be cold; a west wind, warm; a south wind, warm and probably wet (because of the Gulf of Mexico); and an east wind, coming off the Atlantic, warm

Ideal **WEATHER PREDICTION** setup includes satellites, constant-altitude balloons, airplanes, ships, and shore stations (1). Information on wind, temperature, and cloud formations is received by **RADIOTHEODOLITE** (2). Water in **RAIN GAUGE** (3) collects in bucket, weighs down on spring, operates pen, draws line on graph. **WEATHER BUREAU STATION** (4) has rain gauges, anemometers for wind speed, radar on a tower for tracking storms.

CUMULUS (upper left) are fair-weather clouds. CIRRUS (upper right) predict a storm within two days. CIRRO-STRATUS (lower left) probably mean a storm by the next day; ALTO-CUMULUS (lower right), storm in a few hours.

and wet. A northwest wind will be cold and dry; from the southwest, comparatively hot and dry; from the southeast, hot and very wet; from the northeast, cool and wet. Of course, if you live in California, a west wind will come off the Pacific and will probably be cool and may bring light rain; a south wind will almost certainly bring heavy rain. However, in a hurricane the wind blows in great circles as the storm advances. Therefore, in your locality the wind may be blowing in a direction opposite to the direction the storm is traveling. Benjamin Franklin is thought to have been the first American to notice this strange fact.

Scan the Clouds

Clouds are important weather predictors. Clouds are formed usually when hot air rises. The temperature of the air goes down until the saturation point is reached, then the invisible water vapor condenses into tiny water droplets that we see as clouds. These droplets are only 1/2500 inch in diameter. When conditions are right, these droplets join with others and may grow a million times. When they have a diameter of 1/125 inch they are heavy enough to fall, and may come down as rain, although raindrops generally average from 1/50 to 1/5 inch in diameter. If on the way down they freeze, they reach the earth as hail. If the water vapor freezes under the right conditions, snow is formed. It may reach the ground as snow; but in warm weather it will melt on the way down and arrive as rain. Raindrops are usually larger in warm weather.

Clouds have names. High riding, hairy "mare's tail" clouds are called *cirrus*. Cirrus is a latin word meaning "a curl of hair." Cirrus clouds form at 20,000 to 40,000 feet, and are mostly ice crystals. Flat clouds are called *stratus,* a Latin word meaning "spread out." Remember it by thinking of the flat strata in rocks. Big, white, puffy clouds are called *cumulus,* a Latin word meaning "a heap." Think of them as being "accumulated" into heaps. Clouds that rains come from are called *nimbus,* meaning a "rainstorm." It's easy to remember because you have to be nimble when nimbus clouds appear or you'll get wet!

The names are sometimes combined, as *strato-cumulus,* cumulus clouds in layers. Sometimes the word *alto* appears in front of the name. It means that the clouds are formed at a high *alti*tude. This prefix is used to indicate the clouds known as middle clouds.

Storm Warning!

When a storm is coming, the clouds often follow one another in a regular procession. First the hairy *cirrus* clouds appear. They are so high up they are pushed ahead of the storm by the onrushing westerlies that travel faster than the winds nearer the ground. They usually mean that rain is twenty-four to forty-eight hours away. Then come *cirro-stratus,* as the clouds of ice crystals close together in a thin veil. The sun glares through; or at night the moon forms a halo. The clouds lower, the sun grows dim, and *alto-stratus* closes a gray curtain. Then the sun is shut out as *stratus* blankets the sky. You'd better check your tents and make sure everything is under cover, for within six or seven hours, *nimbo-stratus,* dark and dreary, will bring rain.

Clouds also foretell good weather. Everyone loves *cumulus,* the big puffy clouds boys like to lie on the ground and watch change shape. But when the bottom grows black and the top looks like a white anvil, look out! That's *cumulo-nimbus,* the thunderhead. You'll be drenched in a flash, but the rain won't last long. *Alto-cumulus* are little cumulus clouds riding high. They mean fair weather. When they break into smaller cumulus clouds they look like the scales of a fish and are called *cirro-cumulus,* the mackerel sky. They may bring unsettled weather and brief showers.

Folklore and Weather Proverbs

Before there were weather bureaus, people often made up rhymes to help them predict the weather. Most of these were senseless, but others were quite accurate. Some go back many centuries.

Jesus said to the Pharisees, "When it is evening, ye say, It will be fair weather: for the sky is red" (Matthew 16:2).

This is one of the most reliable weather predictors. The sun appears red in the evening when it is shining through dust. The air in the west is dry, and the air that is in the west at night is the air you will get in the morning.

"If the sun sets in a cloud bank, expect a storm."

This is true because weather comes from the west. The storm in the west tonight will be overhead by morning.

"Stars bright, tomorrow all right."

Right! The stars are bright because the air is dry. No rain for at least twenty-four hours.

"When the grass is dry at morning light,
  Look for rain before the night."

Right! The grass is dry because a blanket of clouds overhead kept the ground too warm for water vapor to condense. These clouds will probably bring rain before night.

Don't Miss These Signs!

Other signs will help you predict accurately. There is *bad* weather ahead—

When swallows skim low over the pond. Swallows chase insects. Before a storm the high air is cool and the insects fly near the ground, where the air is warm. The insect-catching birds follow them down.

When the stars are fuzzy or there is a halo around the moon. Cirro-stratus clouds are forming, harbingers of rain within twenty-four or forty-eight hours.

When train whistles and the drone of airplanes seem near and loud.

When distant mountains seem close. Unstable air is taking away the haze.

When forgotten toothaches and old pains throb. Well, anyway, there does seem to be a connection between backaches and lowered air pressure, a precursor of bad weather.

Also beware when smoke from the campfire hangs low over the ground, clouds hang close to the tops of the mountains, the west wind shifts to east or south, and the nights are warmer than they have been.

226

Look out for anvil-shaped cumulo-nimbus, the THUNDERHEAD. It means thunder, lightning, heavy rain; but the storm will pass quickly and the sun shine again.

There is *good* weather ahead—

When swallows fly high. The upper air is warm, the insects enjoy flying in it.

When there is morning dew. A clear, cold night causes condensation near the ground.

Also be glad when the campfire smoke rises straight up, the nights are cold and crisp, spiders spin in the grass, and a light morning fog breaks by ten o'clock.

HOW MANY OF THESE CAN YOU DO?

Check each one when you finish it.

- ☐ 1. Erect a weather vane and rain gauge.
- ☐ 2. Keep a record of the weather (wind, rainfall, sunshine, temperature) for one month.
- ☐ 3. Predict tomorrow's weather each evening for a week. Write down your prediction and next day see how right you were.
- ☐ 4. Get your Pathfinder unit to visit the local weather station.
- ☐ 5. Earn the MV Honor award in *Weather*.

INTERESTING BOOKS ABOUT WEATHER

Reading the Weather and *Understanding the Weather,* T. M. Longstretch (Macmillan Co.)

Describe many weather signs. Helpful to campers.

Weather, Paul E. Lehr, R. Will Burnett, Herbert S. Zim (Golden Press)

Weather (MV Honor booklet)

CHAPTER 21

animals with fur

YOU and the rest of your Pathfinder unit are hiking through the woods. It's an exploratory hike—none of you have ever been along this trail before.

Suddenly you hear what sounds like the *crack* of a rifle. Taken by surprise, everyone stops talking, then starts in again, twice as fast as before, each one giving his idea as to what caused the sound.

Finally your captain raises a hand. "Hush! Beavers! Follow me and we'll find them."

He heads into a deer trail and the rest of you follow, putting into practice all you've ever learned about stalking and concealment.

The deer trail winds through the trees. After a couple hundred feet the captain raises his hand again and whispers, "A beaver lake." Noiselessly, each of you finds a tree or a bush to hide behind, and there in front of you is a beautiful little mountain lake that wasn't shown on the map.

There's not a beaver in sight. But there is a pile of sticks in the middle of the lake that you recognize as a beaver's home.

And then there's a little black nose sticking up through the water—and a beaver comes into view. He swims around in circles. Up goes his head. His whole body undulates gracefully like a seal's, and his tail comes down *thwack* on the water with a great splash, and you know for sure what made the rifle sound that attracted you there in the first place.

Presently out comes Mrs. Beaver and two children, and you watch fascinated for a long time. Among other things, you find out whether the beaver hits the water with his tail only as a danger signal, or whether he does it sometimes just for fun. At last, your captain glances at his watch and whispers, "We've got to leave! It's almost time for supper."

As silently as you came you slip back along the deer trail, then race down the path toward camp. What a story you've got to tell the others! They'll certainly want you to lead them to beaver lake tomorrow!

"Where is the dwelling of the lions?" (Nahum 2:11).

But beavers are only one of the hundreds of different furry animals that live in our country. Unfortunately, most of them stay out of sight so much of the time that people rarely see them. Scientists call them mammals, because they give milk to their young. Their bodies are usually covered with fur or hair, and sometimes with sharp quills.

Mammals seldom come out in the open; many shun daylight. It is up to you to learn how to find them. The Indians of a hundred years ago knew much more about the wild animals than white people do today.

How to Find Wild Animals

First, you must learn to walk silently. It is more fun to go in a group, but you'll have to be careful not to talk. You must practice creeping through the bushes, be willing to lie on a mossy log, or sit for hours on a stump surrounded by overhanging vines as you watch a red fox digging out her hole or bringing food to her young. From a high rock lookout, with a pair of field glasses you may see a mountain lion catching ground squirrels, but it will take great skill to watch such a creature and not be found out. Mountain lions have had much more training in watching than you have, and it is usually they who do the discovering, while you are unaware of their presence. But with some practice you may get to the place where *you* can do the watching. It is certainly worth a try.

Start Small!

When you begin to watch mammals, start with a small animal like a chipmunk or a meadow mouse. A chipmunk is ideal, for he will come out in broad daylight and run around in the grass and bushes looking for seeds to eat. If you sit motionless on a log he will not know you are there. He may actually run over your feet. If you keep a straight face and never make a sound or a movement, he will think you are a part of the log, but if you so much as sneeze, he'll scamper away and hide. Fortunately, chipmunks have short memories and come back soon to go on hunting seeds.

You may watch a colony of meadow mice in a grassy place. These little fellows make tunnels through the thick grass next to the ground, and they live there all their lives. If you can find a place where the tunnels come out into the open, such as under a clump of bushes, you will be able to see all that the mice do.

MAMMALS THAT EAT PLANTS AND INSECTS—Top line: mole, shrew, meadow mouse, white-footed field mouse. Second line: flying squirrel, squirrel, chipmunk. Third line: beaver, woodchuck. Sitting by itself, clinging to the top of the old pole: opossum. Bottom line: rabbit, porcupine, muskrat.

Just Like People

Sit still for an hour or two at a time, watching. The mice run along the trails they have made under the grass and bushes, and you will see them meet each other, perhaps touch noses as they exchange greetings, then after a second or two go their own ways along the trail. Soon another mouse comes along, perhaps carrying some grass in his mouth. Sometimes two mice have an argument when they meet, and you will laugh at what happens—they seem so much like people!

Perhaps someday you will find a porcupine climbing up the trunk of a pine tree. If you are careful not to disturb him you may watch him all day, or perhaps for several days. He may live in that tree for a week or two. With field glasses you can see every move he makes and learn to know the grunting sounds of porcupine talk.

You may be fortunate enough to see a real bobcat on a woods trail. If you stand still he may come to within a few feet of you before turning and walking away. Naturally, in such an experience you'll almost stop breathing from the sheer thrill of having a wild animal so close.

Getting to Know Them

To learn to know the mammals it is important to spend much time observing their habits and to write down in a notebook everything you learn. You can't trust your memory to recall the delightful experiences you have had. So get a convenient notebook and write down everything you see. You may someday write a book about your observations!

Traps

One way to learn about the small animals is to trap them alive. Traps that do no harm to the animals are easy to make from an ordinary mousetrap and a tin can. They can be set out in the woods and baited with rolled oats, and you will soon have a small animal of some kind. You will probably catch white-footed mice most often, but there will be jumping mice, pocket mice, chipmunks, harvest mice, grasshopper mice, red-backed mice, and many others, depending upon the part of the country you live in. Be sure to put some fluffy cotton in the back of the can so the little animal can make himself a bed and keep warm.

Another good way to make live traps is to bury old milk bot-

SMALLER MEAT EATERS—Top: mink. Second line: a little spotted skunk, large striped skunk, weasel (summer coat). Below: Otter. Bottom: badger.

Wilwerding

tles or tall tin cans far enough into the ground so that the very top of the can or bottle is even with the ground. If you want to catch a shrew you merely hang a bit of meat (a dead grasshopper will do nicely) on a string from a small stick extending over the opening of the bottle. The shrew comes along, tries to reach up to get the grasshopper, and falls into the bottle. Wild mice are caught in the same way, except that you put some rolled oats in the bottle or can, and sprinkle a few grains around the opening of the bottle, as well. The oats in the bottle keep the captured animal happy until you come for him. Sometimes a shrew will find your mouse before you do, and will have eaten him up by the time you come along. In such a case, however, you will at least have the shrew! But shrews don't live long without food. Go inspect your trap frequently.

Cages

Once you get a small mammal in this manner you will want to keep him in a cage at home for a few days while you learn more about his habits. An empty aquarium makes a good cage for a mouse, and if you put some mosses, tiny bushes, and other plants in there he will think he is right out in his own woods. Give him some water in a shallow dish and plenty of food, and he will live in good health for a long time.

The important thing to remember in keeping a wild animal is to prevent his being disturbed, as much as possible. Don't put the cage where a lot of people can frighten him, and when you watch him make sure that you do not make noise or sudden movements. Treat him in the same way you would if he were out in the wild. You will learn much from such a small creature.

ANIMAL HOMES

Mammals live everywhere. There is not a spot on our continent where there are no mammals at all. Yet, unless one knows how and where to look, he can travel for weeks without seeing one. Let us notice a few places where we can find them most easily.

Meadows

Animals of meadows and field are hard to find in the daytime, and at night you will need a strong flashlight if you are going to watch them at work. The most common meadow animal is the

LARGE MEAT EATERS—Top: mountain lion, lynx, bobcat. Second: grizzly bear, brown bear. Third: coyote, raccoon, wolf. Bottom: red and gray fox.

W. Iwerding

meadow mouse, with his short ears, long soft fur, and medium-long tail. He eats nothing but grass, and makes narrow tunnels through it next to the ground. You must get down on your knees and part the grass in order to find the runways, but when you do find one and sit beside it for an hour or two you will see several of the little fellows come running by. They work all day long, as well as far into the night. If you follow the runway for some distance you will find branching trails, some of them ending in burrows.

Shrews also live in these runways, and while they eat some of the meadow mice, they prefer the beetles that walk through the runways. But if they get really hungry, and insects are scarce, they will catch and eat a mouse, even though the mouse is three times bigger than the shrew.

Jumping mice may also be found in the meadow, as well as *white-footed mice. Rabbits* are often found in and about meadows and brushy fields. In the West *ground squirrels* will be found in the meadow, as well as *coyotes* and *weasels.* The coyotes and weasels are looking for meadow mice to eat.

Lakes and Streams

Along the shores of lakes and streams you will be sure to find *raccoons* and *skunks, weasels* and *minks,* hunting crayfish, frogs, insects, fish, and other small animals. Since most animals come to the water to drink, such a place is ideal for observing them. But if you want to see them in their natural conditions you will need to build a small platform in a tree above the shore and sit up there on a moonlit night. You can use a strong flashlight or a spotlight, for the light will not bother the animals very much. As long as you keep quiet (and awake) you will have a wonderful time watching the animals come to the shore to drink or to capture food.

A few animals make their homes along the shore. *Muskrats* often dig their burrows into the bank of the stream. *Beavers* do the same in many parts of the country, especially where they do not make dams. They make channels back into the meadow a short distance, or into a woods, so that they can get the bark of small trees for food. Shrews are often found along the margin of the stream, but if you are up in a tree you will have difficulty identifying them, they are so small. If you are really lucky you may see an *otter,* for this animal loves water more than anything else. You may even discover an otter slide, and see these delightful creatures

HOOFED MAMMALS—Top: white-tailed deer, mule deer, black-tailed deer. Second line: elk, caribou, moose. Bottom: pronghorn, bighorn, mountain goat.

Wilwerding

climb to the top, then slide down the muddy bank into the water, just for the pure fun of making a splash.

Woods and Forests

The forest animals are perhaps the most interesting to watch. While you have many trees to hide behind, you won't be able to see so far, either, so you will have to be unusually still and have plenty of patience. *Raccoons, foxes, coyotes, weasels, bears, bobcats,* and *mountain lions* are the common meat eaters of the forest. *Deer, elk,* and *moose* may be found there too, depending upon the part of the country where you are. You will find deer almost everywhere, but elk mainly in the Rocky Mountains and Olympics, and moose in the far north.

But there are many small mammals in the woods. Only *chipmunks* and *squirrels* are out all day long. *Flying squirrels* come out at night, so are seldom observed. Woods mice are out mainly at night, but now and then you may see one in the daytime.

You may often see the mice as you sit around a campfire at night. If you place food here and there for bait you will soon find *white-footed mice* coming up near you by the fire. Lay a line of rolled oats from back in the woods a short distance, and lead it up toward the fire. If you are exceptionally still, the mice may come right up to you. Raccoons will come into your camp at night, even when you are sitting by the fire. It is amusing to see a pair fight for the food you have left out for them. They remind you of selfish youngsters.

Deserts

If you go camping in the desert you will want to make a fire at night and sit beside it quietly, waiting for animals to come near. Be sure to place a variety of food out for them, not too near the fire. Rolled oats will bring in *kangaroo rats, pocket mice,* and *harvest mice,* and also perhaps *desert pack rats* or *wood rats.* Occasionally, you may be fortunate enough to see a *ringtail* or perhaps a *bobcat.* A *kit fox* or *gray fox* may come into the dimly lighted area on the fringe of your campfire, but you will need to have sharp eyes to see him. You might see a herd of *peccaries* (wild pigs) in some parts of the country, but it is a privilege very few campers ever get. Peccaries are interesting to watch, but never scare them! They can do a lot of damage when they are excited. In southern Arizona you may find the huge *banner-tailed kangaroo rat,* the largest of all the kangaroo rats. You will be amazed at the size of this beautiful fellow.

Most mammals take very good care of their young. BISON cows (left) hover over their calves. A COYOTE (right) brings a jack rabbit home for its pup.

High Mountains

Up the slopes of the high mountains you can find many kinds of mammals. There are *red-backed mice, phenacomys* (a mouse that looks much like a common meadow mouse, but lives in trees), several kinds of chipmunk, *mantled ground squirrels,* and often several other kinds of ground squirrel, plus *tree squirrels, weasels, bobcats, mountain lions, bears, martens, fishers, pocket gophers,* and *flying squirrels.* It will take you some time to see all of these, of course, but around a campfire you can coax several of them out into the open with food. The hard part is to sit quietly long enough.

Up here you will find more deer than anywhere else. One hiker on a mountaintop in Utah saw 750 deer in 30 minutes. You will find elk in the Rocky Mountains and Olympics, and in the northern Rockies you may see *moose,* and even *caribou.* There are *mountain goats* and *bighorn sheep* on the windswept slopes, but you will do a lot of hiking to see these majestic animals.

Tropics

Down in the tropical jungles of southern Mexico and Central America you may find still other fascinating mammals. Many kinds live there that are not found in the United States at all. There are six kinds of opposum, for instance, also *kinkajous, coatis (coatimundis), cotton rats* and *rice rats* (these are found in the Southern States as well), plus more kinds of mice that are not found farther north. There are large mammals such as *jaguars, ocelots, margays, jaguarundis, peccaries,* a small deer known as *Mazama* (a little reddish fellow), gigantic *pocket gophers, monkeys,* and *anteaters.* A camping trip to the jungles is a thrilling experience after a person has become familiar with the wild animals of his own country.

LIFE HISTORIES

To really get acquainted with an animal you should make a life-history study of it. This is a study of the life and behavior of an animal from the time it is born until it grows up and has a family of its own. It's great fun and may prove quite valuable.

Biologists have studied the life histories of many wild animals, but there are a great many more that have not been studied in complete detail. It is quite possible for your Pathfinder Club to find out things about wild animals living near your home that no one else in the world knows.

First, of course, you will need to capture a pair of wild animals —meadow mice or ground squirrels, perhaps—and keep them in a cage that is as nearly like their wild home as possible. You should provide nesting material so the animals can make a nest for their young. Be sure to watch everything the animals do and *write it down.*

In a notebook write careful descriptions of the young when they are born. Record their appearance each day or at least every two or three days until they grow up. Notice when the fur begins to appear, when the eyes open, when the teeth begin to grow, when the first sounds are made, when the youngsters first eat solid food, when they begin to run around in the nest or cage, and the time when the mother weans them. Keep a record, and *keep it up to date!* Record all the interesting things the young ones do, and how the mother takes care of them.

All through this study you will be wise to take pictures if you have a camera and proper equipment for closeups. Or you may try your hand at making drawings. When you are through watching the family, you should write up all your notes in story form, and perhaps some magazine will publish it.

CONSERVATION OF MAMMALS

Let Them Live!

Mammals are important! Many of them do a great deal of good by eating harmful insects. Others destroy pests such as mice and rats, and still others provide fur. It is also important to have plenty of wild animals in the wilderness areas where people can go and see these creatures God has made.

What a dismal world it would be if there were no coyotes howling on the barren hills, no bears in the forests, no raccoons in the woods, no prairie dogs on the plains. How sad if there were no

Baby **OPOSSUMS** live in their mother's pouch for weeks; later they hold on to her back whenever she travels. Adults cling to trees with their tail.

kangaroo rats in the desert, no sea lions on the rocky shores, no whales to play in the ocean. We want to know that there are wolves in Canada and Alaska, polar bears on the ice pans of the arctic, mountain goats in the rugged hills of the West. Don't let anyone kill off these interesting animals.

There are immeasurable values to be placed on all our wild animals, and no wilderness area is complete without them. What a thrill it is to peek around a tree trunk and see a moose standing in a marsh eating water lilies! What fun to watch ground squirrels playing with each other among their burrows, or a family of skunks walking single file down a country road in the moonlight!

Get Close to Them

Great men of old felt very close to these creatures God made. David loved to watch animals as he herded his sheep on the hills around Bethlehem. They taught him to trust and depend on God.

He watched the animals and birds drink from the streams that flowed from high springs in the mountains. He noted the constant supply of food in the meadows for animals that lived there; the "trees of the Lord" that provided homes for the birds; the refuge of the high hills; and rock slides for the wild goats and conies.

He saw the forest animals creep forth at night after their prey and go back to their dens at sunrise. He was impressed by the "innumerable" animals of the sea, small and great.

All of these, said David, wait upon God, who gives them their meat in due season. "That thou givest them they gather: thou openest thine hand, they are filled with good" (Psalm 104:27, 28).

241

Five BEAVER (count them) busily working away on their lodge in a swamp.

Cat Eats Mouse

It was not in God's original plan that animals should prey upon one another. Satan has done much to spoil God's purpose for the creatures He made. Yet Satan has not been given full control. God uses some of the curses brought about by sin to keep a balance and check in nature. Sick and old animals, such as deer, fall prey to the big carnivores, and this tends to keep the herd in a healthier condition. Mating fights make for the survival of the stronger animal, which is a benefit to the race. Hordes of harmful rodents and insects are kept in check by many of the smaller meat eaters.

What a privilege it will be in the new earth to see the animal kingdom as it was intended to be in the beginning, not "red in tooth and claw," but controlled, peaceful, and existing for the pleasure of man. What opportunities there will be to do life-history studies there! We can spend several millenniums just studying mammals!

Most of the rodents are harmful in some way or other. All mice are harmful in a general way if they get into gardens and fields, yet when they are out in the forests and woods they do no harm. Even pocket gophers, which are extremely harmful to garden and field crops, do no harm up in the mountains. The European rats and mice that live in our cities, in our homes, and in barns and outbuildings are always harmful, and are the greatest pests among all the mammals. Meadow mice are perhaps the most harmful of the wild mice, but it is not often that they cause much damage. However, sometimes they occur in great numbers so that there may be as many as 80,000 mice per acre—and then they do a great deal of damage.

(Upper row) A FAWN lies asleep; a SKUNK sets out on business; a GOLDEN MANTLED GROUND SQUIRREL, frequently called a chipmunk, fills up his pouches. (Bottom row) A PORCUPINE is startled by the cameraman; a PRAIRIE DOG has its lunch; a BLACK BEAR cub climbs clear of danger.

Who's Guilty?

Ground squirrels and tree squirrels do some damage, but normally it is not great. However, in farming areas ground squirrels may do considerable harm. Tree squirrels are harmful if they are too abundant. Moles are thought by most people to be extremely harmful, but this is not really true. Moles eat insects almost entirely, and when people think moles are damaging their gardens it is actually pocket gophers that are guilty.

Shrews (related to moles) are also great insect eaters, and they do much good by destroying harmful insects. But the bats are the most important of all the insect eaters, for they eat nothing but insects. They especially enjoy mosquitoes and gnats, and eat tons of them every night of the spring and summer months. If there is a bat cave near your home there won't be many mosquitoes around during the summer to bother you.

Skunks are extremely important in destroying insects. They sometimes eat a few chickens and eggs, but if we make the chicken

243

houses tight the skunks will not be able to get in. Badgers help us by eating ground squirrels and mice. And even coyotes do far more good than harm. They may sometimes catch a chicken or turkey, but they normally eat mice, rats, and gophers; and when the coyotes are killed off these harmful rodents multiply so fast that there is often no grass left for the cattle to eat.

Try to become aware of the balance of nature. Many animals accused of being harmful are actually important to us despite the harm they do, because they act as a check on the populations of animals that are much more harmful. It is up to us to learn something about all the animals, and to cooperate with nature in true conservation, maintaining the wonderful balance God has put here.

HOW MANY OF THESE CAN YOU DO?

Check each one when you finish it.

☐ 1. Arrange for your Pathfinder Club to visit the zoo and study the mammals there.

☐ 2. Go with your unit to the nearest national park and ask the park naturalist to tell you about the animals found there.

☐ 3. Make a life-history study of small mammals you have captured with live traps and kept in natural-type cages.

☐ 4. Take photos of mammals in color or black and white.

☐ 5. Study mammal tracks, and make plaster casts of them. (See page 85.)

☐ 6. Stalk a wild animal in his native habitat until you are close enough to make careful observations, then write what you see in a notebook.

☐ 7. Earn the MV Honor award in *Mammals,* then get the advanced Honor.

INTERESTING BOOKS ABOUT MAMMALS

How to Know the Mammals, Ernest S. Booth (William C. Brown Co.)

Field Guide to the Mammals, William H. Burt (Houghton Mifflin Co.)

Field Guide to Animal Tracks, Olaus J. Murie (Houghton Mifflin Co.)

Lives of Game Animals, Ernest Thompson Seton (Charles T. Branford Co.)

Mammals of North America, Victor Cahalane (Macmillan Co.)

Mammals (MV Honor booklet)

You can catch small animals alive without hurting them in a TIN-CAN TRAP. Cut one end from a No. 10 can; fasten it to the movable part of a mouse trap, passing the trigger through a hole in the center of the lid. Poke twig through snow or leaves to find runway; clear a space; set trap by hole.

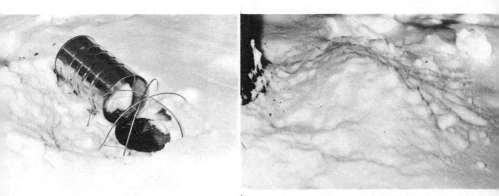

Put wire ribbing over the lid so nothing will keep it from shutting. Cover with aluminum foil and snow during winter. Use twigs and leaves in summer.

Come back next morning, and if you're lucky you'll find a mouse or a shrew. Use peanut butter for bait and put fluffy cotton in the can to make a nest.

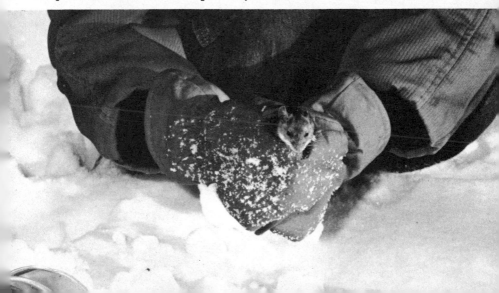

friends of a feather

THE pile of leaves was eight feet high and twenty-four feet across. It was no ordinary pile, however. It had been gathered, and was now being carefully guarded, by a *megapode,* a bird about the size of a chicken that lives in Australia and New Guinea. Every so often the megapode would poke its long beak down into the pile, fill it like lemonade in a straw, pull it out and test the temperature. For there were eggs in that heap, and the decaying leaves were keeping them warm. When the temperature did not please the megapode it scraped away some of the leaves from the top, or added more. After eight or ten weeks one of the eggs hatched, the baby bird tunneled its way out of the pile, and promptly flew away.

A *cardinal* lived among the trees at the edge of a town in North America. One day house builders moved in and cut the trees down. There were many more trees nearby, but the cardinal never flew into them, although on the bare ground it now had no place to hide from hawks and owls overhead. It did not dare go into the woods, because in so doing it would be invading the territory claimed by other cardinals. Next day only its red feathers remained, lying on the open ground just a few feet from the protection of the woods.

How Do You Like Your Eggs?

The *elephant bird* that used to live on the island of Madagascar off the east coast of Africa may have weighed 1,000 pounds and laid an egg that could hold more than two gallons of water. The *ostrich* lays an egg that may be nine inches long and six inches in diameter, with a shell a quarter of an inch thick and large enough to hold a dozen and a half chicken eggs. The *hummingbird* lays an egg the size of a pea.

Can All Birds Fly?

The *kiwi,* in New Zealand, cannot fly, and keeps falling over when it walks. A *loon* flops down on its chest and pushes itself

"Behold the fowls; . . . your heavenly Father feedeth them" (Matthew 6:26).

over the ground. An ostrich can run at fifty miles an hour, and keep up the pace for a considerable distance. A *quail* leaps into the air when frightened and whirs noisily over a hedge and comes down again—and rarely goes more than ten miles from home. The *wandering albatross* soars for hundreds of miles across the southern seas with scarcely a flap of its widespread wings.

A Nest for Each

A *bald eagle* makes a nest of sticks and branches that may be twenty feet high and nine feet wide and weigh a couple of tons—and may use it for twenty-five years in a row. The *oriental swift* builds a nest from its saliva, and the *eider duck* pulls down from its own chest to line the inside of its nest. The *hornbill* makes its home in a tree trunk, and builds up the door with mud when the eggs are laid, so only the bill of the female sticks out. A *humming-bird* builds a nest the size of a silver dollar out of plant down and lichens, held firmly together with spider web.

Telescopic Eyes

Hawks, on the ground, see birds in the sky so high man needs binoculars to find them. The *oilbird,* nesting in caves, makes a high-pitched sound to help find its way in the dark.

Some Strange Actions

Baby birds sometimes chirp inside the egg before they are hatched. When their mother sounds the danger alarm, they stop their noise. The *ruddy duck* weighs scarcely a pound, but in fifteen days it has been known to lay three pounds of eggs. The *honey guide* leads men and animals to trees where bees are making honey. *Bald eagles* and *ravens* fly upside down when they are particularly happy and the wind is blowing right. *Waxwings* may sit in a row on a telephone wire and pass a red berry down the line from one bill to another.

Stones for Teeth

Seed-eating birds deliberately swallow little pebbles and grains of sand to "chew" their food for them in their gizzard. The male hornbill manufactures a skin in its gizzard and wraps food in this before passing it to mamma hornbill sitting in the hole in the tree. A *flycatcher* that swoops down to catch an insect and overshoots its target may stop in mid-air and back up. *Gulls* and *crows* drop clams on rocks to break the shells. And a *woodpecker finch* on the Galápagos Islands pokes a stick or thorn into holes and crevices to make the insects come out.

The killdeer and curlew build **PRIMITIVE NESTS**, only depressions in the rocks or grass. Notice how well the egg color matches the surroundings.

Hummingbirds build delicate **NESTS IN TREES** (above, left). A mourning dove cuddles her babies on a nearly bare branch. Junior (below, left) looks for papa pileated woodpecker. A coot returns to her **NEST ON THE WATER.**

LEARNING ABOUT THE BIRDS

How do people know all these interesting things about birds? There are several good ways to learn. One of the quickest is to read bird books. Better yet, watch the birds and see for yourself what they do. You may even find the books are sometimes wrong!

Watch Them

Bird watching is a good way to begin. Organize a Pathfinder bird hike. Start out early in the morning and "Go West, young man, go West!" Keep the rising sun behind you so it shines on the birds. Take along a bird book such as *Field Guide to the Birds* to help you identify what you see, and a pair of binoculars if you have them. As you get more serious about bird watching you may want to go alone, for groups always make noises that frighten the birds.

Keep a notebook, using a looseleaf book and giving each bird a page to itself. Make a *trip list*—all the different birds you see on one trip. Then start an *annual list*—all the different birds you see in a year. Begin again each January as if you had never seen even a robin before. Then begin work on your *life list*—all the different birds you see in your whole lifetime. Be sure to include in these lists the date when you saw the bird and the State and county where you first observed it.

Bird watching on hikes is tops for learning the names of birds, but it doesn't reveal much about their habits—and the habits are much more interesting than the names.

Build a Blind

To find out how birds live, build a *bird blind*. It doesn't have to be elaborate. Something like a tent three feet across and four feet high will do well. Erecting one in the woods near a bird's nest would make an excellent Pathfinder project. Count off the Pathfinders and rotate, each one taking his turn to spend several hours in the blind. The watcher in the blind has to be absolutely quiet, and must have no end of patience. But the results are satisfying. Keep notes on everything the birds do—when they leave the nest, when they return, what they do when they get back, what kind of food they bring the babies, how often they feed them, how the babies treat one another when their parents are away, how they exercise their wings, when the first feathers appear, and so on. Any Pathfinders in your club who are working on the MV Honor in *Photography* will want to get some pictures from your blind.

250

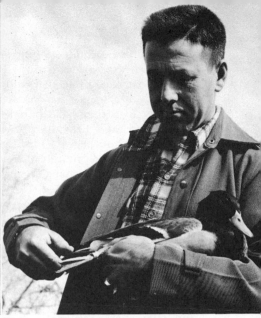

The best way to observe birds close up is to sit patiently in a BIRD BLIND. BANDS are put around the legs of migrating birds to see how far they fly.

You can hang the pictures in your clubroom later as trophies of your accomplishments.

To find out about migration, it is necessary to band birds. Unfortunately for Pathfinders, *bird banding* is illegal unless you have a permit from the Government, and permits are only awarded to persons at least eighteen years of age. In bird banding, birds are trapped alive, and a band is slipped around one of their legs. If at some time in the future that bird is ever found, the finder should write to the Fish and Wildlife Service in Washington, D.C., giving the number on the band and the time and place where the bird was found. This way it is possible to tell how far birds travel and what routes they take. So far about seven and a half million birds have been banded in the United States, and 600,000 of them have been recovered.

Make Them Like You

The most practicable way to find out about birds is to *attract* them to your back yard. Then you can watch them from the window. Provide food and water, and perhaps build birdhouses or plant shrubs and trees, if you have enough room.

Remember that some birds eat seeds, others eat flesh, so provide for both. Seed eaters like cracked corn, broken nuts, peanut butter, bread crumbs, sunflower seeds, rape, buckwheat, hemp, millet, wheat, barley, oats, wild rice, rye, pancakes, raisins, and fruit. Meat eaters like suet and meat scraps.

Don't use metal dispensers in freezing weather, for the birds may freeze to them. Drill little holes in a log and fill them with white beef suet. Provide a variety of food to please a variety of birds. Once you begin a bird-feeding station, you must keep it up. Missing out just one day during snowy weather may cause many of the birds to die that depend on you.

IDENTIFYING BIRDS

There are probably 100 billion birds in the world, and 8,600 different kinds. So it's not likely that anyone will ever be able to identify them all from memory. But practically everyone knows a *robin* and a *sparrow,* and you probably also know a *mockingbird,* a *cardinal,* and a *blue jay.* So you're on your way.

Notice where birds can be found. Don't look for robins swimming on a lake, or mallard ducks nesting in a desert. Scientists who study birds are called ornithologists. They divide birds into families, largely based on where the birds make their homes or find their food. The families are divided into orders. You would be wise to learn to recognize the families and orders of birds in your county.

Water Birds

Water birds are placed into several orders. *Loons* and *grebes* are very awkward when they try to walk, but they are wonderful divers.

Herons, egrets, and *ibises* are long-legged water birds. Look for them along the edges of streams and lakes. They nest in tall trees. In the Everglades National Park in Florida is a great colony of ibises in a clump of mangrove trees out in the water. It is thrilling to visit this colony.

Shore birds make up the largest group of water birds. They include the *sandpipers* and their relatives, as well as *gulls* and *terns, auklets, murrelets, guillemots,* and *puffins.* Look for them along the ocean and in large lakes. During spring and fall migration great flocks of them can be seen in many parts of the country.

NEAR WATER: Top: black tern, bobolink, yellow-headed blackbird, king-fisher. Second line: killdeer, sora rail, spotted sandpiper, Wilson's snipe. Third line: wood duck, mallard, blue-winged teal. Bottom: bittern, coot, least bittern (above coot), loon, pied-billed grebe, night heron. Find them in swamps, rivers.

Wilwerding

The second largest group of water birds includes the *ducks, geese,* and *swans.* This is the best-known group of water birds, but few people really know the different kinds of ducks and geese. It takes careful study to get them well in mind.

Marsh birds make up the other group of water birds. They are the *coots, gallinules,* and *rails.* Coots are common all over the country. Rails are plentiful too, but almost impossible to see, for they hide in the grasses and cattails of the marshes.

Birds of Prey

Hawks and *owls* form two distinct groups. Hawks normally fly about in the daytime, while owls come out mainly at night. However, *burrowing owls* and *short-eared owls* fly in the day. All these birds are flesh-eating, destroying large numbers of mice, rats, and gophers. Some eat small birds as well, but the good they do far exceeds the bad.

Woodpeckers chisel their way into tree trunks hunting insects. Look for their nests in dead tree trunks. With few exceptions most male woodpeckers have a spot of bright red somewhere on their heads.

Flying Jewels

Hummingbirds hover around flower beds, darting in quickly to suck the nectar through their hollow tongues. It's worth a good hunt to find their tiny nests.

Songbirds

Perching birds, generally known as *songbirds,* make up the largest order, with about 5,100 species. There are twenty-three families in the United States and Canada.

Flycatchers are important perching birds, because they eat so many harmful insects. *Kingbirds, scissortails,* and the smaller flycatchers are abundant all summer long in many parts of the country, but when fall comes they migrate to the tropics.

Crows, ravens, magpies, and *jays* are the most intelligent of all birds. They make wonderful pets, though many people call them pests. They do some damage, especially the crows, but they do far more good in every case, so that they should not be exterminated. Crows eat almost any animal or vegetable food. Jays eat the eggs of

UNIQUE SHAPES—Top: bald eagle, crow, great horned owl. Center: great blue heron. On the left of the heron (left to right): meadow lark, song sparrow, whippoorwill, woodcock, pheasant, bobwhite. On the right of the heron (from the top down): flicker, house wren, yellow-billed cuckoo, and mourning dove.

Wilwerding

other birds, but they also do much good, so should not be killed.

The thrush family is greatly loved. *Robins* are the most common members. All thrushes are good singers, except the *bluebirds.*

The blackbird family includes the *redwings,* which may be the most abundant bird in North America. *Yellow-heads, orioles,* and *meadow larks* also belong here.

The sparrow-finch family is the largest in the songbird order. *Sparrows* have dull colors, but are very important because they eat millions of tons of weed seeds. *Finches* have brighter colors than do sparrows, and do much good by eating harmful seeds. *Towhees* scratch around in the dirt under bushes and eat quantities of harmful insects and seeds. *Buntings* are the prettiest members of the sparrow family, and the *painted bunting* challenges the beauty of the brightest tropical birds.

There are many more birds than have been mentioned here. Look over any bird book and you will find other groups to study.

MIGRATION

Along about the time when the slanting sun of autumn is blue with the haze of burning leaves, the quiet of late afternoon may be shattered by the chirping of thousands of small birds flying endlessly southward. Flocks of geese or cormorants arranged in perfect V's wing their way purposefully in the same direction. Fields that all of a sudden in the evening are swarming with nervously hurrying little birds are deserted completely by morning. The fall migration is on.

Unsolved Mystery

Migration is an unsolved mystery. God asked Job if he understood it, and Job could not answer. (See Job 39:26.) Aristotle, a famous Greek of 2,200 years ago, said surely birds just go to sleep in the winter. It is said that in 1703 an anonymous treatise was published in London, saying that migrating birds go to the moon! Many people still believe that little birds cross the ocean on the backs of bigger ones, but this is not so.

Robins usually go just a few hundred miles south. *Redwings* that breed in Alaska come down to northern Texas. The *eastern fox sparrow* flies from Labrador to the southern United States, but these trips are short. *Nighthawks, barn swallows, cliff swallows,* and *thrushes* from northern United States and Canada go down as far as Brazil, and some even farther. *Scarlet tanagers* breed in an area that stretches 1,500 miles across the eastern half of Canada and

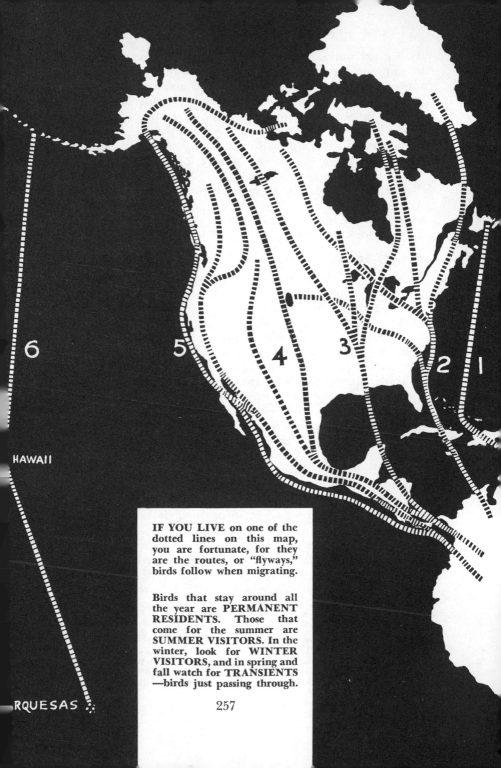

6

5

4

3

2

1

HAWAII

RQUESAS

IF YOU LIVE on one of the dotted lines on this map, you are fortunate, for they are the routes, or "flyways," birds follow when migrating.

Birds that stay around all the year are PERMANENT RESIDENTS. Those that come for the summer are SUMMER VISITORS. In the winter, look for WINTER VISITORS, and in spring and fall watch for TRANSIENTS —birds just passing through.

257

the United States. In the fall they fly south in a band that narrows to just one hundred miles wide across the Panama Canal, then spreads out as the birds hunt food in Colombia, Ecuador, and Peru.

Bobwhites, western *quails,* and some *woodpeckers* don't migrate at all. *Chickadees, juncos,* and some other birds that nest in the Rocky Mountains just move up and down the side of the mountains as the seasons change. But the *arctic tern* really travels. Arctic terns may lay their eggs in the snow just a few hundred miles from the North Pole. Then, as winter comes on, they fly south. Although their exact route is not known, many of them probably cross the Atlantic to Europe, and go down the coast of Africa to spend the winter not far from the South Pole. Thus they travel ten thousand miles, at least.

Height, Speed, and Danger

Most birds fly below 3,000 feet, many of them barely clearing the waves. On the other hand, mountain climbers have heard migrants as they flew over the Himalayas near to Mount Everest at 18,000 to 20,000 feet.

Birds usually take two weeks to a month to go a thousand miles. Some go faster. The speed record was made by a *lesser yellow-legs,* which was banded on Cape Cod and recovered on the island of Martinique in the West Indies six days later. The distance was 1,930 miles. The bird had traveled at least 320 miles a day.

Migration is full of perils. A sudden snowstorm may kill thousands of traveling birds in a few hours. Lighthouses with a steady white light are hit by thousands of birds, but the danger is much less when the light is red or flashes. Some floodlighted monuments, such as the Statue of Liberty, attract hundreds of birds to their death. In recent years the floodlights on some buildings have been turned off during the migrating season.

How do birds know when to begin their journey, and how do they find their way? No one knows. Some leave their summer homes when food becomes scarce, but they may leave their winter homes when food is abundant all around. Some scientists say that it is the changing length of the day that warns the birds that the time has come to go, and this sounds good while the birds are in the north. But how do these birds know when to return, when they

WINGS—Top: (wings short, rounded; tail long) Cooper's hawk; (wings long, narrow; tail long) marsh hawk; (wings pointed, tail long) duck hawk. Second line: (wings broad; tail broad, rounded) red-tailed hawk; (wings long, tail long) turkey vulture; (wings long, pointed; tail forked) swallow-tailed kite. Bottom: herring gull, barn swallow, nighthawk, chimney swift, common tern. Identify by wings and tail.

Wilwerding

spend the winter in the tropics where the length of the days hardly changes at all between one season and another.

Stars or Compasses?

How do the birds find their way? Do their parents teach them? No. The children of some birds leave a week or two before their parents. Do they follow landmarks? If so, how can they fly at night, as so many of them do? Do they have built-in compasses? Magnets were tied to some birds to try out this idea, but the birds still found their way all right. Do they navigate by the stars? Some birds definitely do, for when some were placed in a planetarium and the stars were shone on the ceiling, the birds changed the direction in which they were sitting as the stars moved around the curved ceiling; however, other birds have been seen flying through dense fog without the slightest doubt as to where they were going, and there wasn't a star in sight. It is a mystery God has not yet revealed to man. Perhaps He will tell it to a Pathfinder who tries hard enough to find out.

PROTECTING THE BIRDS

Millions upon millions of passenger pigeons used to inhabit the United States. Now not one is left. There are about sixty *Everglades kites* left in Florida, and that is all. There are approximately sixty *whooping cranes* left in all the world. The *ivory-billed woodpecker* and the *California condor,* magnificent birds, are in great danger of extinction.

Because a bird has pretty feathers, or makes an easy target, or tastes good to eat, millions of them have been slaughtered. Others have been nearly wiped out because men cut down the forests or drain the marshes or invade the mountains where these birds make their homes.

The Case of the Missing Ducks

God knew what He was doing when He made nature the way it is, and men are wise who leave nature alone. People who try to improve on the balance of nature usually regret it. Hunters who wanted more bobwhites to shoot killed off the hawks and owls

COLORS—Top: (mostly black) redwing, cowbird, purple grackle. Second line: (red-black-white) rose-breasted grosbeak, downy woodpecker, red-headed woodpecker. Third line: (brown back, spotted breast) wood thrush, brown thrasher, fox sparrow. Fourth line: (dark head, reddish below) robin, orchard oriole, chewink. Fifth line: (mostly red or orange) scarlet tanager, cardinal, Baltimore oriole. Sixth line: (mostly yellow) goldfinch, yellow warbler, yellowthroat, prairie warbler. Bottom: (mostly blue) bluebird, blue jay, indigo bunting.

Wilwerding

around a certain lake, because these birds sometimes kill bob-whites. But with the owls and hawks gone, the rats and mice increased and ate nearly all the bobwhites' eggs. Boys who were very proud of the ducks that grew on their father's pond every year began trapping the skunks around the lake to sell their skins to buy bicycles. Soon there were no ducks, for the duck eggs were eaten by snapping turtles. When the boys decided to leave the skunks alone, the skunks ate the snapping turtle eggs and the ducks came back.

It is now against the law to kill any wild birds in the United States except crows and a few others. But Pathfinders leave all birds, including the crows, to live their lives in peace.

HOW MANY OF THESE CAN YOU DO?

Check each one when you finish it.

- [ ] 1. Go on a bird walk and make a list of all the birds you see.
- [ ] 2. Set up a bird blind near a nest and keep a record for two weeks of everything the birds do.
- [ ] 3. Build a birdhouse and set it up in your back yard.
- [ ] 4. Put a bird bath in your back yard and keep it supplied with water all summer.
- [ ] 5. Set up a feeding station in winter and keep it supplied with food till spring.
- [ ] 6. Take three photographs of birds.
- [ ] 7. Earn the MV Honor in *Birds*.

INTERESTING BOOKS ABOUT BIRDS

A Field Guide to the Birds and *A Field Guide to Western Birds*, Roger Tory Peterson (Houghton Mifflin Co.)
Two very good books for helping you identify birds on a bird walk.

Field Guide to Bird Songs (Houghton Mifflin Co.)
Two 12-inch LP records of bird songs to accompany *A Field Guide to the Birds*.

1001 Questions Answered About Birds, Allan D. and Helen G. Cruickshank (Dodd, Mead & Co.)
A book you will enjoy, for it answers so many questions.

Check-list of North American Birds (American Ornithologists' Union, Cornell University, Ithaca, N.Y.)
The official list of all North American birds.

Birds (MV Honor booklet)

A coconut **BIRD FEEDER** is easy to make, but don't use in freezing weather. Birds may stick to the cold metal. A wooden shelf tied to a tree is better then.

The feeder located on a pole turns with the wind. Keep feeders well stocked. A tray set up outside the window brings the birds close for easy watching.

your slighted friends

L OOK out! It's a snake!" someone screams, and at once you know that he is not a Pathfinder—or hasn't been for long, for Pathfinders soon lose their fear of snakes as they learn the truth about them.

For instance, "Look at its fangs!" someone will yell when he sees a snake. "Naw, that's its stinger," someone else corrects him. Actually, the "forked fangs" are the snake's tongue, and when the snake sticks it out it is smelling. In the roof of the snake's mouth are two small pits known as the Jacobson's organ. The tongue picks up the little particles in the air that make up odors, takes them into the mouth, and puts them on the Jacobson's organ, and that's the way the snake smells. The tongue is so soft that you can scarcely feel it when it is flicked against the pupil of your eye.

The snake is one of the most misunderstood creatures on the earth. It was forced to play a part in the Garden of Eden in bringing sin into the world. Many people fail to recognize what was included in the curse placed on the serpent, and this has brought about many false notions concerning snakes.

"But," exclaim many voices, "doesn't the Bible say the serpent was cursed?" It does. It also says the ground was cursed, and yet man eats freely of the fruit of it. People fear spiders almost as much as they do snakes, yet the spider did not come directly under the curse.

Squeezed or Crushed?

Did you ever hear someone say, "I don't like the way snakes crush the bodies of animals before they eat them"? This is not true. The snakes that get their food by constriction include several valuable species such as the *Red Rat Snake,* the *Fox Snake,* the *Pilot Black Snake,* besides others that feed largely on rodents. (Rats and mice, squirrels and rabbits, are rodents.) The constrictors do not crush their prey. No bones are broken. The coils of the snake tighten quickly around the body of the mammal, interfering

"Be ye therefore wise as serpents" (Matthew 10:16).

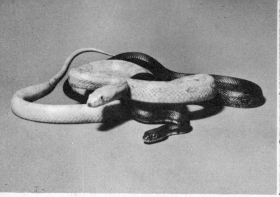

When white is black! Both snakes in the left picture are **PILOT BLACK SNAKES**. The white one is an albino. The **RUBBER BOA** (upper right) is a harmless constrictor. The **BULL SNAKE** (lower) is fifty-three inches long.

with the action of the heart and lungs, usually resulting in a quick death.

Wrap-around Tails

The constrictors are good climbers and use their tails to hold on while climbing trees and along beams in old buildings.

"Pilot black snakes drop from rafters and beams onto the shoulders of human beings and choke them." Not true. This fantastic idea is encouraged by people returning from foreign countries who bring back wild stories of *boa constrictors* and *pythons* hanging from trees waiting to draw jungle travelers to a horrible death in the branches. Such stories are made up, and no Pathfinder believes them.

Win Friends for Snakes!

Snakes are rapidly losing their place in the balance of nature. Something must be done to protect them. Public opinion must be changed. Say something good about snakes every time you have a chance.

It is a good idea to question all stories that place the snake in a bad light. The use of such terms as "dreadful reptile" and "horrible creature" shows that the storyteller does not appreciate the balance in nature. Snakes are God's creatures as much as the birds are. They are as valuable and, in many instances, as beautiful. Snakes can enter the small runways of destructive, disease-bearing rodents and help to keep their numbers down. In wintertime field mice destroy trees by eating the bark under the snow. Trees provide food, shade, and beauty and also prevent soil erosion. Thus the rodent-eating snakes protect the trees and prevent erosion.

POISONOUS SNAKES. Cottonmouth moccasin (upper left) lives in southern streams and marshes; is a muddy color and has white inside its mouth. Coral snake (upper right) has yellow bands separating red and black bands, which distinguish it from the harmless scarlet king snake. Copperhead (lower left) lives in the Eastern States; it has a copper-brown color with an hour-glass design. Rattlesnakes (lower right) come in various colors. All have rattles.

Ignorance Kills

"I kill every snake I see, because some are dangerous." What a mistake! Anyone who kills a snake because it is a snake proves he's just plain ignorant.

Actually, only a small proportion of all the snakes in the world are dangerous to man. And most of these are in the tropics.

Four Poisonous Snakes to Look Out For

There are four kinds of poisonous snakes dangerous to man in the United States. They are divided into two groups, pit vipers and coral snakes.

The *pit vipers* can be recognized by two deep cavities, one on each side of the head, behind and below the nostrils. *Rattlesnakes, copperheads,* and *cottonmouth moccasins* are pit vipers. Their venom damages blood cells and blood vessels. It is injected into the snake's victim through hollow fangs located in the front of the upper jaw.

Rattlesnakes are the most widely distributed pit vipers, and are found in all the States except Alaska and Hawaii. In almost every instance they should be considered valuable because of the large number of rodents they destroy. They are dangerous, and close contact with them should be avoided. They are not aggressive. You can enjoy nature and camping in areas where rattlesnakes are abundant if you use common sense. You should be much more concerned over the danger from traffic accidents.

Coral snakes make up the second group. Their fangs are short and have a groove in them for the venom to flow along. They are not movable like the fangs of the pit vipers. The venom paralyzes the nerves and damages the action of the heart and lungs. It is similar to cobra venom, and the death rate from coral snake bites is high. Certain harmless snakes have bands of red, black, and yellow. The coral snake is the only one on which the red touches the yellow.

Poisonous snakes must always be considered dangerous. Respect them, but do not fear them. Fear may cause a person to panic when he sees a poisonous reptile, and this could end in a wild flight from the scene and bring you in contact with other poisonous specimens hidden close by.

You owe it to yourself and to the snakes to be able to recognize quickly any poisonous snake native to the area in which you live or through which you intend to travel. Write to the conservation department of your State for a pamphlet telling of the poisonous snakes native to the State and where they have been found. Send the same request to any large museum of natural history situated in the State. The local public library will have books describing the snakes you want to identify.

Everyday Snakes

Garter snakes are the most common snakes in the United States. There are several kinds. They are usually found near water and feed on earthworms, frogs, toads, salamanders, and fish. Some will try to bite if approached in the wrong manner, but the bite is no more dangerous than the scratch of a thistle.

Don't call the garter snake a "grass snake"! This name can best be applied to the beautiful slender *green snake*. It likes fields and high ground where it feeds on insects, grubs, and spiders.

Two other common small snakes are the *DeKay* and the *red-bellied*. Another beautiful but very shy creature is the *ring-necked snake* with a dark gray, bluish, or black body and a yellow or orange collar. It hides beneath stones, stumps, and bark during the day. Earthworms, some slugs, and insects furnish food for this large group.

These common snakes are most interesting to observe. Snakes do not eat vegetable food and therefore do not damage crops. All snakes are meat eaters. A *garter snake* was once seen swallowing a small leaf of lettuce, but close investigation revealed that the lettuce had been lying in a dish of raw ground beef set out for turtles. Particles of meat on the lettuce caused the snake to pick it up. King snakes and members of the racer family frequently eat other snakes, but they kill only for food.

ALLIGATORS (above) are common in Florida and Louisiana; may lay a hundred eggs in decaying vegetation, and leave them to be hatched by the sun's heat. A hike through woods in Maryland is bound to turn up at least one BOX TURTLE (right).

Some Snakes Are Very Valuable

The *fox, corn, pilot black,* and other rat snakes do much more good in eating rodents than they do harm in disturbing bird life.

"The milk snake milks cows." Wrong again! Milk snakes have no desire for milk. More than 70 per cent of their diet consists of destructive rodents. They are members of the king snake family.

The Longest Snakes

The *bull snake* is probably worth its weight in gold. It cleans out nest after nest of destructive, disease-bearing rodents. The bull snake averages about five feet in length and the *indigo snake* eight feet; these two are the longest snakes in the United States. Both of them become very gentle in captivity.

High Speed Snakes

"We ran all the way back to camp and the snake followed right behind us." So goes the story of the pre-Pathfinder. The chances are he never looked back after he started running. Snakes seem to travel swiftly, but actually they are slow. A *Florida racer* holds the speed record in the United States. It was timed traveling 3.7 miles an hour. The *blue racer* can do 2.5 miles an hour. With its smooth scales glistening in the sun, the racer is a shining example of the dry cleanliness and beauty of all snakes. It feeds on both cold and warm-blooded creatures, including some bird life, but the good it does outweighs the harm.

OTHER REPTILES

Lizards

For speed in the reptile world, go watch the lizards! The *six-lined race-runner* has been timed traveling eighteen miles an hour. Other kinds have reached a speed of fifteen miles an hour. Lizards are more difficult to catch than snakes, because many of them have exceptionally good eyesight and most of them are extremely quick.

Do not attempt to grasp a lizard by the tail, because many kinds have the ability to leave the tail wriggling in your fingers while they scurry away to grow a new one.

Most lizards have legs. An exception is the *glass snake,* which looks like a snake but is really a lizard. It is supposed to shatter like glass when struck, after which the pieces unite again when the danger is past. The only truth in this story is that this lizard can lose its tail as some other lizards do.

You can recognize the glass snake as a lizard by its eyelids. Most lizards have them. Snakes do not. Snakes sleep with their eyes open. Some lizards can do this because the lower lid has a transparent window in it that the lizards can see through when their eyelids are closed.

The *Arizona Gila monster* and its cousin, the *Mexican Gila monster,* are the only two poisonous kinds. The Gila (pronounced heela) monster's venom comes from glands in the lower jaw and affects a victim's nervous system. Whether or not human beings have ever died from it is a matter scientists are not agreed upon.

Lizards are beneficial to man because they feed so largely on insects. Watching *skinks* and *chameleons* will bring you hours of enjoyment. And you will find the *geckos* irresistible.

Turtles

A reptile with a shell is generally known as a turtle. If lizards hold the record for speed, turtles hold the record for slowness. They also hold the reptiles' old-age record. A tortoise brought to the island of Mauritius in 1766 was accidentally killed in 1918. Its estimated age was 200 to 250 years. However, the greatest age that can be proved is 152 years. Even the common *box turtle* may live more than a hundred years. The giant *leatherback* sometimes weighs 1,500 pounds.

Turtles are usually divided into three groups. Those that live exclusively on land are known by the term "tortoise." The American Indian ate turtles having hard shells and gave them the name "terrapins." This name is in common use wherever turtles are

The **COLLARED LIZARD** (left) gets its name from the rings around its neck. **HORNED TOADS** (upper right) are really lizards too. Don't miss the baby! **CHUCKWALLA** (lower right) blows up like this to protect himself from enemies.

sold in food markets. The term "turtle" is sometimes applied only to the group that spends its life in the water, but generally it is used for all shell-backed reptiles.

It seems that some turtles can distinguish colors. Most reptiles and mammals see only black and white. The turtle seems to have a degree of intelligence equal in certain respects to that of a rat, which is considered a very smart animal.

Turtles have no teeth. Instead, they have a horny ridge something like a bird's bill. The common *snapping turtle* can inflict a serious bite when it's out of water, even cutting through a broom handle in one snap. But in the water it has just one desire, to get away.

Alligator or Crocodile?

Scientists usually place alligators and crocodiles in two separate families. A simple, quick way to distinguish between the two is to compare the shape of the heads. The alligator's snout is broad like the toe of a lumberman's boot, while the snout of a crocodile is narrow like the tapered toe of a lady's shoe.

The *American alligator* is found in Southern States from central Texas to the eastern coast of Florida. The *American crocodile* is found in extreme southern Florida.

BRING THEM BACK ALIVE

To really know these creatures of the wild, you must come in contact with them. The experience will remove much foolish fear and will give you no end of enjoyment.

The best time to hunt for snakes, lizards, and turtles is between the hours of eight and ten on a sunny morning. Not all kinds of snakes will be taking a sunbath. Look under rocks and stumps for snakes that do their feeding in the late afternoon and evening. Take along one or more clean cloth bags in which to carry the specimens you capture.

Poisonous snakes do not make good pets, because of the danger involved.

It is better to begin your snake collection with specimens that live near your home. The garter snake is a good one. Catch it with your hands. Some snakes will crawl into your hands if you approach them the right way. Do not use a forked stick, as it is likely to cause injury. Always be gentle with the creatures God has placed here for your enjoyment and learning. Do not hold the snake tightly in your hands. Always move slowly and calmly.

A Cage for Snakes

A glass aquarium tank can be made into a cage suitable for all kinds of small reptiles. A wood framework covered with fly screen can be made to fit the top.

You can keep a specimen up to six feet long in a box-type cage measuring 28 by 12 by 12 inches, if you take it out for exercise once or twice a week. Use glass for the front. Let one half of the back be made into a door. Hardware cloth or window screen should be used for the top, which also is on hinges. Nervous snakes have a tendency to rub their noses against the screen if it is used in place of glass at the front. A sore, sensitive nose will keep a snake from feeding.

Keep the cage dry. Lay several layers of newspapers on the floor, and body wastes can be removed by rolling up the papers. The floor and walls should be scrubbed regularly with hot water and soap. Gently rub olive oil on the snake's skin occasionally, to keep mites away.

An aquarium makes a good SNAKE CAGE. Put in a stick and some leaves and a heavy water dish. Place quarter-inch mesh wire screen on top, well weighted.

Do not attempt to keep reptiles unless you have a steady source of natural food for them. Be sure to read all the literature available in the library on the feeding habits of the kind of snake you plan to keep.

Some snakes will not eat if they are disturbed by movements near the front of the cage. And you will discover that it is a good plan not to handle your snake for about 36 hours after it has had a good meal. Water should be provided at all times in a low, heavy dish not likely to tip when the snake crawls over it.

If your snake does not feed within a month, let it go near where you found it, and catch another. It is not advisable to force feed a snake, because of the danger of injuring its mouth.

Don't Frighten Your Visitors

Be careful not to show your snake in such a way that your visitors become frightened. One of the objectives of your nature project is to win friends for reptiles.

The better you become acquainted with your friends, the more you appreciate them. The same is true of reptiles. So keep a scientific record of each one. For example, if the specimen is a snake, the record should include both the scientific and common names, the sex, the date it was captured, where, by whom, when offered food, what kind, when food was eaten, how much, monthly record of weight, girth, and length, and when skin is shed.

Shoot It With Your Camera

If it is not convenient to keep live specimens, you can become better acquainted with reptiles by photographing them. Use color film if you like, or if you do your own developing make enlargements and tint them with oil colors. A little practice will develop skill and will cultivate a keen sense of observation. One must notice the different colors very carefully in order to paint an accurate color picture. You will find this one of the best ways to appreciate the wonders of nature. A good collection of tinted photographs of snakes, lizards, and turtles will be valuable.

HOW MANY OF THESE CAN YOU DO?

Check each one when you finish it.

☐ 1. Go on a hike looking for snakes, turtles, and lizards.

☐ 2. Catch a snake, keep it in a cage for a month, and make a daily record of everything it does.

☐ 3. Scatter some inch-thick boards on the ground in the woods, put a piece of old linoleum over them, leaving the sides open. Check in a week or two to see whether any snakes have come to live there.

☐ 4. On a hike, have each unit catch a lizard, then let the lizards race to see which ones goes the fastest.

☐ 5. Earn the MV Honor award in *Herpetology*.

INTERESTING BOOKS ABOUT REPTILES

Field Book of Snakes, K. P. Schmidt and D. D. Davis (G. P. Putnam's Sons)

A Field Guide to Reptiles and Amphibians, Roger Conant (Houghton Mifflin Co.)

Snakes Alive, and How They Live, Clifford H. Pope (The Viking Press)

The Reptile World, Clifford H. Pope (Alfred A. Knopf)

Snakes in Fact and Fiction, James A. Oliver (The Macmillan Co.)

Amphibians and Reptiles of Western North America, Robert C. Stebbins (McGraw-Hill Book Co., Inc.)

The National Geographic Magazine for September, 1954, has a splendid illustrated article on snakes, by Doris M. Cochran.

Reptiles (MV Honor booklet)

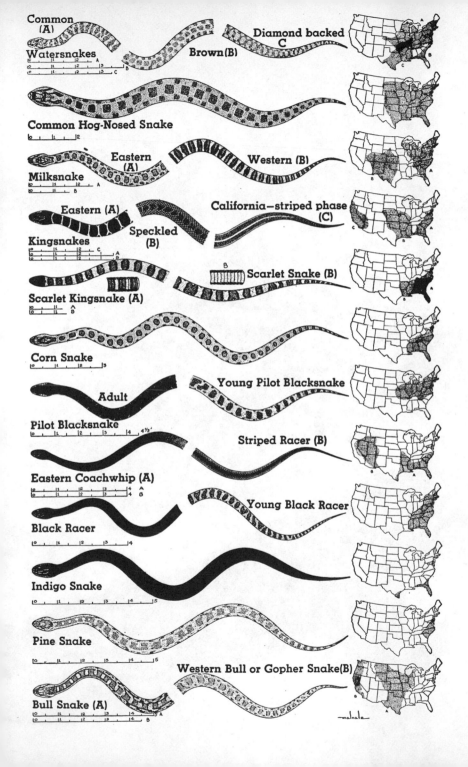

Common (A)

Diamond backed C

Watersnakes

Brown (B)

Common Hog-Nosed Snake

Milksnake

Eastern (A)

Western (B)

Kingsnakes

Eastern (A)

Speckled (B)

California—striped phase (C)

Scarlet Kingsnake (A)

Scarlet Snake (B)

Corn Snake

Adult

Young Pilot Blacksnake

Pilot Blacksnake

Eastern Coachwhip (A)

Striped Racer (B)

Black Racer

Young Black Racer

Indigo Snake

Pine Snake

Bull Snake (A)

Western Bull or Gopher Snake (B)

friends that hop and crawl

ALMOST always the first creatures that a person finds along a creek or around a pond are the amphibians. These are the creatures that hop and crawl. Toads, frogs, and salamanders are amphibians. They all live at least a part of their life in the water. Every boy knows that a tadpole is just a frog that hasn't grown up yet. Toads and salamanders also have tadpole stages that live in the water.

The first warm, rainy nights of spring bring the amphibians out in great numbers. This is a good time to catch them and study them. Even as the birds return from the Southland bringing song by day, the peepers, tree frogs, meadow frogs, American toads, and all their "kith and kin" fill the night air with choruses of spring.

Leading a Double Life

Amphibians lead a double life—partly on land, partly in water. They usually begin as an egg, then become a tadpole, and finally an adult. The eggs are usually laid in the water, but many amphibians lay their eggs in moist places on land. In fact, the common *dusky salamander* wears its eggs around its neck like a sticky necklace of jelly, and everywhere that "mamma" goes the eggs go too.

Every Pathfinder, sooner or later, wants to see the jellylike egg masses of amphibians in shallow ponds and puddles. A closer look identifies the frog's egg masses as being in clumps, the toad's in long strings, and the salamander's in smaller bunches of larger eggs. Salamander egg masses are also rather greenish in appearance. These eggs are laid during the spring rains, the time when the amphibians mate. The salamanders would probably like to sing out as they woo their mates, but only the frogs and toads have voices.

A female *American toad* may lay at one time a string of eggs 72 feet long, weighing $5\frac{1}{2}$ times the weight of the female and containing 10,000 eggs. A *bullfrog* female may lay even more black-and-white eggs at one time. By contrast some of the salamanders may lay only two. The eggs of frogs and toads hatch in three to

"And God created . . . every living creature that moveth" (Genesis 1:21).

277

FROG EGGS

TOAD EGGS

ADULT FROG

ADULT TOAD

A TADPOLE'S LIFE

Both frogs and toads have a tadpole stage. And both begin as eggs laid in water. Frog eggs are laid in a *mass* of jelly, but toad eggs are laid in a *string* of jelly. The eggs develop into the tadpoles, which swim in water. Gradually, the legs form, the tail is absorbed into the body, and the adult shape is perfected. Most frogs keep on living near the water, but toads may wander a long way off.

twelve days, depending on how warm the weather is. It takes almost a full month for salamander eggs to hatch. The baby salamanders stretch out as they grow and look quite different from the stubby-headed frog and toad tadpoles. Frilly, fringed gills stick out on each side of their heads. The tiny *black toad* tadpoles are ready to become toads in about two months, while bullfrog babies live as tadpoles for two whole years.

Growing Up

The process of becoming grown up is an interesting one. As the hind legs appear on a tadpole the tail begins to disappear. The tail is actually dissolved into the body and used as food during this pe-

278

riod of change. The gills disappear and lungs develop so that the tadpole becomes an air-breathing creature. Then the front legs push out, and the head broadens to form the wide mouth of the adult. The wriggling tadpole has grown up.

Frog or Toad?

Frogs and toads are so closely related to each other that they look very much alike, but they also look different. An *American toad* is quite different in appearance from a *green frog*. Yet a *tree frog,* or *tree toad,* whichever name you choose to call it, looks like both and can't properly be called either one. Most toads and frogs, however, can be told apart by the condition of their skin and where they are found. Toads have an almost dry, warty skin and may be found in dry or moist places some distance from water, whereas the frog has a smooth skin moistened by many mucous glands and is usually found near a body of water, where it can jump to safety, using its long hind legs.

Where to Find Them

Tree frogs are usually hard to find. But in the Southland they are easier to find than in any other part of the country. At night they are attracted to the lights of filling stations along the highways. At times hundreds and even thousands are attracted from the big swamps crossed by the new highways.

The most common member of the frog family in the United States is the *leopard frog,* named for the big spotted cat. These handsome frogs are green with blotches on their backs, usually arranged in more than two rows, and with the undersides of their hind legs white. They are protected by law in many States, especially during the breeding season, because of the many hunters who hunt them for their legs.

The largest frog in this country is the bullfrog. There is nothing quite like its deep bass voice, reverberating at dusk across a moun-

INTO THE WATER goes a leopard frog above a hellbender; a spring peeper sings high in the tree. A toad croaks on the bank and a bullfrog hides on the bottom. A tiger salamander crawls out of the water, a tree frog climbs a tree, and an eel-shaped caecilian curls her body around her eggs.

The common WOOD FROG (left) hides in rotten logs; may be hard to find. PICKEREL FROGS (right) congregate in large numbers around small ponds.

tain lake. Its call is a resounding "jug-o'-rum." The body of a large female bullfrog may be 8 inches long and more than 3 inches wide. Hind legs sometimes stretch 10 inches or longer. This is really a huge amphibian when compared with the tiny little *chorus frog* just 2/5 of an inch wide and only 5/8 of an inch long. These littlest frogs, however, make up in voice what they lack in size.

The male *common spring peeper* can be heard for a mile. The green frog's "tchung, tchung," sounds like a plunked banjo string.

The leopard frog is usually found in farm ponds and open meadow streams, while the green frog seems to prefer the woodland streams, where it sits on the bank, all but invisible against the green foliage. It is difficult to tell a small bullfrog from a large green frog, but it can be done by looking for the two raised ridges that run down each side of the green frog's back. The bullfrog never has these ridges.

Look Into Their Eyes

The American toad is one of nature's homeliest creatures, yet it has a personality that more than makes up for its looks. A close examination will reveal eyes that are among the prettiest in nature. Hold the back end of a flashlight against your nose and shine the beam into the toad's eyes. You'll see why the great poet Shakespeare compared them to precious jewels.

Toads eat large numbers of insects that are harmful to man; however, they also eat beneficial insects such as honeybees when they have an opportunity. When a toad finds a beehive with an opening close to the ground, he sits beside the hole and with his sticky tongue snaps up every bee that comes along until he is so full he can't hold any more.

Few animals care to eat toads. Foxes, raccoons, and skunks dearly love to eat a big frog but not a toad. Toads are well protected by a pair of large glands on the back of the head called "parotids." When an enemy grabs a toad, two or more fine jets of milky fluid squirt from the parotids into the animal's mouth. Immediately the animal releases the toad, for he has just gotten a mouthful of one of the bitterest substances known. With a lot of spitting and sputtering Mr. Enemy heads for the nearest water to wash the horrible stuff from his mouth. One or two lessons are enough; he'll never touch a toad again.

The *wood frog* is a handsome fellow with brown to yellow skin and a black mask over the eyes. It is rare, but is well worth searching stream banks for. You will find him only in the shadowy regions of the deep woods and never far from the stream where he grew up.

The common American toad has a cousin called the *spadefoot toad*. This darker-colored cousin is named for a little digging claw on the inside of each hind foot. If you find one of these fellows in the fields you're a sharp-eyed Pathfinder, because few spadefoots are found even though they are fairly common throughout the country. Spadefoots hunt food only while we are sleeping. During the day they stay burrowed down under the ground in some place where the soil is soft. A spadefoot's eye indicates that it is a creature of the night, for its pupil is vertical, like a cat's.

SALAMANDERS

The *red-spotted newt* is a good example of a salamander. It has a life history very much like that of frogs and toads, yet its appearance is quite different from either of these relatives. A salamander's legs are quite small in comparison with its body and it always has a tail. The newt uses its tail to propel itself through the water.

The newt hatches from a solitary egg that has been laid on a piece of submerged vegetation. At first it has gills for breathing, like a fish. But after three months it is an inch long and leaves the water to become an air-breathing creature. The gills disappear and the

SPADEFOOT TOAD (left) has "spades" on back legs to dig itself into the soft earth. The eyes of the AMERICAN TOAD (right) flash in light at night.

color changes. Even the salamander's name changes; it is now called an *eft*.

In the water the newt was an uninteresting brownish color with a few scattered black and orange-red spots; now it has become a beautiful shade of salmon pink or orange. The darker red spots on the sides are ringed with a thin border of black. The newt wears this coat for about three years, as long as it is a "landlubber."

Then it heads back to the water and stays there the rest of its life. Once in the water it develops an olive-green color against which the red spots contrast brightly. A fin develops on top of the tail. The newt does not redevelop gills, but must continue to breathe oxygen in its lungs as it did on land, so it has to surface frequently in order to replenish its oxygen supply.

The beautiful *long-tailed salamander* is usually found on rocky banks in association with *dusky salamanders*. The long-tailed salamander is a bright yellow specked with black chevron marks on the sides and tail. The dusky, on the other hand, is chocolate brown. Both of these salamanders belong to a large family that have neither lungs nor gills. All their oxygen is absorbed directly through the skin from the atmosphere.

The *mud puppy,* also called *water dog,* is one of our biggest salamanders, being about 9 inches long and as big around as a crab apple. It never comes out on land, but stays in the water, breathing with a pair of large, bushy gills. The "mamma" mud puppy has quite a time finding a suitable homesite in the river or quiet stream where she lives. Each egg is suspended from a jelly stalk attached to the underside of a large flat stone. If no stones are found the mud puppy constructs a sunlit sand nest by making a depression in the sand with her tail. She protects the eggs from fish and other enemies until they hatch, six to nine weeks later. The mud puppy has a long life span of at least 23 years. Biological supply houses sell hundreds of mud puppies every year to college biology laboratories to be used for dissection and study.

HOW MANY OF THESE CAN YOU DO?

Check each one when you finish it.

☐ 1. Hold a Frog Olympics. Mark out a big circle in a clearing as a jump arena and let each contestant have his frog jump three times. The longest series of three jumps wins the contest. Bullfrogs jump best. The national record is 16 feet, 4 inches.

☐ 2. Collect some bullfrog tadpoles (any tadpole two inches or

SALAMANDERS. A red-spotted newt (left) in the eft stage. The long-tailed salamander (right) has no lungs or gills; it gets air to breathe through skin.

more in length is most likely a bullfrog tadpole) and keep them in an aquarium until they change form and become adults. Feed them oatmeal flakes and watch the tadpoles spew out the pieces from their gill openings on the sides of the head.

☐ 3. Build a terrarium of woodland plants and stock it with several newts; red efts on the land part and adults in the water part. Feed them small grasshoppers and flies.

☐ 4. Build an amphibian home zoo. Try to collect every species found in your area, even the rare ones. When you get tired of caring for your zoo, present your animals to your city zoo; they'll probably be glad to get them.

☐ 5. Start a collection of preserved amphibians. Preserve your animals in the isopropyl alcohol that you can buy at any drugstore. Collect only one specimen of each kind unless the males and females are different in appearance. Animals should not be collected and killed indiscriminately.

☐ 6. Earn the MV Honor award in *Amphibians*.

INTERESTING BOOKS ABOUT AMPHIBIANS

Handbook of Frogs and Toads of the United States and Canada, Albert H. and Anna A. Wright (Comstock Publishing Associates, Ithaca, N.Y.)

A Field Guide to Reptiles and Amphibians, Roger Conant (Houghton Mifflin Co.)

Amphibians and Reptiles of Western North America, Robert C. Stebbins (McGraw-Hill Book Co., Inc.)

A Natural History of North American Amphibians and Reptiles, James A. Oliver (D. Van Nostrand Co., Inc.)

Handbook of Salamanders, Sherman Bishop (Comstock Publishing Associates, Ithaca, N.Y.)

Amphibians (MV Honor booklet)

six legs, four wings

IF ONE pair of house flies began to reproduce in April, and each following generation continued to reproduce, and if every egg hatched and every baby grew up, by the fall of the year the earth would be covered with a layer of flies four and a half feet deep!

Now remember that the house fly is just one kind of insect. There are at least a million different kinds, and many of them reproduce faster than the fly. The only reason we have not been destroyed long ago is that God provided enemies to keep the insects under control. Birds are a great help, so are bats and other mammals. But the greatest help of all are other insects. A wise Pathfinder wants to know which insects are his friends, and which he should try to destroy.

The Damage They Can Do

The club is having a corn roast. You tear the leaves from a fresh cob—and find the kernels half eaten by an *ear worm* or by a *European corn borer*. That's proof enough that insects damage man's food supply. Fortunately, not all the cobs are spoiled, thanks to the *chalcid wasp* that every year lays eggs in every corn borer it can find.

The *spring grain aphid* causes millions of dollars' worth of damage to grain, but farmers let swarms of *braconid wasps* loose over their fields and they lay eggs inside these aphids. The immature wasp lives in the aphid, eating the aphid's insides, and emerging only when it becomes an adult.

Some years ago it was found that the *cottony-cushion scale* was killing the orange trees in southern California. A worldwide search revealed that in Australia this insect was killed and eaten by the *ladybird beetle*. Some of the beetles were imported into California. They multiplied rapidly, brought the pest under control, and saved the trees. Now every winter they migrate to the mountains, where they are shoveled up by the gallon and brought back to be sold to orchardists and alfalfa farmers.

"Pleasant words are as an honeycomb" (Proverbs 16:24).

So the damage the harmful insects were doing was controlled when men discovered helpful insects that were their natural enemies. But there are still many other harmful insects for which no one has found an effective control.

Japanese beetles, which came to the country on iris roots imported into New Jersey in 1916, lay their eggs in the ground, and the adults, in huge groups, attack grass and plants.

The *boll weevil* first attacked cotton fields in the South around 1892. The adult lays eggs in the cotton boll, and the larvae then eat the developing cotton, doing a quarter-billion dollars' worth of damage or more in some years. *Bark beetles* destroy trees, *peach moths* and *codling moths* ruin fruit, the *Mexican bean beetle* swarms over bean leaves, the *pea aphid,* which used to be content to eat wild vetch, now is doing tremendous damage to peas.

Some of these insects have become a menace because farmers have grown the same crops on the same land year after year. Others are a menace here because they are removed from the natural enemies that keep their numbers down in their homeland. What can be done to reduce the damage they do? It's a billion-dollar question. Perhaps someday a Pathfinder will find the answer. It could be *you.*

INSECTS GOOD AND BAD

There are so many different kinds of insects in the world that it is impossible to get acquainted with them all. However, it isn't hard to see that some—like wasps, bees, and hornets—are quite similar to one another, yet very different from, say, moths and butterflies. Scientists who study insects have divided them into groups, and the best way to start learning the insects is to know the groups —or orders, as they are called. Most of the orders are based on the shape and appearance of the wings. Beginning with insects that have no antennae, and those that have no wings—the *silverfish,* which lives indoors, and the *springtail,* which uses its tail to jump into the air—there are twenty-five orders.

Grasshoppers and Crickets

Notice how straight the wings of a grasshopper stretch out behind when it is resting. Grasshoppers and crickets have been put in the order Orthoptera, which means "straight wings."

Look at your watch, then tell your friend exactly what the temperature is. Here's how. Count the number of times the black *field cricket* chirps in fourteen seconds, and add 40; or listen to the greenish-white *tree cricket* chirping from a branch, and add 42.

HELPFUL INSECTS. The praying mantis (left) and the lady beetle (top) eat harmful insects. Silk comes from the cocoons of silkworms (bottom).

Crickets sing all night; so do *katydids*. They rub the file on one outer wing against a scraper on the other. *Grasshoppers* sing all day, rubbing a back leg against a wing. A *praying mantis* is silent. With its movable head, and eyes that change color, it stealthily stalks other insects, catching them in its forelegs and eating them like corn on the cob. Then it licks itself clean. Flash a light into a dark corner of an old house, and a *cockroach* will probably scurry away. Pick up a twig, and it may turn out to be a *walking stick*.

Termites

Tear off the bark from a dead log and you may see a hundred *termites* rushing for shelter. Because they are white they are often called "white ants," but they have no relation to ants. They are social insects, with a queen, a king, and workers and soldiers. Part of the nest may be in the ground, and the termites build mud tubes to reach up to the food they want to eat. Though many eat wood, they cannot digest it, and in their stomachs live little creatures that digest it for them. Termites do good by clearing away dead trees and old logs, but do a lot of damage in wooden houses. The *compass termite* in Australia makes "ant hills" or "termiteria," that always point north and south. *Eutermes termites* erect cement buildings 20 feet high and 12 feet around.

COLLECTIONS. Keep your insects where friends can see them. Butterflies (left) are in Riker mounts—shallow boxes with glass tops, filled with cotton. Long pins hold mosquitoes in the U.S. Government collection (right).

Dragonflies and Damsel Flies

On a sunny day you will see a *dragonfly* or a *damsel fly* flitting over a pond. The damsel fly lays its eggs against decayed plant stems at the bottom of a pond, but it is too light to break through the film on the water's surface. Look for a male damsel fly pushing a female through this film—and the female then turning upside down and pulling the male through. The nymphs (young) of both insects live in water, moving around by jet propulsion. You can tell the adults apart by the wings—the dragonfly keeps them out when resting, the damsel fly folds them up.

May Flies and Lice

May flies are very delicate insects that may spend as much as three years in the water as larvae, then live as adults only a few hours or days, lay their eggs, and die without eating.

There are three orders of lice—biting, sucking, and chewing. Biting lice include the *hen louse,* on chickens, and the *dog louse* on dogs.

The "cootie," properly known as the *human body louse,* is a sucking louse that spreads typhus fever, trench fever, and other serious diseases among humans who don't keep themselves clean.

Among the chewing lice is the *book louse* that sometimes does a lot of damage to expensive libraries.

True Bugs

Some people call all insects "bugs," but scientists call only one order of insects true bugs. Many of them at first glance look like beetles, but that is because the front half of two of their wings is thick and horny. So scientists call them Hemiptera, "half wings."

288

These CICADAS have just come out of the ground after a seventeen-year sleep. The upper one has already shed its skin and shows its new, glassy wings. They will lay their eggs and be dead before the short summer is over.

At a pond or slow-moving river you will find the *water boatman,* the *back swimmer* (that may bite), and the *water strider,* which sometimes roams at sea far from land. In the water you may see a young *water scorpion,* hanging head down and waiting for a baby May fly or an immature damsel fly to come close enough to be caught. Or you may see the *giant water bug,* which grows two inches long in the United States and four inches long in South America. It eats tadpoles, frogs, fish, and even garter snakes. Females of some water bugs glue their eggs to the backs of the males.

Assassin bugs may bite severely, and *stink bugs* eat caterpillars and beetles and let out a bad smell when disturbed. *Chinch bugs* are harmful to wheat, and you'll likely find *squash bugs* on the leaves of melons and squash.

Bedbugs, alas, have disturbed many a person's sleep, and related species live on bats, poultry, and swallows.

Cicadas and Aphids

Cicadas and aphids differ from the true bugs in that their wings are all made of the same clear, filmy material. They are called Homoptera, "same wings." You'll have no trouble at all knowing that the cicadas are around. All through the long, hot days of July and August you can hear the "seventeen-year locust" singing noisily in the tops of the trees. But who can solve the mystery of these strange creatures?

Their eggs are laid in the tips of the branches. (When you see a few dead leaves at the end of several branches of a tree you can be pretty sure a cicada has laid eggs there.) Soon the eggs hatch, and the larvae go down to the ground, tunnel in the earth, and live off the roots. From time to time they shed their skins. Finally, after seventeen years they emerge, climb up onto a tree trunk, crawl out of their skin, and fly off for a few weeks, to mate and lay their eggs and sing raucously, like their parents, in the tops of the trees.

You can easily find their hollow skins on tree trunks. Every seventeen years great swarms come forth in the northeastern States. In the South it's every thirteen years. And down through the centuries some have "got their clocks wrong," so there are always plenty around every summer. But who tells the shapeless, little larvae, buried deep in the ground, when it is time to come up?

Though cicadas are noisy, *aphids* never make a sound. They grow best on the juicy green leaves on the tops of plants. They have two little tubes inside that produce a sweet fluid called "honeydew," and ants stroke them till they give up this fluid much as men milk cows. When the aphids have eaten all the fresh greenery on one plant, the ants carry them to new "pasture" on other plants.

Copycats and Caddis Flies

Scorpion flies are copycats because they look for all the world like scorpions, even sitting with their long tail bent forward and frightening ignorant people. But there is no sting on the end of their tail, such as a scorpion has, and they are quite harmless.

The "doodle bug" looks for all the world like a damsel fly when it is grown. As a larva it is called the *ant lion,* because it eats ants. It digs a cone-shaped hole in sandy ground and when ants walk by they fall into the hole and cannot get out, because the walls make miniature "land slides" when the ants try to climb up.

Caddis flies are not copycats, but they are in the next order of insects. Their larvae live at the bottom of rivers and make homes for themselves by sticking leaves or stones, sand or gravel, together with silk. Each different species of caddis fly makes a different kind of home.

Moths and Butterflies

Moths and butterflies belong to the order Lepidoptera, which means "scale wings," because their wings are covered with brightly colored scales, very much like the shingles or tiles on a roof.

There are several chief differences between moths and butterflies. Moths usually fly at night, rest with their wings held flat or folded against the body, and have antennae that are either smooth or feathery, but do not have knobs on the ends. Butterflies usually fly in the daytime, rest with their wings erect, and have knobs on the ends of their antennae.

MOTHS. Top line: Pandora sphinx, Luna moth, promethea. Second line: polyphemus, io moth, cecropia. BUTTERFLIES. Third line: great spangled fritillary, common sulphur, cabbage butterfly, mourning cloak. Fourth line: admiral, viceroy, and question mark. Bottom line: tiger swallowtail, wood nymph, and monarch. All these are reproduced one half their natural size.

The most beautiful moth in North America is the pale-green *Luna moth*. The *cecropia* and *polyphemus* are much more common, and almost as good looking. The larvae of the *peach tree borer* drill holes in peach trees. The *codling moth*—the "worm" in apples —lays its eggs only in the twilight, and some orchardists have managed to reduce their numbers by turning on bright lights as twilight approaches then turning them off suddenly when the night is too dark for egg laying. The larvae of the *American tent caterpillar* build tents in trees, then follow one another along roads of silk threads as they march around the branches eating the leaves. Certain of the *hawk moths* are sometimes called the "hummingbird moths" because they hover over flowers the way hummingbirds do. *Measuring worms* are really moth larvae that have legs only on the very ends of their bodies. They bring the back up to the front, making a loop, then stretch the front out ahead as if they were measuring the twig they are on. *Tiger moths,* when young, are the *woolly bears* which some people think forecast mild or cold winters by the color of bristles on their bodies. The larvae of certain of the *owlet moths* are called army worms, because they sometimes crawl across the country in great numbers. The larvae of the *clothes moth* can frequently be found in the closet, eating clothes.

But the *yucca moth* is found only in the deserts of the Southwest. This remarkable moth is the only insect in the world equipped to pollinate the flower of the yucca. Without the yucca moth, there would soon be no yucca seeds. And without yucca seeds, there would soon be no more yucca moths, either, for yucca seeds form the only food the larvae of yucca moths will eat.

The first butterfly in the year is usually the *mourning cloak.* *Swallowtails* linger around flowers, sucking nectar. The *monarch* is famous for its habit of migrating great distances. It protects itself from the birds by producing an evil-tasting fluid in two glands on its wings. The *viceroy* lacks these glands but protects itself by looking very much like the monarch, fooling the birds. Certain of the *tortoise-shell* butterflies also migrate sometimes. And don't overlook the little *blues* and *coppers,* small but brilliant in the sunlight.

Flies and Mosquitoes

Flies and mosquitoes have only two wings and so belong to the order Diptera, "two wings." Most insects have four wings.

Kill every mosquito and fly you can. They are not only a nuisance, they spread disease and death. Female mosquitoes must drink the blood of a mammal, bird, or human. When the *anopheles mosquito* sucks up the blood of a person who has malaria, the para-

MIMICS. Some insects are copycats, or mimics. Walking sticks (left) look for all the world like dead twigs; the leaf insect looks just like a leaf.

sites that cause this disease get into the mosquito. They tunnel through the wall of the mosquito's stomach and multiply rapidly, then travel in the mosquito's blood to the salivary glands in the mosquito's mouth. When the mosquito bites a healthy human, these parasites go out in the saliva into the human's blood, where they multiply rapidly, eat the red blood cells, and give the victim fever chills. Anopheles live in some Southern States and in the tropics. The *aedes mosquito* carries yellow fever. Fortunately, the common *culex mosquito* in North America does not carry either disease.

Mosquitoes breed in water—stagnant ponds, puddles, rain water that collects in the crotches of trees, and in cans left lying around by careless campers. Clean up the stagnant water, and you'll clean out the mosquitoes.

Flies breed in filth. They get germs on their feet. If they get on your food they track those germs across it.

Sand flies fly in swarms on beaches. *Midges, gnats,* and *punkies* swarm under trees in the twilight and bite fiercely. *Robber flies* sit on a twig or a blade of grass waiting for some other insect to pass by, then swoop down and catch it in mid-air. *Bee flies* hover over flowers and look like bees but aren't; they are quite harmless.

ANT GARDENS. This ant nest has been cut in half and the holes show the places where the ants were growing their fungus gardens. The ant nest was found to be eight feet deep.

Beetles

There are about a quarter million different kinds of beetles! Two wings are usually thin and the beetle uses them to fly with. The other wings are hard and form an armor plate or sheath to protect the flying wings. So the beetle order is called Coleoptera, "sheath wings."

The *tiger beetle,* like the real tiger, pounces suddenly on its prey. Look in the damp earth under a rock and you'll likely find a *carabid beetle,* which eats other insects. One kind of these, the *bombardier beetle,* emits a foul-smelling spray when disturbed. On a pond or a slow-moving stream you will find the four-eyed beetle, the *whirligig,* which has two eyes to see what's going on above the water and two under its chin to watch out for enemies—mostly crayfish—under the water. Whirligigs in large swarms swing and swirl on the water like skaters on ice.

The *rove beetle* rides piggyback on a termite and snatches the termite's food just as it is about to eat it. The *carrion,* or *burying, beetle* is believed to bury the bodies of small dead animals as food for larvae.

The *deathwatch beetle* taps its head against the side of its runway in a log or rafter, and used to make superstitious people think it was announcing the death of one of their loved ones. The *click beetle,* when laid on its back, springs onto its feet again with a "click." The *giant stag beetle* grows to be two inches long and feeds on honeydew as the ants do.

Scarab beetles have the strange practice of living in dung and rolling it up in little balls and burying it for food for their young. The Egyptians used to consider the scarab holy, and worshiped it as a god.

Finally, there is the *firefly* that can do something human scientists cannot do—make light without heat. Some fireflies flash in unison. In many species the female does not fly, but stays on the

DIGGER WASP (upper left) digs holes in which to lay eggs. The HONEY-BEE (upper right) carries pollen on its legs. TERMITES (lower left) seek new homes while they have wings. The man (lower right) measures a fifteen-inch tube that termites built so as to reach the wooden floor of a house.

ground and glows—looking for snails. When it finds one, the males drop in for dinner.

Ants, Wasps, and Bees

Ants and wasps and bees belong to the twenty-fifth order, the Hymenoptera, which means "membrane wings." Look at their wings and see what delicate, filmy, membranous things they are.

Most of them are social insects; they live in large societies.

Ants have kings and queens, workers and soldiers. *Army ants* of the tropics do not spend much time in a nest, but march across the land eating everything they come to, dead or alive. *Black ants* are common in the woods, nesting in the soil or in wood. *Fire ants* bite with a sting that burns like fire. They destroy crops and have been invading the Southern States. *Harvester ants* eat seeds, causing considerable loss to farmers. *Fungus ants* grow fungus in their nests, and when the queen moves to a new nest she takes a little piece with her to start a fungus garden in the new home. *Formica ants* build anthills. A European ant invades the nests of *red ants* and takes the ants off as slaves. *Honeypot ants* stuff themselves full of honeydew till they are as round as marbles, and they are then eaten like candy by Australian natives. *Carpenter ants* are the large ants you'll find in the woods. Among other things, they like to eat young praying mantises, and will watch praying mantis eggs for days, checking occasionally to see how soon they will hatch, so they will be on hand when the babies come out. The *Argentine ant* is the pest that gets into houses and does so much damage to food.

Some wasps are social, others are not. The *gall wasp* is not. It lays eggs in the stems of plants. Something in the egg—or else something about the larva that hatches from it—irritates the plant, and it grows a swelling, or "gall," around the larva. The *yellow jacket* makes cells of paper in which it lays eggs.

White-faced hornets certainly are social—and organized! Beware! Their large, paper nests can be found hanging in trees. Leave them alone. Even in the winter they may contain a sleeping hornet that will come buzzing angrily out if the nest is brought into a warm house.

The *mud-dauber wasp* gathers mud by a pond or stream and fashions an egg cell like a water pitcher. It paralyzes some insects with its sting, places them in the pitcher, attaches an egg to a thread of silk and suspends it from the neck of the pitcher so the egg swings clear of the insects, then seals up the top of the jug. When the egg hatches, the larva reaches down and eats the insects, which, being still alive, are quite fresh.

Bumblebees are often seen around red clover, for they are the only insect that can reach down into that clover's deep flower and get the nectar. They make nests in abandoned mouse nests or rodent burrows.

Honeybees, as everyone knows, are social. With their air-conditioned hives and finely organized teamwork, they make beeswax and honey and pollinate billions of flowers, making themselves of tremendous value to humanity.

AN INSECT'S BODY

Count the Legs

Some people confuse insects with spiders. When in doubt, count the legs. A spider has eight legs; insects, *six*. Insects also have *three body sections*—head, thorax, and abdomen. And in nearly all cases they have *four wings*.

A caterpillar may seem to have twelve legs, but six of these are false.

296

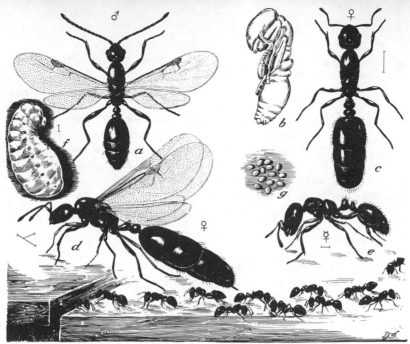

AN ANT'S LIFE. The queen ant (*c*) lays eggs (*g*), which are cared for by the workers (*e*). The eggs hatch into white larvae (*f*), which grow until the larvae become pupae (*b*) and sleep. Usually workers come out of the pupae, but sometimes winged males (*a*) and females (*d*) hatch from them. These fly off and mate; then the female drops her wings and starts a new colony.

Stomach, Brain, and Muscles

Anyone who has been bitten knows an insect has a mouth. Many do not realize that insects also have stomachs, and glands that produce digestive juices, and intestines, where the food is absorbed into the body after it is digested.

An insect has a brain, too, and nerves, along which messages are sent to control the muscles. Muscles? Oh, yes. A human has about five hundred; a grasshopper, about nine hundred.

The skeleton is rather different. It is outside the body. The skin is hard, and is called an exoskeleton. It cannot change its size as the insect grows, but splits every so often, letting the insect crawl out and grow a new, larger one.

Insects breathe. A grasshopper does it with little tubes that open along the sides of its body. The grasshopper closes the back holes and sucks air in through the front ones. The air goes down the tubes, which branch everywhere, getting smaller and smaller. Then the grasshopper closes the front holes and forces the air through the tubes and out the back holes.

297

An insect has blood, and a heart to pump it around, though the blood vessels are not nearly so complicated as ours.

Finally, an insect can fly, which we cannot. A dragonfly, with four wings, can stop two wings and proceed "on two motors" if it wishes. A fly, which has only two wings, can beat them in a figure-of-eight motion to keep itself in one position in the air. Some kinds can change the pitch of their wings and go forward, back, up, and down more skillfully than any man-made airplane. A scientist studying the flight of flies noticed on the back of the flies two bumps that look like posts with knobs on top, and are called halteres. When he cut one haltere off, the fly could go only in circles. When he cut both halteres off, the fly could not fly at all. In the halteres are little holes with hairs sticking into them. The wind goes through these holes as a fly flies, and it is believed that the hairs tell the fly how fast he is going.

Amazing, isn't it, what equipment God has built into the insects!

HOW MANY OF THESE CAN YOU DO?

Check each one when you finish it.

- ☐ 1. Catch a caterpillar and watch it change into a butterfly or moth.
- ☐ 2. Make a collection of at least fifteen insects.
- ☐ 3. Make an ant house.
- ☐ 4. Earn the MV Honor award in *Insects*.
- ☐ 5. Earn the MV Honor award in *Moths and Butterflies*.

INTERESTING BOOKS ABOUT INSECTS

The Insect World of Jean Henri Fabre, Jean Henri Fabre (Dodd, Mead & Co.)
   Full of interesting stories about insects.
Field Book of Insects, Frank Lutz (G. P. Putnam's Sons)
   A standard book for identifying insects.
Insects, Herbert S. Zim and Clarence A. Cottam (Golden Press)
   Well-illustrated book in the Golden Nature Series.
A Field Guide to the Butterflies, Alexander B. Klots (Houghton Mifflin Co.)
The Insect Guide, Ralph B. Swain (Doubleday & Co., Inc.)
Insects and *Moths and Butterflies* (MV Honor booklets)

HARMFUL INSECTS. Top: some aphids sucking the juices from a rosebud; a silverfish. Middle: a young grasshopper eating a corn leaf; a boll weevil on a cotton boll. Bottom: clothes moth, Japanese beetle, and gypsy moth.

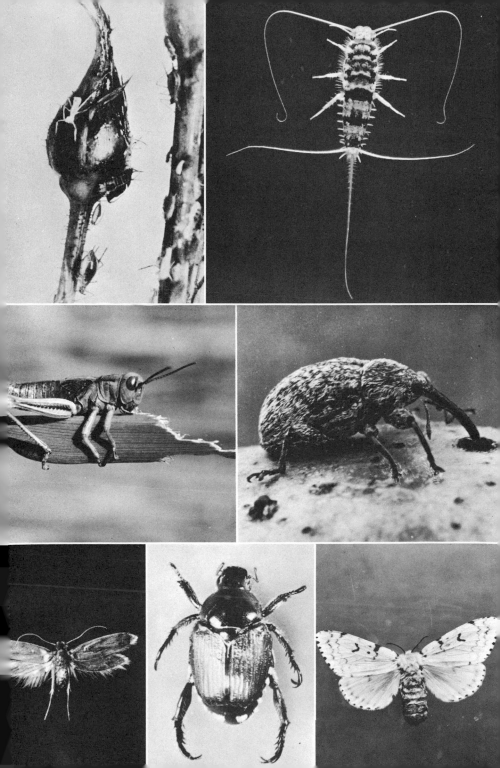

trappers with eight legs

BILL was not a Pathfinder. He had found a hole at the bottom of a grassy hill on the edge of some woods, and he was sure a wild animal lived there. Having just gotten a flash camera for his birthday, he determined to sit by the hole that night and photograph the animal coming out.

He told Bob about his discovery, and Bob, who was a Pathfinder, came over and examined the hole, stood up, and said, "There's no animal living there. You'll be wasting your time if you try to get a picture here tonight."

But Bill insisted, and that night he spent many dark hours waiting for an animal that never showed up.

Next morning he asked Bob how he had known so definitely that there was no animal there. "It looked like a perfectly good hole to me."

"It was a good hole," Bob said, "but it hadn't been used for months." He pointed. "See that spider web going right across the middle? It's dusty, and there's no spider around. If some animal were still living here, it would break the spider web when it went in or out, and the spider would have to renew it so often it wouldn't have a chance to get dusty. A dirty old web like that proved to me that no animal had gone through the entrance in a long, long time."

Amazing Creatures

Say "spider" and most people shudder! Yet spiders are among the most amazing creatures God made. And contrary to popular belief, most of them do not make webs.

There are *trap-door spiders,* for instance, that dig burrows in the ground with a trap door on top. Some tunnels are just one straight hole, others have branches, and each branch is closed by another trap door.

The female lives in the burrow, and after the baby spiders hatch from the eggs, they may live with her during the winter. The

"The spider taketh hold with her hands, and is in kings' palaces" (Proverbs 30:28).

tops of the doors may be camouflaged to make them harder to find.

Tarantulas, many of which are large and hairy, sometimes run about in the tops of trees in the tropics. Some also dig burrows, closing the top with just a few strands of silk when they are at home. They eat beetles and grasshoppers, and may even dine on frogs, lizards, and small snakes "in season." The female often sits in the doorway of the burrow turning her egg sack round and round in the sun to keep the eggs warm. Her greatest enemy is the "tarantula hawk," a wasp that paralyzes her with its sting, then drags her off to a hole in the ground and lays an egg on her body.

Then, there are *turret spiders,* which build a rampart, or chimney, around the top of their burrow, and sit on top of it to catch insects as they go by. The *ogre-faced spider* weaves a net about the size of a postage stamp, folds it up, then sneaks up on its enemy and hurls the net over it.

Hunters and Fishers

Look for *wolf spiders* hunting insects in the roots of prairie grass. *Pardosa* carries her egg sack around with her, and when the babies hatch, they climb aboard mamma for the first week of their lives. And if one pardosa mother kills another pardosa carrying babies, the babies of the dead mother scramble onto the living mother. *Tiger wolves* have yellow stripes; *sand wolves,* when chased, seem to disappear right into the sand. Actually, they open their camouflaged trap doors, slip inside, and slam the doors behind them.

Fisher spiders live near water. They sit on the bank, with their front two feet resting on the water. When a fish—even two inches long—swims by underneath, down goes the spider, grabs the fish, poisons it, then hauls it ashore for the picnic.

The *raft spider* in England (there is a spider in America that may do the same) builds a raft by sewing leaves together. Then it climbs aboard and drifts down the stream, only getting off occasionally to run across the water to catch some insect that looks appetizing.

Another fishing spider, the *pisaurid,* takes very good care of her babies. Just before they hatch she makes a nursery for them by sewing leaves together. The babies don't seem to mind that the leaves are usually poison ivy!

The *water spider* lives under the water. It breathes—as all spiders do—through holes in its sides, so it takes air down with it in bubbles attached to hairs. It stretches out a web under the water, then fills it full of air, and lives in this "diving bell."

The **TRAP-DOOR SPIDER** lines a hole with web and makes a trap door at the top, then sits in the doorway waiting to pounce when her prey comes by.

Jumping spiders have better eyes than most spiders—they can probably see a foot in front of them. They creep up on their prey, then leap on it like a cat. *Crab spiders* can often be found in flowers. They look like tiny crabs and can walk sideways, the way crabs do. They can also change their color from white to light yellow, depending on the color of the flower they are on. Crab spiders wait for insects to land, then sting them while they are sucking nectar.

The *spitting spider* sneaks up on a fly, then, from a quarter inch away or more, spits sticky glue all over it. *Bolas,* the cowboy spider, is an ugly-looking thing, but some scientists think she smells like a flower. She gets her dinner by sitting on a twig, producing a short length of silk, and putting a blob of glue on the end. When a moth comes near, she swings this "lasso" around her head, takes aim, and hits the moth with the glue. Then she winds in her cord and eats. If a moth doesn't come by in fifteen minutes or half an hour, she eats the rope and the glue and starts over.

Web Spinners

There are, of course, spiders that spin webs. The simplest web is made by one of the *stick spiders*. It is just one single strand stretched across a path. But the middle part is kept sticky, and gnats often land there.

SPIDER WEBS like this one are usually renewed every night or two. When you find one, come back again and check on it every few hours, and sooner or later you will see the spider spinning a new one—a fascinating sight.

Agelena, a grass spider, builds a web shaped like a funnel. Above the web she stretches some invisible lines, then she sits in the bottom of the funnel to wait. Soon a grasshopper leaps over the funnel, bangs into the unseen wires, gets confused, and falls onto the web. There's nothing sticky about it, but when he tries to get off he feels like a man stumbling through deep snow being chased by a bandit on skis. For the spider it's dinnertime.

Indoors you'll have no difficulty finding the tangled cobwebs of the *house spider.* Outside, under hedges, you may find the tangled webs of its cousin, *theridion.* These webs are not as tangled as they seem. Under the hedge, thin, highly elastic, sticky lines run down to the ground. A crawling insect bumps into one. He struggles, the line breaks, and being elastic, it hauls him up into the air. He continues struggling, his feet beating the air, and bumps into other sticky threads until he is well and truly caught. Then the spider comes down for lunch.

The *triangle spider* spins a triangle-shaped web. Finally, most beautiful of all, are the orb webs spun by the garden spiders. Everybody who says he has no use for spiders should watch one of these webs being made. It isn't hard to do—the spiders renew them every night or two. When the web is finished, drop an insect into it, watch the spider tie him down, wrap him up, and sting him. When the web is finished, the large, long-legged, brightly colored *orange argiope, silver argiope,* and *banded argiope* usually stretch themselves out in the center of the web. But *arenia* makes herself a bedroom of leaves off to one side and stretches a telephone line from the web to her couch, to wake her up when an insect arrives.

Fearful Lovers

When it's time for love-making, the male spiders have to be careful. All spiders are very shortsighted, and if the male is not careful he may be eaten before he has explained the purpose of his call. Males of the web-making spiders tug gently on the lady's web, like a suitor knocking on his girl friend's door. *Hunting spiders* have marks on their chest and arms, and as they approach the female they wave their legs and dance to show off the marks. Some spiders drum on the floor with their front feet. And at least one kind of spider wraps a fly in silk and presents it—like a box of chocolates—as a gift on the first date.

In many cases the males are eaten by the females, but far more often they get away safely.

Those Eight Legs

You will hear some people call spiders insects. There are many differences, however. The easiest to see is the number of legs. Spiders have eight. Insects have six.

Moreover, spiders do not fly, their bodies are divided into only two parts instead of three, they spin silk for almost everything they do, and they have eight simple eyes and no antennae.

Though spiders do not have wings, they sometimes go sailing. On a calm, sunny day in spring or fall you may see a spider crawl up to the top of a blade of grass or the tip of a fence post, and there begin letting out silk. As the strands get longer, suddenly the spider takes off, going almost straight up. It is called ballooning, and almost all spiders do it. It helps to keep them from living too close to one another. They choose a calm day when the earth is warmer than the air, and warm air currents, going upward, take the tiny spiders with them. They may come down a few yards away—and try again—or they may come down on ships more than two hundred miles from the nearest land.

Spiders and Man

The spider's silk is of tremendous value to her. She uses it constantly as a dragline. She makes different kinds for the framework, for the scaffolding, and for the sticky part of her web. She uses it to truss up her victims, and, soft and fluffy, to line the sac for her eggs. The web is stronger for its size than steel wires, and lasts for years. It ought to be good for human use. But it isn't.

Boys in the New Hebrides use spider silk for fishing lines—and ground up spiders for bait. Men in the Solomon Islands trick the *nephila spider* into weaving her web inside a bamboo loop, then use the web as a fishing net. Makers of telescopes in the past have used the fine threads across the lenses of their instruments, but since World War I this practice has been diminishing. And in emergencies the funnel web of the grass spiders has been used as a bandage—though it is dangerous because of the many germs. In the tropics, the *huntsman,* or "banana spider," is often encouraged to live indoors to keep down the roaches and other disagreeable insects. The web would really become valuable, though, if it could be used like the silkworm's for making clothes. It has been tried. A few stockings have been made, and a dress or two. And the material is said to be beautiful. But it takes 663,522 spiders—more or less— to make a pound of silk—and when a lot of spiders are kept together, there are soon only one or two left. They eat one another.

About the Black Widow

Nearly all spiders have a poisonous bite, but they usually won't bite a human even if he tries to make them; and in the United States only one common spider has a bite that is poisonous to humans—the *black widow*. Her poison may well be the most deadly venom produced by any poisonous animal.

Fortunately, she doesn't want to bite humans. When she does, she is able to inject only a little venom, because she doesn't have much to start with. The poison attacks the nerves. There is sharp pain that moves around the body and settles in the legs and abdomen. The patient feels sick to his stomach, dizzy, weak, and may find it hard to breathe. Fortunately, hardly anyone ever dies from the bite, and now there is a good cure, an injection of calcium chloride. When bitten, call the doctor at once.

Better yet, don't get bitten. Know what the black widow looks like—a very shiny black marble with long thin legs. Usually there are red marks on the stomach—a red dot or a red hourglass—but these may be hard to see. Clean out sheds and around woodpiles, and especially check privies and latrines when camping. The chances of being bitten are about the same as being struck by lightning; the danger of dying, very much less.

Get acquainted with the spiders! God packed a lot of wonderful

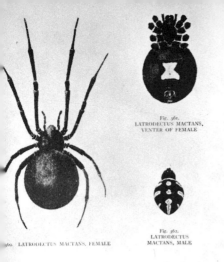

Fig. 361.
LATRODECTUS MACTANS,
VENTER OF FEMALE

The **BLACK WIDOW** is the only common poisonous spider north of Mexico. Fortunately, it is easy to recognize. Look for the shiny black body, the long thin legs, and the red spots on the abdomen.

Fig. 362.
LATRODECTUS
MACTANS, MALE

360. LATRODECTUS MACTANS, FEMALE

things into them, and He hoped we would take time to find out about them.

HOW MANY OF THESE CAN YOU DO?

Check each one when you finish it.

☐ 1. Watch a spider leaving a web.
☐ 2. Drop an insect into a spider's web and report to your Pathfinder Club on what happens next.
☐ 3. Find a spider's egg sac and cut it open to see how it is made.
☐ 4. Cut a strand from a web and see how much weight you can hold with it.
☐ 5. Make a collection of twelve different kinds of spider.
☐ 6. Earn the MV Honor award in *Spiders*.

INTERESTING BOOKS ABOUT SPIDERS

The Life of the Spider, Jean Henri Fabre (Dodd, Mead & Co.)
Mr. Fabre conducted some very interesting experiments with spiders.
Spiders, Bertha Morris Parker (Row, Peterson and Company)
Interesting and easy to understand.
American Spiders, Willis J. Gertsch (D. Van Nostrand Company, Inc.)
More technical.
The Life of the Spider, John Crompton (New American Library of World Literature, Inc.)
An excellent book for teacher to read to the class at school.
Spiders (MV Honor booklet)

wildflowers

ONE of the best things about wildflowers is that you can study them on a Sabbath walk. Some Sabbath soon, when church is over, have the whole family go down by a lake or stream for the afternoon.

By Rivers and Marshes

Walk around the water. Along the banks you should find tall, straight *cattails,* and out in the water the *yellow pond lily* or the *bladderwort,* that has traps underwater for catching small fish. Here, too, you'll find *arrowhead,* with large leaves shaped like arrowheads, and roots the Indians used to eat. *Jewelweed* may be here also, with spotted orange flowers and a seedbox that bursts open when you touch the trigger, scattering seeds four feet away. Look here, too, for *forget-me-not,* with thick fleshy stems and pale-blue flowers, and yellow *fringed loosestrife,* that got its name from the old belief that animals would stop striving with or fighting one another when these flowers were tied around their necks. Very early in the spring you should find the *skunk cabbage,* whose large spotted leaf emits a most terrible smell when it's torn. Bend down and see the little flowers hiding inside this leaf.

In the Woods

On another Sabbath afternoon, especially early in the year, walk through the woods before the leaves are on the trees. *Trillium* and *hepatica* will be racing to see who can first announce the arrival of spring. Not long after, in moist woodlands, *Jack-in-the-pulpit* will be preaching his first sermons. His pulpit doesn't look much like an Adventist pulpit, but it does look very much like the pulpit in churches that build a canopy over the place where the speaker stands.

In damp areas there are almost sure to be *violets* close to the ground, and baggy *Dutchman's breeches* hanging upside down on a line to dry. On rocky hillsides *wild columbine* will be standing tall,

"Solomon in all his glory was not arrayed like one of these" (Matthew 6:29).

holding flowers that look like comets with small yellow heads and bright-red tails. *Showy lady's-slipper* can be found in damp woods, while the *pink lady's-slipper,* sometimes called *moccasin flower,* inhabits dry sandy woods. Both seem too beautiful to be wild, with a flower like a purse that bees must crawl inside to get either pollen or nectar.

Fields and Roadsides

But the real masses of flowers come in the summer and autumn. Walk along a country lane and see whole fields white with *daisies* that are good for making daisy chains, or yellow with *buttercups* that are supposed to tell whether you like butter when they are held under your chin. (If you do, your chin reflects yellow, so it's said!) Out West the *California poppy* blankets a hillside in orange, accented by purple *lupines,* which got their name from *lupus,* the wolf, because farmers once thought they ate all the minerals out of the soil. There will be *dandelions* everywhere, with a name that means "lion's tooth," and *black mustard,* which has tall yellow flowers and black, spicy seeds.

In purple patches look for *heal-all,* and not far away, pink *bouncing bet* or *soapwort,* the sap of which makes a lather when mixed with water. *Queen Anne's lace* makes a field white with large heads of greenish-white flowers. It is also called *wild carrot.* Pink *shooting star* has a scientific name that means "the twelve gods," and you'll find the poisonous *nightshade,* which has a blue or purple flower not unlike a shooting star and is closely related to tomatoes and potatoes.

Honeysuckle, clambering all over wayside fences, is covered with flowers that seem more fragrant in the evening when the moths begin to fly. The common *yarrow* can be told easily by its white and yellow flowers and fine, fernlike leaves. *Clover* rears small round heads of pink or white in low grass. *Common milkweed,* with round clusters of purple flowers, is the favorite food of monarch caterpillars. And *morning-glory,* escaped from well-kept gardens, closes its pink-and-white trumpets at sundown. *Fireweed,* brilliantly red, is first to grow on burned-out hillsides.

Suddenly, as summer turns to autumn, fields and open woods are bright with *goldenrod,* whose fluffy seeds are good for starting fires. And in sunny fields is *black-eyed Susan,* like a large daisy with a brown center and a fringe of orange.

Wildflowers everywhere, and different in every changing season! With such variety a Pathfinder hike or a Sabbath walk is always an interesting adventure.

INSECT EATERS. Both of these plants eat insects. The leaves of a Venus flytrap (left) snap shut like the jaws of a trap. Once an insect has flown into the hood of the cobra plant (right), it cannot get out again, and growing weary, it falls down into a fluid at the bottom and is digested by the plant.

LEARNING THEIR NAMES

In order to know flowers well, learn to recognize four different parts. Hold a buttercup in your hand. Under the flower notice some green "petals." They are not petals, but sepals. They form the *calyx,* which covered the bud before it opened. The yellow petals make up the *corolla.* Count the sepals and petals. On buttercups there are five sepals and usually five petals. The number varies on different flowers. Look down into the buttercup. There is a circle of hairs with dust on them. The hairs are the *stamens,* the dust is pollen. Right in the middle of the buttercup is a round green knob, the *pistil,* which contains the ovaries, where the seeds are made. Look, then, for these four parts—calyx, corolla, stamens, and pistils. It also helps to notice the leaves and what the fruit looks like.

Some Families to Begin With

Start out learning these ten common families. It will be easier to learn others once you've made a beginning. The following characteristics are general, though there are exceptions:

Members of the *lily family* have three sepals and three petals, six stamens, and three parts to the pistil. Usually the sepals have the same color as the petals, so that the flower looks as if it has six petals. Some of the common lilies you will enjoy finding are *tiger lily, trillium, adder's-tongue, Solomon's-seal,* and *desert lily.* Asparagus, chives, and onions belong to this family too.

311

The *pink family* can be identified by their opposite leaves, swollen nodes, and notched petals. Members include *chickweed, bouncing bet, campion, catchfly,* and *sweet William.* Carnation is a cultivated member of this family.

The *buttercup family* members have many stamens and many pistils. Besides the yellow *buttercups* you will want to know the *anemone,* the *hepatica, crowfoot, columbine, baneberry,* and *marsh marigold.*

The *poppy family* have two sepals that drop off as the flower opens, many stamens, and several compartments in the pistil. You may find *bloodroot, celandine poppy, California poppy,* and *prickly poppy.* Notice in many poppies the holes in the seedboxes for the seeds to fall through.

The *mustard family* are easy to learn, because the members have four sepals, four petals, six stamens, and two parts to the pistil. Get acquainted with *black mustard* (yellow blossoms), *peppergrass, water cress, spring cress, shepherd's-purse, toothwort,* and *sea rocket.* Turnip, radish, cabbage, and cauliflower belong here.

The *rose family* have many variations, but all of the members have many stamens. Try to find the *wild rose, cinquefoil, avens, wild strawberry,* and *steeple bush.* You will discover that many of our fruit trees, such as apples and peaches, are also roses. So are raspberries, cherries, prunes, plums, almonds, apricots, and several others.

The *bean family* have flowers that are not wheel-shaped. They have an irregular flower, two lateral petals and two lower petals united to form an upturned keel. Some bean relatives are *beach pea, partridge pea, wild indigo, lupine, vetch, clover, trefoil, wild licorice,* and *locoweed.* Of course, green peas are in this family, and so are alfalfa and peanuts.

The *mallow family* members have a funnel-shaped flower and many stamens united together around the pistil. Try recognizing the *common mallow, rose mallow, hollyhock, hibiscus,* and *marshmallow,* from which marshmallows used to be made. Cotton is the most important member of this family.

The *violet family,* like the bean family, have flowers that are not wheel-shaped. There are five sepals and five petals, one of which has a spur, and five stamens. Some of the violets are *bird's-foot violet, blue violet, long-spurred violet, white violet, yellow violet,* and *wild pansy.*

Top: rhododendron, columbine, azalea. Middle: California poppy, skunk cabbage, pink lady's-slipper. Bottom: fringed gentian, trillium, and trailing arbutus.

Look out for POISON IVY (above and at left)! It grows as a shrub and also as a vine that climbs trees. POISON OAK in the Western States is similar, but grows only as a shrub. Do not touch the leaves or the stem at any time of the year. It is in touching that the poison gets onto the skin. Identify both poison ivy and poison oak by the fact that the leaves grow in GROUPS OF THREE. "Leaflets three, let them be." Wash yourself with plenty of warm water and yellow soap when you get home from a hike.

The *composite family* has a blossom made up of many tubular flowers forming an inner disc and several ray flowers that look like petals around the edge. This is a very large family and you may meet *black-eyed Susan, sunflower, aster, daisy, devil's paintbrush, dandelion, coneflower, Spanish needle,* and *goldenrod.*

HOW MANY OF THESE CAN YOU DO?

Check each one when you finish it.

☐ 1. Make a collection of fifteen wildflowers, carefully pressed and named.

☐ 2. Go on a Pathfinder plant hike and see who can name the most wildflowers.

☐ 3. Collect seeds from ten different wildflowers and try growing them.

☐ 4. Take apart the seedbox of a morning-glory and examine it closely.

☐ 5. Earn the MV Honor award in *Flowers.*

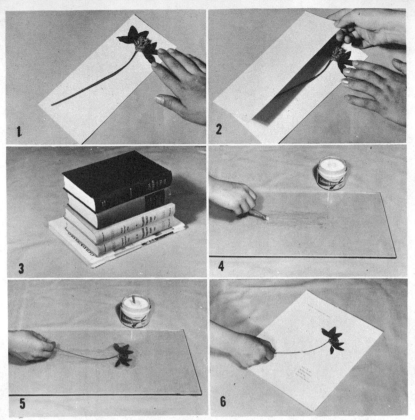

MAKE A COLLECTION of wildflowers: 1. Lay a flower on blotting paper with leaves and petals as flat as possible. 2. Put second piece of blotting paper over it. 3. Set magazines on top; add some heavy books. After two or three days, spread a thin coat of paste on glass. 4. Lay dry flower on it. 5. Lift flower; paste it in scrapbook. Label with name, date, place where it grew.

INTERESTING BOOKS ABOUT WILDFLOWERS

Wild Flower Guide, Edgar T. Wherry (Doubleday & Co., Inc.)
  Has many lovely pictures.
The Macmillan Wild Flower Book, Clarence J. Hylander and
  Edith Farrington Johnston (The Macmillan Co.)
  Magnificent pictures of five hundred Eastern flowers.
Field Book of American Wild Flowers, F. S. Mathews (G. P. Putnam's Sons)
  A very helpful book for identification.
Flowers, Herbert S. Zim and Alexander C. Martin (Golden Press)
  A Golden Nature Guide with good pictures, easy descriptions.
Flowers (MV Honor booklet)

forest sentinels

YOU and the Pathfinder Club are on another hike. Your goal this time is to see as many birds as possible, so your trail leads across a field and through some woods, because you know that birds nest in *trees*. Presently you are hungry and you get your lunch out of a paper sack made of wood that came from *trees*. The lunch includes an apple and an orange, both of which grew on *trees*. For dessert you munch on a candy bar, first ripping off the cellophane wrapper —which was made from *trees* too. The candy is full of chocolate and almonds, both of which grew on *trees*. Lunch over, you are thirsty. Fortunately, there is a little stream nearby, and your counselor explains that the water is there because the roots of the *trees* and the humus from the *trees'* leaves form a sponge that has been storing up water from the winter snows. Later in the afternoon you canoe on the lake. The canoe may be made of metal, but the paddle is made of wood—from *trees*. And in the evening all the club sits around a campfire, and while the director tells stories, the campfire detail keeps adding to the flames logs from cut-down *trees* to keep the fire and the fun going as long as possible.

How many ways trees help us!

Surely no human being would ever carelessly damage one!

Trees Have Many Enemies

Yet trees have many enemies, and man is the worst of all. Farmers, eager to get clear land on which to grow crops and make money, have destroyed millions of acres of forests, often just burning the lumber as waste. Careless foresters, cutting down large trees, have let them fall on smaller ones, making them useless for lumber. Or they have cut out all the trees from a hillside without leaving any behind to provide seeds for new growth. Trees that took centuries to grow are sometimes whacked down in a few minutes to make way for a road or to widen a street. Thoughtless friends of the trees may kill them by blazing the trunk to mark a trail. This injury to the bark opens the door for diseases to enter. For this reason, too,

"As the days of a tree are the days of my people" (Isaiah 65:22).

only pre-Pathfinders use trees as targets for throwing knives and axes. Pathfinders know better.

Insects are the tree's next worst enemies. Some insects, to be sure, help by pollinizing and even pruning. But others, such as the pine beetle, the spruce budworm, the tussock moth, the gypsy moth, and the brown-tail moth, kill trees by the hundreds of thousands or make their wood useless for lumber, usually by boring holes in the trunk and branches.

Disease does untold damage. Millions of chestnut trees have died from the chestnut blight, a disease that has destroyed practically all these magnificent trees and which no one has found a way to stop. Dutch elm disease is killing off large numbers of the stately American elms that line city streets, and blister rust is killing the white pines of the Western forests.

Fire destroys millions of acres every year. Lightning starts some of these fires, but God usually provides rain with the lightning to put out such fires. More often, forest fires are caused by careless humans who leave campfires smoldering, or who throw away matches and cigarettes still burning, or who break glass bottles and leave the shattered glass fragments to provide lenses through which the sun's rays are focused onto dry grass to start new fires.

Every Pathfinder is careful with fire, remembering the rules: Break your match; light fires only in safe places and drown them afterward; acquaint other campers with the dangers of smoking on the trail.

Fortunately, a new day is dawning. Foresters are beginning to look on the trees as a "crop." Only mature trees are cut, and younger ones are carefully left to grow to full size before being harvested. Billboards and signs and Smokey the Bear impress campers that a forest fire ruins a campsite for many years to come. Burned-over and cut-over areas are being planted with young trees—and Pathfinders can help in this. Free trees for such purposes are often obtainable from the State Department of Agriculture. Progress is being made in stamping out diseases and insects. For all this Pathfinders can be thankful.

Getting to Know the Trees

When you first go to a new school, everybody in the classroom looks like everyone else. But when you get to know the students they all seem so different you can hardly believe you were confused at first. It's the same way with trees. At first they all seem the same. But if you'll get acquainted with them, they will all seem different, and you won't have any trouble at all distinguishing them.

TREES NEAR HOME are the best ones to learn first. All these grew within two blocks of one Pathfinder's home, and there are many more in the same area. Beginning at the upper left corner and going around to the right, they are pin oak, American holly, catalpa, cucumber or magnolia, sugar maple, basswood, Norway spruce, birch, Norway maple, and red cedar. How many trees are you able to identify within two blocks of your home?

BARK is an easy clue for identifying many trees. Starting at the upper left, there are the flaky WHITE OAK, stringy CEDAR, smooth BEECH, crocodile-like TULIP POPLAR, muscular MUSCLEWOOD, and jigsaw SYCAMORE.

Chances are that at school someone introduced several of the students to you. Get someone to introduce the trees to you. It's the best way to learn their names.

Some students are blond, some are brunette. Some are tall, some are short, some fat, others thin; some have blue eyes, some have brown. By these differences you identify them. Do the same with the trees.

Look for height, shape, leaves, and fruit.

How *tall* is it? A tree a hundred and fifty feet tall might be a redwood; it couldn't be a maple.

What *shape* is it? Is it pointed like an arrow, or does it spread out like a vase? Compare a pine and an oak.

Are the leaves long like a needle? or are they flat and broad? If they are flat, are the edges rounded? Do they have sharp spikes sticking out of them? or are they cut into little teeth like the edge of a saw? Check the veins. Is there one vein down the middle, with other veins branching off? or do all the veins come together at the bottom, where the leaf joins the stem? Is each leaf all by itself

SHAPE is another good clue for identification, and it is especially valuable in the winter. There is no doubt that each tree at the top is the same as the one under it. On the left is the red oak; right, one of the many hickories.

(simple)? or is each leaf made up of several smaller leaflets (compound)?

Finally, "By their fruits ye shall know them." Does the tree have acorns? Are the seeds in cones? Do they have wings? Are they nuts? Are they like berries?

Don't try to learn all the trees in the world at once. Begin with the ones near home. You probably know some of them already. And when you know about two dozen well, you'll be something of an expert in your community.

Trees are usually divided into two great groups, those that do not lose all their leaves at once and those that are bare and leafless during the winter. The first of these are called evergreens, and the others, deciduous. We will discuss some of the evergreens first.

TREES WITH NEEDLES AND SCALES

Pines

Pine trees have leaves that look like needles. They are more abundant in the West and in southern Canada. But there are several kinds in other parts of America too, so you can get acquainted with some no matter where you live. The needles are often wrapped together at the bottom in bundles. Both the eastern and western *white pine* have five slender needles in a bundle. The *sugar pine* of the West also has five needles in each bundle, but the sugar pine can easily be distinguished from the white pine by the extremely large cone the sugar pine produces.

Pines that have three needles to a bundle include the *pitch pine* of the Northeast, the *longleaf pine* and the *loblolly pine* of the Southeast, the *ponderosa pine,* the *Jeffrey pine,* and the *knobcone pine* in the region of the Rocky Mountains. The longleaf pine can easily be recognized by its needles, for they are usually more than a foot long. The ponderosa can be recognized by its bark, which is reddish, the color of cinnamon.

Pines with two needles in a cluster include the *jack pine* so common in northern Michigan, the *red pine* native to the Northern States, the *slash pine* and the *shortleaf pine* of the Southeastern States, and two that have been imported—the *Austrian* with long needles and the *Scotch* with short needles. The *lodgepole pine* of the Rocky Mountains and the Pacific States also has two needles. The *pinyon pines* of the Southwest have from one to four needles.

Spruces and Firs

These are the symmetrical evergreens that are used so often for Christmas trees. Both spruces and firs bear their needles singly instead of in bundles. The needles of the spruces grow all around the twig and are squarish. The needles of most firs seem to grow only on two sides, making the twig appear flat. The needles are also flat and blunt at the tip. If there are cones on the trees, you can identify the spruce by the fact that its cones hang down. Fir cones remain erect and shatter when ripe.

Red and *white spruce* are found in the Northeastern States, *black spruce,* transcontinental in scope, *blue spruce* in Colorado, *Engelmann spruce* high up in the Rocky Mountains, and *Sitka spruce* in the North Pacific region.

The *balsam fir* of the Northeastern States, with its fragrant needles, the *white fir* of the Western States, and the *alpine fir* that grows in cool moist places along the upper slopes of the Rockies—these are the best-loved firs.

Hemlocks

The *eastern hemlock,* found most abundantly in the Appalachian Mountains and on the northern borders of the Eastern States, is a graceful tree with small, flat, blunt needles that have two white lines on their underside. *Western hemlocks* are similar. The West

WHITE PINE

LODGEPOLE PINE

PONDEROSA PINE

PINYON PINE

DOUGLAS-FIR

HEMLOCK

SPRUCE

TRUE FIR

REDCEDAR

SEQUOIA

REDWOOD

YEW

also has the so-called *false hemlock,* more commonly called *Douglas fir.* It has needles that look like the needles of some of the spruces. It can be recognized by the leaflike growths that project between the scales of the cones. These magnificent trees are second in size only to the sequoias, and their tall, straight trunks provide much of our finest lumber.

Sequoias

The *redwoods* and the *big trees* of California are different species of the *sequoias.* Societies have been organized to protect them, and thousands of tourists each year visit the cathedrallike groves of redwoods in northern California and the ancient big trees of Sequoia National Park. The redwoods are the taller, reaching in a few cases more than three hundred feet. They have small needlelike leaves. The trunks of the big trees are much larger in diameter, and the branches have scaly leaves.

Cedars, Junipers, and Cypresses

The word *cedar,* as it is commonly used in speaking of cedar chests, cedar posts, and cedar pencils, may refer to the *white cedar,* but this tree ought to be called the *arbor vitae.* Sometimes *cedar* means the *red cedar,* but this should be called *juniper.* Arbor vitaes have tiny cones, and leaves that look like fish scales. The junipers may have tiny needles or they may have scalelike leaves. Their cones look a lot like blueberries.

The *common juniper* is a low-spreading bushlike tree, but many ornamental arbor vitaes and junipers have been imported, and they grow in a large variety of shapes and sizes.

The *bald cypress* of the Southern swamps is a valuable tree. Lumber from it is very enduring and is used in places where other lumber would rot quickly. The yellowish-green needles drop as winter comes on, leaving the tree bare, which is why it is called "bald." These trees can be identified by interesting growths that extend upward from the roots and protrude above the water. These are called knees by the people of the South.

TREES WITH BROAD LEAVES

Willows and Poplars

Willows frequently grow beside streams or lakes. They grow fast and easily—even from a live branch pushed into the wet soil. Probably the most common is the *sand-bar willow,* which seems to start growing very quickly on newly formed sand bars. The *black willow*

SWEETGUM

SYCAMORE

OSAGE-ORANGE

HORSECHESTNUT

SUGAR MAPLE

BASSWOOD

MAGNOLIA

DOGWOOD

ASH

is a much larger tree, and gets its name from the blackness of its bark. The *weeping willow,* with its hanging branches, is thought to be the one on which the children of Israel hung their harps when they wept in memory of Zion. The *pussy willow,* with its furry catkins, is a welcome sign of spring.

Poplar trees probably are more appreciated than any other tree in America, because they grow in the great treeless areas where most other trees won't grow. The *quaking aspen* is found over a larger area of America than any other tree. Aspen leaves tremble in the slightest breeze, because the leaf stems are flat. The *cottonwood* has triangular-shaped leaves. The *bigtooth aspen* is named for the large teeth in the edges of the leaves. The *balm of Gilead* and *balsam poplar* have fragrant leaves, but are not so well known as other poplars.

Maples

Most of the maples grow in the Eastern States. However, there are some very beautiful ones in the West, such as the *Rocky Mountain maple,* which has leaves with three very distinct lobes. The West also has the *big-leaf maple,* which grows right along the coast from California to British Columbia.

In the East, however, there are four or five maples that everyone can easily become acquainted with. The *sugar maple* and the *black maple* are very much alike, and they produce most of the maple syrup that is sold for pancakes. The *silver maple* is silver on the underside of the leaf. The *red maple* is found in swamps, and turns a beautiful red during autumn. In the northern part of the United States, especially around the Great Lakes and north of them into Canada, you may find the *striped maple* (or *moosewood*), that has white stripes on greenish bark.

One maple that has immigrated to North America is the *Norway maple.* The best way to identify it is to break off a leaf. If a white, milky juice oozes out, it's a Norway maple.

Buckeyes

Drill a hole downward through the center of a buckeye, run a string through with a knot on one end, and get your best Pathfinder buddy to do the same to another buckeye. Hold up your buckeye on the end of its string and let your buddy take a whack at it with his buckeye. Then tell your friend to hold out his buckeye on the end of its string while you take a swing at it. Take turn about, one shot each time, till one buckeye shatters. Count the number of buckeyes your buckeye breaks before it is broken. The buckeye that breaks

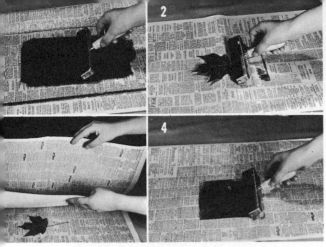

Family: MAPLES (Aceraceae)

Common Name: Sugar Maple

Scientific Name: Acer saccharum

Location: Montgomery Co., Md.

Make a LEAF PRINT: 1. Get a supply of printer's ink from a newspaper office and spread it on glass with a rubber roller. 2. Place a leaf upside down on newspaper and roll the inked roller over it. 3. Place the leaf, ink side up, on fresh newspaper, place plain paper over it, and then another sheet of newspaper over that. 4. Roll ONCE. 5. Label print, and save in a scrapbook.

the most buckeyes is the champion. This game is very popular among boys in England. They use horse chestnuts instead of buckeyes, and call them conkers.

You won't have any trouble identifying horse chestnuts and buckeyes, because the leaves are made up of several leaflets that radiate from the leaf stalk and look somewhat like a palm tree. And when the fruit is ripe it lies on the ground looking out of its prickly husk like the eye of a buck peering from behind its hairy eyelids. The difference between the horse chestnuts and the buckeyes is that the horse chestnuts usually have seven leaflets and the buds are sticky. The *Ohio buckeye* has dry buds and usually only five leaflets.

Nuts to Eat

Black walnuts grow in the eastern half of the United States, and *English walnuts* in California orchards. Both make delicious eating. Black walnuts are large and beautiful trees with leaves that contain anywhere from nine to twenty-three leaflets. The shell of the nut is deeply furrowed and hard and is surrounded with a fleshy material that makes it look almost like an unripe peach. The lumber of the black walnut is very valuable, but it is scarce now since so many of the trees have been cut down for building houses and making furniture. The English walnut has a smoother shell that is not so hard to crack, and there are thin partitions inside the nut. Besides these two walnuts, there are four other species of walnut in the Southwest, but they are not common. One has a very small nut only half an inch in diameter.

The *butternut* tree looks very much like a walnut, except that the bark is a little smoother. The leaves, also, look like walnut leaves. But the butternut fruit is a long, slender nut and can easily be distinguished from the walnut. It is said that Indians used to boil the nuts to get the fat that would rise to the surface like butter.

Hickory trees are found largely in the eastern part of the United States. There are four species you would do well to remember. The most important is the *shagbark hickory,* which is a large tree with bark that scales off in sheets. The nutshells are hard but worth the effort of breaking, for the nuts are very edible. The *shellbark hickory* differs in that there are fewer leaflets, and the twigs have an orange color. The fruit is larger than that of the shagbark. The *mockernut hickory* and the *bitternut hickory* have smaller nuts that are more easily cracked, but bitter.

Birches and Their Relatives

This group includes the birches, alders, hornbeams, and hazelnuts. The birches are medium-sized, graceful trees with simple leaves and catkins. The *paper birch* is the most popular. It grows throughout most of Canada and the northern part of the United States. The bark is almost pure white and peels easily. The pioneers frequently used it for writing paper and the Indians used it for making canoes. The *yellow birch* is similar to the paper birch except that the bark is a rather dirty yellow. The *river birch* of the Southern States has a cinnamon-colored bark, and grows along the edge of streams. The leaves of all these birches are very much alike.

The alders may be small shrubs to medium-sized trees and usually grow near streams or on the shores of lakes. Included among them are the *red alder,* the *thinleaf alder* that grows in the West, and the *Sitka alder* that grows in the western part of Canada.

The hornbeams are found mostly in the eastern part of the United States. The *hop hornbeam* has thin gray-brown bark, broken into shaggy plates. The leaves are very finely toothed. The *American hornbeam* is sometimes called *blue beech, ironwood,* or *musclewood,* and has very smooth blue-gray bark. Bulges in its trunk look like rippling muscles of a champion wrestler.

Ashes

The ashes can be recognized quickest by their seeds, which have wings and hang in clusters. (But remember that maples and elms also have winged seeds.) Next, notice the leaves, which are nearly

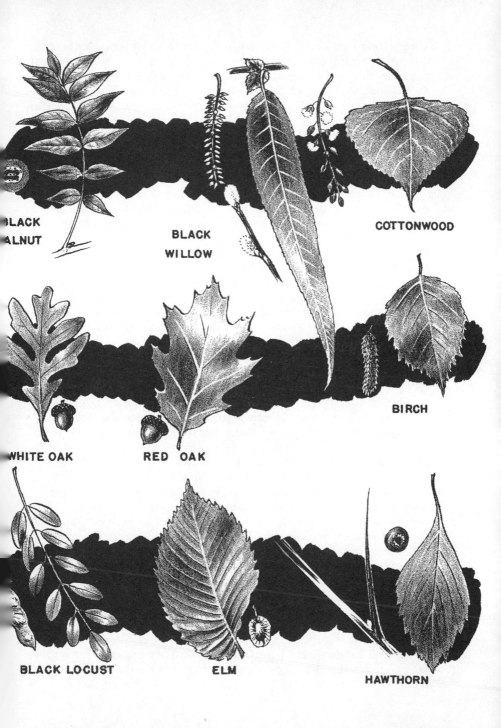

BLACK
WALNUT

BLACK
WILLOW

COTTONWOOD

WHITE OAK

RED OAK

BIRCH

BLACK LOCUST

ELM

HAWTHORN

always compound and come out of the stem on opposite sides. It is difficult to tell one ash from another unless a person has a manual to guide him, but the most important is the *white ash,* which grows throughout the Eastern States. To distinguish between the white ash and the others it is necessary to see the little winged fruits, also to notice the number of leaflets on each leaf, and to see whether the leaflets have stems or not. Most ashes are designated by colors, such as *green ash, black ash, red ash,* and so forth.

Chestnuts and Beeches

Unfortunately, most young people today will never see a *chestnut,* for most of these great trees have been killed by disease. However, there are a few left in the East, and some hybrid varieties have been planted that may withstand the disease. The leaves are simple with large pointed teeth on the edges. The nuts usually come by two's in a hairy, prickly bur. The trees are found only in the eastern part of the country. The *beech* is found only east of the Mississippi. It is a beautiful, low tree that spreads out considerably. It has a thin, smooth, light-gray bark, that can be spotted easily in a forest among other kinds of trees, and is a popular place for carving initials. Inside the burs are small, triangular nuts that are very edible and well worth looking for when you're hungry on a hike.

Oaks

Oak trees grow all over the United States, and they can be identified by their acorns. No other trees produce acorns, and this is the best clue for identifying them, because the leaves are of many different shapes and sizes. The best-known oaks can be placed in two large groups: those that have leaves with rounded, smooth edges, and those that have leaves with sharp bristle tips. Among those having smooth, rounded leaves are the white oaks: the *eastern white oak,* and the western *California white oak* and *Oregon white oak.* Besides these, you can find the *bur oak,* the *post oak,* and the *chestnut oak,* all having smooth, rounded lobes on their leaves.

Among those having sharp lobes are the *northern red* and *southern red oaks,* the *black oak,* the *pin oak,* and the *scarlet oak.*

The *willow oak* will probably fool you the first time you see it. The leaves are long and narrow, as you'd expect willow leaves to be. But the tree produces acorns, so it's an oak.

Elms

Several kinds of elms grow in the Eastern States. The important ones are the *American elm,* which grows into a very beautiful

A FOREST FIRE is a very tragic thing. Once-beautiful woodland becomes an eyesore of burned stumps. Many animals are killed or left as homeless orphans. Pathfinders are always careful about their fires.

tree with a spreading top; the *slippery elm,* sometimes called the *red elm,* which is not so large a tree as the American elm and has leaves that are very rough; and the *rock elm,* which can easily be distinguished from the others by the many ridges of a corky substance that grows on its smaller branches. All of these have leaves that are finely toothed and not quite symmetrical (one half of the leaf does not go as far down on the leaf stem as the other does).

Magnolias

Magnolias grow wild in the Southeastern States. *Tulip trees,* which are relatives of the magnolia, are found throughout the entire eastern part of the country. Most magnolias have large simple leaves and huge white flowers. The fruit is shaped like a cone, and out of the cone come seeds that hang down on slender threads.

Papaws and Root Beer

If you're quick you may be able to top off your supper on a fall hike with a few creamy *papaws.* But you'll have to be quick, because opossums, squirrels, raccoons, and foxes like the banana-shaped fruit too and will probably beat you to it. Let the first frost cure them before you try eating them. Papaws are quite common in the East. Their leaves are rather large and are wider at the end than they are at the base. The beautiful blossoms are the color of mahogany.

Strip off the outer bark from the root of *sassafras* and boil it in water, cool the water, and you'll have root beer! Sassafras grows all over Eastern United States. It's easy to identify, because the leaves have four interesting shapes—a left-hand mitten, a right-hand mitten, a mitten with two thumbs, and just plain oval like an egg. Sometimes sassafras is a small shrub, sometimes a large tree.

Related to the sassafras are the *California laurel,* which grows on the West Coast, and the *bay tree,* both of which give off a spicy smell when the leaves or twigs are crushed. *Red bay* grows in the southern part of the United States.

Sweetgums and Sycamores

The *sweetgum tree* is found throughout the southeastern part of the United States, and has been grown successfully as far north as Michigan. The leaves are star shaped. The bark is gray-brown and deeply furrowed with narrow ridges. The wood takes a high polish and is often used for floors and boxes. When the bark is injured, sap oozes out. It is golden and sweet and—some people think—good to chew. That's why the tree is called sweetgum.

The *sycamore* is probably the most massive tree in the East and sometimes lives five or six hundred years. Indians used it for dugout canoes. It is common throughout the eastern States.

The Rose and Pea Families

More trees are related to the rose than you can imagine! Among them is the *mountain ash,* that has clusters of orangelike berries hanging from the ends of its limbs. The *shadbush* that you can find in the woods, bearing white flowers early in the spring, and the *hawthorns,* that grow everywhere, are also members of the rose family. Most hawthorns have been difficult to identify because there are so many varieties, but one thing they all have in common is that they produce a small applelike fruit, and have thorns. That's why some of them are called thorn apples.

Cousins to the roses are the peas, and they have quite a large family too. In Southwestern United States you'll find the *acacia* and the *mesquite.* There is the eastern *redbud,* with showy red flowers that blossom before the leaves come out in the spring, and the *Kentucky coffee tree,* south of the Great Lakes. All over the Eastern States you'll find the *honey locust* with thorns that hunters sometimes use as pins or spears, and the *black locust,* which is sometimes

FOREST MANAGEMENT. Modern foresters look on wood as a crop, and they plan to have a new harvest of it every twenty years or so. They may log out only certain areas of a forest at one time (upper left), thus preventing erosion. They train high school students how to drill holes to determine the age and health of trees (upper right). They collect seeds from the most promising trees (lower left). The axman topping the tree is about 130 feet in the air.

used for fence posts. All of these trees produce a beanlike pod, and they all have compound leaves like the leaves of the sweet pea.

Sumac

Sumacs are so different in different parts of the United States! For instance, in the Southwest grow sumacs that have just a simple leaf, but most of the sumacs in the eastern and northeastern parts of the United States have compound leaves. Best known is the *staghorn sumac*. Its new stems branch like antlers and are very hairy, like the new horns of a stag. The fruit is a cluster of red berries.

In the swamps of the Northeast grows the *poison sumac*. Be-

You can make a LEAF SILHOUETTE easily by pinning a leaf securely to a piece of paper and spraying around it with the paint from a pressure can.

ware! It has compound leaves similar to the staghorn's, but its fruit is made up of clusters of white berries. Leaves and stems are as poisonous as poison ivy or poison oak!

HOW MANY OF THESE CAN YOU DO?

Check each one when you finish it.

☐ 1. Learn twenty-four local trees.
☐ 2. Make a collection of twenty pressed leaves, properly labeled, either for yourself or for your club museum.
☐ 3. Make a leaf-print collection of ten leaves.
☐ 4. Plant a tree.
☐ 5. Learn to make blueprints of leaves.
☐ 6. Learn to make leaf prints, using blue-line paper. (Obtain from an architect supply store.)
☐ 7. Learn to make spatter prints of leaves.
☐ 8. Earn the MV Honor award in *Trees*.

INTERESTING BOOKS ABOUT TREES

Field Book of American Trees and Shrubs, F. S. Mathews (G. P. Putnam's Sons)
    The standard book on American trees and shrubs.
A Field Guide to the Trees and Shrubs, George A. Petrides (Houghton Mifflin Co.)
Trees, H. S. Zim and A. C. Martin (Golden Press)
How to Know the Trees, H. E. Jaques (Wm. C. Brown Co.)
How to Know the Western Trees, Harry Baerg (Wm. C. Brown Co.)
Forest Trees of the Pacific Slope, Sudworth (U.S. Dept. of Agriculture)
Trees (MV Honor booklet)

when accidents happen

PART FOUR

in emergency

HELP!"

Any Pathfinder who hears that cry wants to rush over at once and give assistance. It is the kind thing to do.

But it is wise to ask first, Are there adults around who could give better help? Then if there are no adults near, ask yourself, Do I know what to do and can I do it? If you cannot give the right kind of aid, do not attempt to help. You might make matters worse. But study this chapter so you will know what to do another time.

For someday an injured person's life may depend on YOU.

The suggestions given here are for first aid only. Always send for a doctor at once, and tell him what has happened so he can bring with him the equipment or medicine he will need.

Treat for Shock

Almost every injured person should be treated for shock, no matter what his injuries are. This kind of shock is not electric shock. Doctors call it traumatic shock. A person feels weak and dizzy, his skin is pale and moist, his pulse is weak, his breathing shallow, and he may be sick to his stomach.

The treatment is important but simple—*keep the patient lying down, keep him warm.* Lay the patient down, usually with his head low. Keep him warm with a blanket all around him, unless the weather is hot. If he is conscious, give him a little water or something warm to drink.

Electric Shock

Do not touch a victim of electric shock while the current is still surging through his body, or you may be electrocuted. Shut off the current if possible. If not, pull away the fallen wire that is touching the victim, or push or pull him from it. At this point do not touch the wire or the victim with your hands, but always use a dry object that does not conduct electricity—a wooden pole, a rope, or a tree limb. Be *sure* it is *dry!*

For hoisting a stranded person up a cliff, make a sling by passing a rope under his armpits and knees, and fastening it with a bowline-on-a-bight knot.

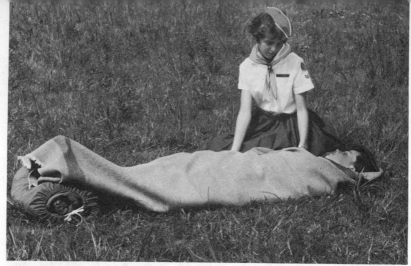

Treat for SHOCK. Lay the victim down, with his feet slightly higher than his head. Keep him warm by spreading blankets or coats over and under him.

Treat the victim for shock (*lay down, keep warm*); and if breathing has stopped, start artificial respiration immediately after the electric current has been disconnected. Send for the doctor or your town's rescue squad.

Drowning

If a swimmer shouts that he is drowning, do not swim out to him! Throw him a rope or hold out a wooden pole where he can reach it. If he is too far from shore, go after him in a boat. Swim out ONLY if you have taken a course in lifesaving.

Artificial Respiration

When a person stops breathing, treat for shock (*lay down, keep warm*), and begin artificial respiration as quickly as possible. Two methods that the American Red Cross recommends are the mouth-to-mouth method and the Hogler-Nielsen back-pressure-arm-lift method.

In mouth-to-mouth, kneel down beside the unconscious person and see if there is anything in his mouth. If there is, wipe it out with your fingers or with a cloth over your fingers.

Tilt his head back and pull on his jaw until his chin juts out. This moves his tongue so it will not block the air passages. With one hand, keep his chin in position. Place your mouth over his mouth, pinch his nose shut with the other hand, and blow.

Then turn your head aside and listen for air coming out.

Repeat the process twelve times a minute for adults, blowing

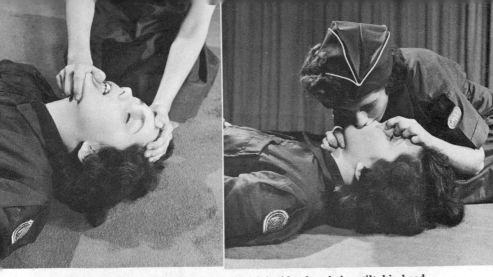

To give **ARTIFICIAL RESPIRATION**, kneel beside the victim, tilt his head back, and pull up on his chin. Be sure his mouth is empty. Place your mouth on his mouth, pinch his nose, breathe in vigorously. Turn your mouth aside to let his air out; then breathe into the victim again, twelve times a minute.

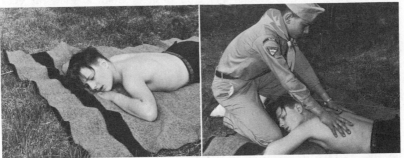

Or use the **HOLGER-NIELSEN** method. Lay the victim face down, with his cheek on his hands, mouth open. Be sure his mouth is empty (upper left). At his head kneel on your right knee and place your hands on his back with your palms between his armpits (upper right). Rock forward till your arms are vertical, applying steady pressure on his chest (lower left). Slide your hands along his arms and raise his elbows till you just begin to lift him (lower right). Let the arms down, repeat the process twelve times a minute.

SPRAINED-ANKLE BANDAGE. 1. Place the middle of a folded triangular bandage under the instep, bring the bandage up, and cross it behind the sprained ankle. 2. Bring the ends around and cross them in front. 3. Push the ends under the bandage on both sides of the shoe. 4. Fasten with a square knot.

vigorously each time. For children, place your mouth over the child's *mouth and nose,* blow twenty times a minute. However, don't blow as hard as with adults.

In the Holger-Nielsen method, place the victim face downward, with his hands overlapping under his cheek, elbows out. Clear his mouth. Kneel close to his head and place your hands on his back, with the palms lying just below an imaginary line running between the armpits. Rock forward until your arms are nearly vertical, and let the weight of the upper part of your body exert steady, even pressure downward on your hands. Slide your hands out to the victim's elbows and draw his arms upward and toward you, applying enough lift to feel resistance and tension at his shoulder, but not enough to change his position. Then lower his arms to the ground.

Repeat this cycle about twelve times a minute.

Whichever method you use, continue the treatment for an hour or two. Stop only when the victim begins to breathe on his own, or when a doctor says there is no more hope.

Bleeding

Most of the accidents Pathfinders have to treat are no more serious than a cut finger. Simple wounds like these can be washed under a faucet, then protected with a Band-Aid.

BLANKET STRETCHER. Lay a blanket on the ground and place a pole on it four inches more than one third the width of the blanket from the side. Fold the blanket over. Place second pole four inches in from the end of this flap and fold again. Always test a stretcher before carrying the victim in it.

TWO-MAN CARRIER. Clasp hands to make seat or make back rest with arms.

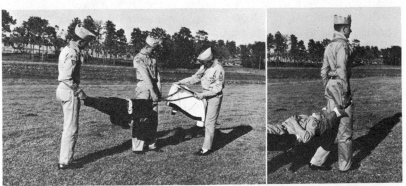

OTHER METHODS. For coat stretcher, pass poles through sleeves; fasten buttons. If injuries are not serious, put arms under knees, armpits; use chair.

More serious bleeding may need a gauze dressing held firmly in place by a long bandage.

To stop bleeding, place a gauze square—or several thicknesses of a clean handkerchief—over the wound and press firmly with your fingers or the palm of your hand. If this does not stop the bleeding, it may help to apply pressure against an artery bringing blood to the wound. One important pressure point is on the inside of the arm halfway between the shoulder and elbow. Another is below the groin on the inner half of the thigh. Use your fingers on the arm pressure point, the heel of your hand against the other.

If bleeding still does not stop, you may have to apply a tourniquet above the wound, but do this only when absolutely necessary.

Snake Bite

Do four things for victims of poisonous snake bites—*constrict, clean, cut, suck.*

First, of course, treat the victim for shock (*lay down, keep warm*), and send for the doctor.

Then *constrict* the blood flow to keep the poison from spreading, by wrapping a narrow band around the arm or leg about an inch above the bite. Make it snug, but not too tight. Don't use a tourniquet.

Clean the wound, possibly using water from a canteen.

Cut. Sterilize in the flame of a match the sharpest knife blade you have and make a cut a quarter inch long and an eighth of an inch deep in each fang mark, cutting the long way of the limb. Do not cut crosswise.

Then *suck.* Use the suction cup of your snake-bite kit, if you have one and it gives good suction. Otherwise, suck with your mouth. Rattlesnake poison will not hurt you if you swallow it. Rinse your mouth well occasionally.

Get the patient to a doctor as quickly as possible, transporting him on a stretcher. Continue treatment as you go, and put ice on the wound, if available. The patient will most likely get better.

Treat a bite from a nonpoisonous snake like any other cut.

Burns

If you should see a house burning, first make sure there is no one inside. Shout, pound on the door, get the people out! Then send for the fire department.

A person whose clothes are burning should be made to lie down. Wrap him in a wool blanket, overcoat, or carpet.

The pain of simple burns and scalds can often be relieved by

342

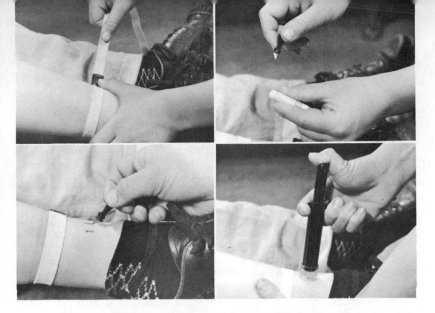

WHAT TO DO FOR SNAKE BITE

IF YOU HAVE A KIT (above). Apply a constricting band about two inches above the fang marks. Make it snug, but not too tight. Wash bite area with soap and water if possible. Sterilize a knife blade in disinfectant. Make a quarter-inch cut, eighth-inch deep, in each fang mark and two more similar cuts half an inch up the leg, cutting the long way of the leg. As the limb swells, move the binding up and cut again. You may have to make many cuts.

IF YOU HAVE NO KIT (below). Make a constricting band by folding a handkerchief till it is narrow. Tie it around the limb. Select sharpest knife blade available and sterilize it in a match flame. Make cuts the same as you would with the knife in a kit. Then check the inside of your mouth to be certain there is no wound in it. Suck. Spit out the poison, Rinse mouth often.

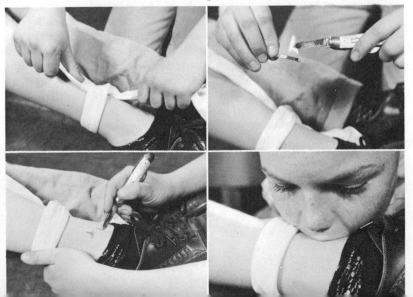

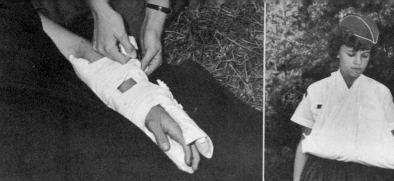

Apply TWO SPLINTS to a broken arm. Use almost any light, stiff material the width of the arm and reaching from the elbow to the finger tips. Pad them, and keep in place with two bandages around both splints and arm. For a SLING use a triangular bandage. Tie the ends behind the neck. Raise the fingers slightly higher than the elbow. Tie a knot or use safety pin at elbow.

soaking the injured part in cold water. Then cover the burn with a gauze dressing or clean handkerchief at least four layers thick.

Burns that produce blisters are more serious. Be ready to treat the victim for shock (*lay down, keep warm*) if the blistered area is at all extensive. Use no antiseptic, do not break the blisters. Apply a gauze dressing and bandage lightly.

Deeper burns are usually very serious. Call the doctor at once. Treat for shock, and cover the burned area with gauze and a bandage if it is small, or with a sheet if it is large, to keep out the air.

Broken Bones

Broken bones should be treated with great care, or what may have begun as a fairly routine injury could finish up a serious wound with lifelong damage.

A break in the arm or lower leg should be splinted.

For splints use boards, sticks, mop handles, a pillow, a folded newspaper—almost anything stiff and fairly light. To make the splint more comfortable, pad it with soft material such as folded clothing, cotton batting, even handfuls of grass or straw. Then tie it with a cravat bandage, necktie, belt, or torn sheets.

Breaks in the thigh bone should be left for the rescue squad. And if there is reason to suspect that the victim may have broken one of his back or neck bones do not move him the fraction of an inch. Damage to the spinal nerve might kill him instantly.

Study First Aid

The directions given in this chapter only touch on what a Pathfinder should know about treating accident victims. One of the most valuable awards you can earn is the MV Honor in *First Aid*.

WHEN ICE BREAKS. Extend your arms onto the ice, kick your legs in the crawl stroke till your hips are at the edge, then carefully roll onto the ice.

Make a **HUMAN CHAIN.** Crawl toward the victim with someone holding your ankles and someone else holding his. Grasp the victim by wrists, snake back.

AN ICE CROSS is two boards locked together. It is excellent for spreading your weight so the ice will not crack. A ladder is good, and easier to find.

picture credits

There are nearly 575 illustrations in this volume. On these two pages are listed the names of the people who provided the pictures. In addition to the many Pathfinders appearing in the photographs, special mention should be made of Robert Davis, Ronald Hudson, Philip Harper, Jerry Rochester, and other members of the Sligo Pathfinder Club, Takoma Park, Maryland, and of G. Ray James and members of the Sanitarium, Forest Lake, and Orlando Pathfinder Clubs of Florida, who spent many days posing patiently for the photographer. The Boy Scouts of America graciously contributed many pictures appearing in their *Scout Field Book*. Members of the art department of the Review and Herald helped substantially with the sketches. To one and all, a hearty Thank you.

(The numbers refer to the pages. The letters refer to the pictures on a page, counting alphabetically, left to right, top to bottom.)

American Forest Products Industries, K. S. Brown, 333 (D)
American Red Cross, 314
Harry Baerg, 213, 215, 279, 323, 325, 329
C. R. Beeler, 123 (C, D)
Boy Scouts of America, 46, 53, 111, 112 (A, C, E), 113, 114, 118, 119, 120, 121, 202, 203 (A, C-F), 231, 233, 235, 237, 253, 255, 257, 259, 261, 275, 291, 345
W. E. Burns, 124 (A), 127
Charles Carey, 135 (C-H)
Lee Carter, 39, 87, 178
Gladys Clarke, 313 (G)
Desmond Cummings, 137
Columbia Union College Biology Department, 280, 281, 283
Jack Darnell and Crutcher Studio, 172, 175, 177
A. Devaney, 218, 276
Paul DeBooy, 33, 35, 161 (A)
Herb Ford, 13 (A)
Freeman Studios, 50
John D. Freeman, 22
Harry Garlick, 336
Esther Henderson photo from Frederic Lewis, 313 (D)
Herbert Photos, Inc., 304
J. Byron Logan, 11 (A), 14, 16, 17, 19, 21, 51 (B), 100, 112 (B, D, F), 128, 159 (C), 203 (B), 207, 339 (A, B), 343
Lawrence Maxwell, 2, 8, 11 (B, C), 24, 27, 29, 30, 31, 36, 37, 38 (A), 40, 42, 43, 47, 54, 55 (A), 57 (A-C, E-G), 61 (A, C, E), 62, 64, 65 (B), 66, 67 (B, C), 69, 74, 76, 77, 78, 79, 81, 82, 85, 89, 90, 91, 93, 99, 102, 103,
105, 107, 123 (A, B, E, F), 124 (B), 125 (B-E), 126, 130, 131, 132, 133, 134, 135 (A, B), 138, 140, 141, 143, 145, 146, 147, 149 (A, B, D, E), 152, 158, 159 (A, B), 162, 167, 168 (A-C, E, F), 169, 171, 179, 245, 273, 315, 319, 320, 321, 327, 334, 338, 339 (C-F), 340, 341, 344
Moody Institute of Science, 311
Kenneth Moore, 266 (B)
T. A. Moran, 136
Mt. Wilson and Palomar Observatories, 208, 216 (A, B)
Josef Muench, 316
National Park Service, 198, 201, 313 (C)
Ralph H. Anderson, 308
Jack E. Boucher, 227 (A)
F. J. Francis, 313 (B)
National Wildlife Federation, 313 (F)
G. Newman, 246
Bill Oliphant, 165 (A)
Boyd Olson, 110, 168 (D)
Don Palmer, 55 (B), 57 (D), 65 (A), 67 (A), 94, 96, 97, 98, 115, 180, 182, 183, 185, 189, 191, 193 (B), 194 (A), 195, 196
© 1900, by E. A. Perry, 313 (A)
Carl E. Petterson, 278
© Pontiac and General Motors, 72
Pope's Studios, 13 (B)
H. Armstrong Roberts, 116, 288 (A)
Don Roth, 13 (C), 155, 157
C. H. Seitz, 186
Grant Tolles, 224
U.S. Department of Agriculture Photo, 204, 205, 284, 287, 288 (B), 289, 293,

346

347

index

349

350

351